I0125279

Party Switching in Israel

SUNY series in Comparative Politics

Gregory S. Mahler, editor

Party Switching in Israel
A Historical and Comparative Analysis

CSABA NIKOLENYI

SUNY
PRESS

Cover image from Shutterstock: an Israeli voting booth in a polling station during national election day in Israel. Elections in Israel are based on nationwide proportional representation. Ashkelon, Israel, February 10, 2006.

Published by State University of New York Press, Albany

© 2023 State University of New York

All rights reserved

Printed in the United States of America

No part of this book may be used or reproduced in any manner without written permission. No part of this book may be stored in a retrieval system or transmitted in any form or by any means including electronic, electrostatic, magnetic tape, mechanical, photocopying, recording, or otherwise without the prior permission in writing of the publisher.

For information, contact State University of New York Press, Albany, NY
www.sunypress.edu

Library of Congress Cataloging-in-Publication Data

Name: Nikolenyi, Csaba, 1971– author.
Title: Party switching in Israel : a historical and comparative analysis / Csaba Nikolenyi.
Description: Albany, NY : State University of New York Press, 2023. | Series: SUNY Series in Comparative Politics | Includes bibliographical references and index.
Identifiers: LCCN 2022021028 | ISBN 9781438491615 (hardcover : alk. paper) | ISBN 9781438491622 (ebook) | ISBN 9781438491608 (pbk. : alk paper)
Subjects: LCSH: Party affiliation—Israel. | Political parties—Israel. | Political candidates—Israel. | Israel. Keneset—Rules and practice.
Classification: LCC JQ1830.A979 N55 2023 | DDC 324.25694—dc23/eng/20220830
LC record available at https://lccn.loc.gov/2022021028

10 9 8 7 6 5 4 3 2 1

אֲנִי לְדוֹדִי וְדוֹדִי לִי

("I am my beloved's and my beloved is mine")

—Song of Songs 6:3

Contents

Illustrations

Figures

Tables

Acknowledgments

The original idea of this book was conceived during a lunch conversation with Shaul Shenhav at the Mount Scopus campus of the Hebrew University of Jerusalem where I spent a sabbatical leave on a Forsccheimer Visiting Fellowship in 2007–2008. Over the next several years, we presented several papers together and published an article on the "Constitutionalization of Party Unity in India and Israel" in *The Journal of Legislative Studies*. The Department of Political Science at the Hebrew University remained a very important intellectual home where I returned on many occasions and where I was always welcome to discuss and debate ideas. In addition to Shaul, I owe special gratitude to Reuven Hazan and Gideon Rahat for reading and commenting on various drafts of my work and always offering helpful comments and clarifications.

My research benefitted greatly from academic visits at the School of Politics and International Relations, and the Centre for European Studies at the Australian National University in Canberra and the O.P. Jindal Global University in Sonipat, India. My hosts Ian McAllister, Jacquline Lo, and Rohee Dasgupta provided me with an ideal environment to pursue my comparative work. Collecting and organizing the large amount of data for this research required the able assistance of several wonderful student assistants at Concordia University. I am especially indebted to Jonathan Punski and Reuven Perez for their dedicated work and help that allowed my work to progress.

Researching the politics and the history of legislative party switching in Israel allowed me to make Jerusalem our home, where working in the collections at the National Library of Israel was of indispensable value. During my many visits at the Knesset, I received invaluable help from several individuals: Gila Eldar, director of the Knesset Library; Arbel

Astrachan, legal advisor of the Knesset Commmittee; Inda Novominksy, director of the Knesset Archives, and her predecessor Rivka Marcus. My work would not have been possible without the support of a research grant awarded by the Social Sciences and Research Council of Canada as well as logistical and financial assistance provided by the Concordia University's Faculty of Arts and Science and the Azrieli Institute of Israel Studies. I owe special gratitude to Rafael Chaiken (formerly of SUNY Press), Michael Rinella and Diane Ganeles (currently of SUNY Press) as well as to the anonymous reviewers of my manuscript whose careful reading and insightful comments helped me sharpen my writing, argument and analysis. I remain responsible for any remaining errors of omission and commission.

The journey of writing the book was not only a professional but also a personal experience in a very deep and meaningful sense. Along the way, I have benefitted from the support of our friends and families in Montreal and Israel. I owe my special and affectionate gratitude to Lazar and Jewel Sarna who shared the warmth and the hospitality of their home and family; their care and encouragement have been and will remain a never-failing source of inspiration and confidence. My in-laws, George and Csilla Gondos, have lovingly shared in all our adventures, growth, successes, and failures.

My most intimate and deepest gratitude is reserved for Andrea with whom I have shared a life of love, affection, and learning since our youth. This book was nurtured to fruition by her never-ending support and belief in me.

I dedicate this book to Andrea, the love of my life.

Introduction

Israel's twenty-third government was brought to an unceremonious end on March 15, 1990, when the Knesset majority voted Prime Minister Yitzhak Shamir's government out of office less than a year and half following its investiture. This was an event of historic proportions because no Israeli government had been defeated on an opposition-sponsored no-confidence vote in the country's legislature ever before. Although the government had started its term as a national unity coalition that included both Likud and Labor, the country's two largest parties at the time, it had lost its majority when Labor entered into an understanding with the ultra-orthodox religious Shas party to bring it down and replace it with a new coalition of Left and religious parties. Eventually, the Labor-Shas deal, which became popularly known in Israel as the "stinking trick," backfired and led to Shamir's return to power at the helm of the twenty-fourth government formed by a narrower coalition of Right and religious parties, leaving Labor squarely in the opposition benches.

Government instability was already a well-known and recurrent feature of Israeli parliamentary life ever since the creation of the State. As such, there was hardly anything unusual about the fact that the coalition of parties that formed the government after the general election would change, leading to the investiture of a new government.

However, what was extremely unusual about the events that transpired in the Twelfth Knesset was the pivotal role that defectors played in determining whether Shimon Peres of the Labor Party or Yitzhak Shamir of Likud would become the next prime minister. During the three months that ensued between Shamir's defeat in March and his eventual return to power in June, the Israeli public watched in dismay as one Knesset member after another defected from their parties in an effort to position

1

themselves as kingmakers between the rival claimants to power. The eventual outcome of the government formation game was indeed determined by a handful of defectors who successfully demanded, and received, ministerial positions in the new government as a reward for betraying their parties.

The Israeli public did not take kindly to this turn of events, and in one of the largest ever public protests in the country's history it demanded the political class to introduce fundamental reforms to restructure the system and the operation of government. The "stinking trick" reminded Israeli voters of the case of Rahamim Kalanter, a one-time member of the Jerusalem city council whose famous defection from his party in 1956 saved the crumbling coalition headed by Mayor Gershon Agron and gave birth to the highly pejorative term *kalanterism* in the Israeli political lexicon. What was particularly problematic about both kalanterism—the phenomenon of Knesset members moving from one party to another in exchange for positions or material benefits—and the "stinking trick" was that the defectors involved received executive appointments in exchange for crossing the floor, which reinforced the public perception that the voters' mandate was negotiable among their representatives and up for grab to the highest bidder. Although kalanterism remained a relatively isolated phenomenon in Israeli national politics until 1990, the "stinking trick" brought it back to the center of the public spotlight and debate.

A central element of the reforms that followed the upheaval in the Twelfth Knesset was the introduction of the direct election of the prime minister, which was expected to insulate the office of the head of government from the ill effects of partisan horse-trading.[1] The immediate effect of the reform was the transformation of the Israeli political system from pure parliamentarism to a hybrid presidential-parliamentarism;[2] however, it proved to be a short-lived experiment, and the direct election of the prime minister was rescinded by the Fifteenth Knesset in 2001. Nonetheless, the change of the government system left behind several long-term effects that can still be detected in the ongoing fragmentation, volatility, and personalization of the Israeli party system.[3] In addition to the direct election of the prime minister, the Knesset also responded to the public's demand for reform in yet another way: by passing an anti-defection legislation that was supposed to make it ever less attractive for Knesset members to leave the party that they had represented in the previous election. In contrast to the brevity of the direct election of the prime minister, the anti-defection legislation, a package of several interconnected laws, has proved to be a lasting reform institution. Although its different components have been amended several times since its inception, the legislation has remained an integral part of the architecture of Israeli political institutions, and as such has had profound consequences, both expected and unintended, for the stability of the political parties in the Israeli parliament.

The Argument

This book tells the story of the emergence of Israel's anti-defection law and the consequences it has had on the stability of political parties, as well as on governments in the Knesset. *My central argument is that whereas the law has successfully insulated government stability from the potential hazard of party defections, it has simultaneously given rise to new forms of strategic calculations on the part of elected parliamentarians that have actually resulted in a relative increase in the rate of party switching as well as a weakening in legislative party stability.* In other words, the Israeli anti-defection law has sacrificed party stability in favor of ensuring that governments will no longer fall as a result of defections.

In the vast majority of established democracies around the world, political parties are in charge of managing their own internal processes and mechanisms by which they secure the compliance of their parliamentary representatives, sanction indiscipline where and when necessary, and deter deputies' ultimate form of dissent, which is to exit the party altogether. Therefore, the adoption of an anti-defection law in a stable democracy, where party competition is already institutionalized, such as Israel, is a puzzle in and of itself. It is true that over the past few decades, a growing number of new democracies, where political parties and the party system are still relatively less institutionalized,[4] have adopted formal legislation, and often constitutional provisions, to strengthen parliamentary parties against their own members' exit option.[5] Such anti-defection laws set out concrete penalties for individual parliamentary deputies who change their partisan affiliation during the inter-election period, but in exceptional circumstances they may entirely ban party exit. However, while the adoption of anti-defection measures may seem reasonable in new democracies, in established democracies with an institutionalized party system the adoption of anti-defection legislation is not only puzzling but is often described as a violation of fundamental political rights and freedoms of the individual deputy.[6]

Informed by the classic Burkean theory of the free mandate, established democracies rarely adopt legal, let alone constitutional, restrictions on their parliamentary representatives' freedom to choose and change their partisan affiliation after the election.[7] Quite the contrary, a significant number of established democracies actually provide constitutional protection for the freedom of individual parliamentarians' mandate from excessive party control in order to ensure that the voters' interests and preferences will not be subordinated to those of political parties.[8] This practice is widely supported by the international legal community, which has produced a number of reports, documents, and position papers that share the consensus according to which the freedom of elected deputies' mandate, including their freedom to choose their party affiliation even after the election, takes precedence over the interests and the unity of political parties.[9]

Nonetheless, as the case of the Twelfth Israeli Knesset shows, the protection of the free mandate may come at a high cost if members of parliament change their partisan affiliation on a scale, or in a manner, that leads to loss of public trust in the legitimacy of the electoral and representative institutions. Defections and floor-crossings may create or reinforce the popular perception that legislators are unprincipled and opportunistic actors motivated by the selfish pursuit of personal gains. In extreme cases defections may even trigger acute political crises causing deep decline in the legitimacy of the system of government. Viewed in these terms, anti-defection laws may also be understood as legal instruments whose primary objective is to regulate political parties and legislators in order to protect the legitimacy and the integrity of the political system rather than measures adopted to limit the freedom of individual deputies.

Why Israeli lawmakers responded to the aftermath of the "stinking trick" by formalizing and institutionalizing the regulation of party unity even though the prevailing view in most established democracies, echoed by several leading Israeli jurists, supports the freedom of individual lawmakers is one of the major puzzles that the book will investigate. The puzzle becomes even more interesting when one considers the history of the Israeli anti-defection law: following decades of unsuccessful calls to adopt such legislation, the eventual passage of the legislation in 1991 was succeeded by a series of amendments and changes, which shows that far from losing any interest in abandoning the formal regulation of party unity, the Knesset has remained seriously committed to regulating it. Prior to 1991, several instances of defections led Israeli lawmakers to demand that some kind of formal regulation be taken against such, allegedly unscrupulous, parliamentary behavior. The recurrent trope in these demands was that since Israeli voters gave their mandate to political parties, by virtue of the fact that on election day they vote for a closed list of candidates, and not to individual representatives, Knesset members should have no right to change the number of seats that parties secured directly from the electorate. In their own defense, defectors would often argue either that they personally were responsible for bringing a substantial number of voters to support the party or that the party has changed its position on issues that it has promised to the voters during the election campaign. As such, they would claim that their defection actually served the interest of the public to by punishing a party that steered too far from what it had committed itself to represent in the last election.

Although the anti-defection law has been amended on several occasions, it has consistently retained at its core a mixed delegate-trustee mandate of representation, which combines the free agency of the individual representative with political parties' ownership of the voters' mandate. This mixture, however, has created normative ambivalence with regard to the question of who actually owns the voters' mandate: the individual Knesset member (MK) or the party on whose ticket he or she was elected. Instead of making a clear choice either in favor of the free mandate or in favor of the party government model of representation, the Israeli anti-defection law sought to strike a middle ground between the two models. On the one hand, the law established clear penalties for defections, which suggests a movement toward the partisan end of the mandate continuum. On the other hand, the law has also created loopholes and conditions that continued to keep the exit option open for legislators dissatisfied with their party's directions and decisions. In this sense, the anti-defection law has maintained the freedom of individual legislators to exercise their exit option, albeit under more circumscribed conditions than what was the case before the legislation had taken effect.

By refusing to punish defections in a categorical manner and, instead, establishing precise conditions under which defections can go unpunished, the anti-defection law has created an institutional foundation for the weakening of the cohesion of legislative party groups. Prior to the passage of the legislation, disgruntled Knesset members would quit their parties whenever they estimated that the circumstances were appropriate. However, once the anti-defection law stipulated the precise conditions under which defections were not penalized such disgruntled parliamentarians had a strong incentive to defer their defections until those conditions were met. In the meantime, they would provoke deeper internal dissension within the party, which would cause a severe loss of cohesion and institutional stability.

In addition to prolonging intra-party dissent, a second important unexpected consequence of the Israeli anti-defection law has been its failure to reduce the actual number of defections. Figure I.1 provides firsthand evidence that the number of elected Knesset members who have changed their party affiliation since the anti-defection law came into effect: party switching per Knesset has increased from an average of 7.5 before to 12.4 after the adoption of the anti-defection law.

Moreover, the types of defections have also changed dramatically: direct floor-crossings from one party group to another have been eliminated; the establishment of single-member party groups has dropped to a negligible number; and the overwhelming majority of defections have been collective in nature and have taken the form of creating new legislative party groups. The increase in the number of new party formations

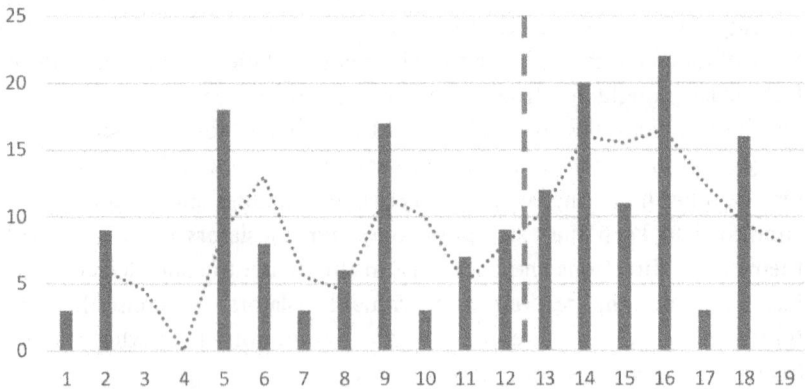

Note: The vertical dashed line separates the time series between the years before and after the adoption of the anti-defection law. For source and details, see the Appendix.

Figure I.1. Party switching per Knesset, 1949 to 2015.

has also led to a sharp increase in the rate of the fragmentation of the legislative versus the electoral party system. Using the effective number of parties index,[10] figure I.2 compares the level of party system fragmentation in each Knesset at the start of its term with the level of fragmentation at the end of the term. Put simply, since the Twelfth Knesset, the legislative party system has been consistently more fragmented at the end of the term than it was right after the last election.

The failure of the Israeli anti-defection law to reduce legislative party fragmentation is related to the countervailing effects of the Israel's extreme proportional representation electoral system.[11] Well known for its favorable treatment of small political parties, the electoral system in and of itself creates an inherent obstacle to legislative party unity. The combination of a historically low electoral threshold coupled with a regime of generous state funding for political parties has made it historically quite easy for dissatisfied politicians to split from their parent party and set up new ones with a realistic expectation to win representation in the

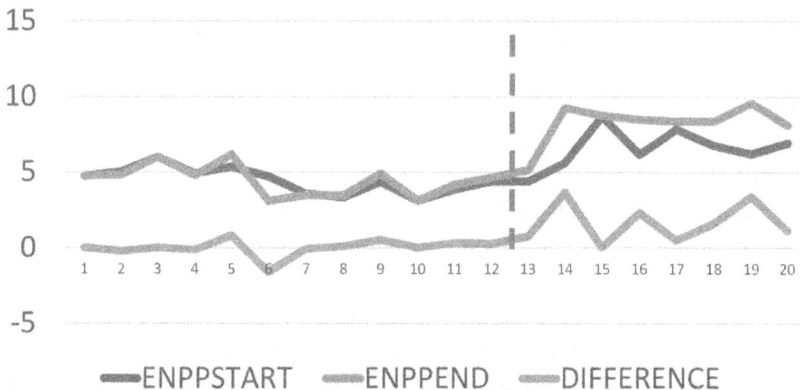

Note: ENPPSTART refers to the effective number of parliamentary party at the start of each Knesset; ENPPEND refers to the effective number of parliamentary parties at the end of the same Knesset. The effective number of parties, also known as the Laakso-Taagepera index, is calculated by dividing into the unity the sum of the squared percent of all parties' seat share that won at least one seat in the Knesset. The vertical dashed line separates the time series between the years before and after the adoption of the anti-defection law.

Figure I.2. Inter-election changes in the number of parties in the Knesset, 1949 to 2019.

Knesset in the next election. For the anti-defection law to have a strong bite it would have had to be defined much more sharply and it would have had to forbid defections and party exit categorically in order to counteract the fissiparous tendencies that stem from the electoral system and the party funding rules. Instead, the very legislation that is supposed to keep parliamentary parties stable and united actually acts to reward intra-party minorities and factions as long as they satisfy the relatively weak conditions set out in the law.

An Overview of the Chapters Ahead

The presentation of the argument unfolds as follows. Chapter 1 provides a theoretical background to the study of rules and laws established to keep legislative parties together. As the chapter will show, although the scholarly literature on party switching has become a growth industry, scholars to date have paid scant attention to the ways in which anti-defection laws, the legal instrument with the explicit and direct intended effect on party switching, operate. Moreover, anti-defection laws have also been neglected by scholars who study party laws, legislation by which the state regulates the activities of political parties. Whereas the state regulation of particular areas of party life have been more thoroughly studied, such as party finance, others, such as legislation aimed to keep parliamentary parties together, have remained by and large neglected.

Chapter 2 provides a historical overview of party switching and its attempted regulation both before and since the adoption passage of the anti-defection law in 1991. It shows that in spite of the frequency of party switching, the Knesset remained consistently reluctant to adopt formal legislative measures against them until the "stinking trick" de-stabilized Yitzhak Shamir's national unity coalition government and the defectors became king-makers in the government formation drama that followed. In stark contrast to the dramatic events in the Twelfth Knesset, none of the successive legislative amendments to the anti-defection law were triggered by deep political crises. Quite the contrary: the history of the anti-defection legislation shows that governing coalitions have gained a very strong legal instrument in this legislation to shore up their strategic political needs. As such, the stability of the anti-defection law has become quite vulnerable to the shifting realities of Israeli coalition government.

Chapters 3 to 7 are dedicated to an in-depth exploration of the five main consequences of the Israeli anti-defection legislation for (1) the frequency of switching, (2) the type of switching in terms of the number of parliamentarians involved, (3) the timing of the switch and (4) the direction of party switching in terms of the government-opposition divide, and (5) the electoral consequences of party switching. Chapter 3 explains the counter-intuitive finding that the frequency of party switching has actually increased rather than decreased in the aftermath of the law taking effect. The chapter expands on the argument that not only does the anti-defection law have specific features encouraging party switching but it also interacts with other institutional mechanisms, specifically the electoral system and the proliferation of intra-party candidate selection primaries, that further incentivized party exit. The chapter illustrates the interaction of these processes through a case study of the disintegration of the Likud party in the Fourteenth Knesset.

Chapter 4 examines the rise of collective party switching, as opposed to solo exits, since the adoption of the anti-defection law. The chapter specifically argues that the number of Knesset members involved in a given switch has been consistently a reflection of the institutional provision in the anti-defection law that allowed one-third of a party group to split away with no penalty. Although the one-third provision was originally intended to be a proxy measure for an ideologically driven party split, it has instead become a focal point toward which party switchers strategically converged. The chapter provides three cases studies to show the mechanics and the ambiguities in the application of the "one-third" condition: the formation of the Yi'ud (Destiny) party in the Thirteenth Knesset, the disintegration of the Pensioners' Party in the Seventeenth Knesset, and the split in the Israeli Labor Party in the Eighteenth Knesset.

Chapter 5 studies the puzzling preponderance of pre-electoral party switching in Israel. Comparative studies suggest that the electoral cost for party switching should be higher in close proximity to the next election, which should therefore lead more legislators to switch party earlier in the term. In the Knesset, however, the anti-defection law has had very specific built-in provisions that actually facilitated and encouraged pre-electoral party exits. In most cases, this meant that intra-party dissension and conflict would fester throughout much of the legislative term, making parties less united and less cohesive, and would become formalized at the pre-electoral stage. The chapter presents four cases, two solo and two collective switches, to illustrate the causes and dynamics of the pre-electoral timing of party switching.

Chapter 6 explores the directionality of party switching. It shows that the overwhelming majority of switches have taken place among the opposition parties, both before and since the adoption of the anti-defection law. As such, the anti-defection law has not had any particular effect on the direction in which MKs switch. However, through a detailed case study of the gradual disintegration of Prime Minister Ariel Sharon's successive coalition governments in the Sixteenth Knesset, leading to the highest number of MKs switching parties since the adoption of the anti-defection law, the chapter shows the important role that the anti-defection legislation played in prolonging the tenure of a rapidly weakening coalition government.

Chapter 7 examines the electoral consequences of party switching both for individual MKs as well as for the new party groups they form. The chapter shows that for individual Israeli legislators the electoral cost of party switching has increased since the anti-defection law took effect, which is surprising given that the actual rate and frequency of switching has increased over the same period. The seeming contradiction is resolved by looking at the electoral consequences of party switching for the new party groups that are created: new party groups often survive and do well in the next election, however, the MKs who are elected from its list may not be the same ones who carried out the formation of the group in the first place. In this regard, first-term rookie MKs are particularly vulnerable and are re-elected only half as frequently as their more experience colleagues.

Chapter 8 shifts the discussion to a comparative context by situating the Israeli case in the context of three other contemporary democracies that have adopted anti-defection laws in order to maintain the political integrity of their elected legislators: India, South Africa, and New Zealand. This chapter shows that the Israeli legislation is indeed comparatively mild in terms of its sanctions, which resulted in its failure to eliminate defections. At the same time, by institutionalizing the mixed delegate-trustee model Israel has successfully combined its simultaneous commitment to fostering party stability without compromising the political freedoms of individual parliamentarians.

A Note on Terminology

Throughout the book several technical terms are used to denote various forms of party switching. The generic term "party switching" refers to any change in an elected legislator's party group during an inter-election period. Technically, this could include the full-scale amalgamation of multiple party groups creating a new one. However, since the anti-defection law was not concerned with such changes but rather with regulating MKs *exiting* from their party group, I use the term "party switching" in the sense of "party exit" and will, therefore, use the terms interchangeably. As such, I define party exit as an event when an *elected member of the Knesset leaves his or her parliamentary party group, either alone or together with other members, before the next general election with one of the following three outcomes: (1) the switching MK becomes a Single MK in the Knesset, (2) the switching MKs form a new party group, or (3) the switcher(s) join an existing party group.*

A "defection" is a specific form of party exit as defined in the anti-defection law and its various amendments, as discussed in chapter 2. Similarly, a "split" is also defined in the anti-defection legislation as a form of party exit exempted from the penalties meted out for defectors. While party amalgamations are not covered in my analysis, there are a few instances when a small party group collectively merges into another larger party group. Such cases are counted as forms of exit since the parties involved are not creating a new "third" party. The appendix presents a list of all party switches in the Knesset, both collective and solo, that meet this definition.

Chapter 1

Conceptual and Comparative Considerations

This chapter establishes the scholarly context for the study of party switching and its regulation. The first section situates the study of anti-defection laws in the context of the literatures on party cohesion and party switching. The second section casts a broader comparative view and surveys the global proliferation of anti-defection laws. Although such laws have been on the rise with a growing number of states adopting some version of it, most of these cases can be found in new or non-democracies. As such, Israel remains one of the few exceptional cases of an established democracy that has adopted an anti-defection law that is still in effect. The third section discusses the concept of *kalanterism* in the broader context of the two classic models of legislative representation: trusteeship versus delegation models. It shows that *kalanterism* falls within the trustee model of representation, which accords maximum freedom to elected representatives and which is the norm in most contemporary democracies.

Party Cohesion and Party Switching

Legislators in parliamentary systems form, and enter, political party groups in order to realize advantages from collective action such as the formation, termination, and scrutiny of governments, or advancing policies via the legislative process on behalf of their electoral constituents. In fact, as Giovanni Sartori points out, the effectiveness of parliamentary systems of govenrment require *"parliamentary fit"* political parties, "that is to say parties that have been socialized (by failure, duration, and appropriate incentives) into being relatively cohesive and/or disciplined bodies. . . . disciplined parties are a *necessary condition* for the 'working' of parliamentary systems."[1]

Given the profound significance of party unity for parliamentary government, conventional wisdom in the legislative and coalition theoretic literatures assumed parties to be unitary actors. This assumption, however, has been brought into question over recent years by scholars who point to variation in the ability of parties to maintain unity of action among their members. The analytical distinction between party cohesion, "the extent to which, in a given situation, group members can be observed to work together for the group's goal in one and the same way," and party discipline, "a special type of cohesion achieved by enforcing obedience or . . . a system of sanctions by which such enforced cohesion is attained"[2] reminded legislative scholars that party unity could not be taken for granted: parties may arrive at the legislature with a certain degree of cohesion that obtains as a result of the party's own historical, institutional, or sociological characteristics,[3] but at times party unity needs to be compelled by leaders invoking disciplinary measures.[4] The relationship between cohesion and discipline is not linear. Whereas sanctions normally need be applied only when, and because, cohesion falters,[5] too little or too much cohesion may actually make the use of party discipline either pointless or redundant.[6]

A rapidly growing area of work in the literature on party cohesion is party switching,[7] defined by Heller and Mershon as "any recorded change in party affiliation on the part of a politician holding or competing for elective office."[8] Party switching is a well-known feature of legislative politics in a number of states, many of which have adopted constitutional or other legal measures to curtail and limit such behavior.[9] These measures can range from a severe constitutional ban on any switching activity to a more lenient rule in the operating procedures of the legislature to require a switching member to spend time as an Independent before entering his or her new host party group. The impact of a switch on the legislative party system may be essentially of three types: a switch may increase, decrease, or leave intact the degree of partisan fragmentation in the legislature.[10] In turn, changes in the format and the fragmentation of the legislative party system may have further important consequences, including the allocation of portfolios and other coveted legislative positions, such as mega seats,[11] among political parties as well as the composition and the duration of the government.

The relative timing of party switches may shed light on politicians' motivations to give up their existing labels and adopt a new one. Mershon and Shvetsova break down an inter-election period into three distinct phases in order to track the temporal distribution of party switches.[12] Drawing on the rational choice assumption that legislators are motivated by office-, vote-, and/or policy-seeking considerations, they distinguish among switches that are related to the formation of a new government (office-seeking switches); those that are related to expectations regarding the next elections (vote-seeking switches); and those that happen in-between (policy-seeking switches). They find that a midterm conditioning effect encourages legislators to shy away from switching their party label too soon after the last general election or too close to the next one.

Several scholars have pointed out that party switching may carry considerable electoral costs.[13] Although loyalty to an unpopular party label can be electorally damaging as well, Klein reports that it is more common to find legislators in new, as opposed to established, European democracies to switch from parties that cannot guarantee them re-election.[14] In contrast to these claims, both Fell and Gherghina report that the electoral cost of switching can be significantly mitigated by the strategic consideration of the destination party or the switching legislator's past legislative experience, while Hamzawi finds evidence that legislators' decision to switch is policy motivated once they determine that their current party able is electorally harmful.[15] Yoshinaka's work on party switching among American legislators has shown the central importance of ambition as a motivational driver of defections. While party switching is costly in electoral terms in the United States, the promise of Congressional committee assignments can shift ambitious legislators' calculation in favor of switching.[16] Party-level characteristics have also been linked to party switching. Heller and Mershon find evidence that Italian legislators tend to flee from more disciplined party groups, while Volpi finds that authoritarian parties and parties with unstable value label were prone to suffer more defections.[17]

The literatures on party cohesion and party switching attribute a central role to political institutions as independent variables. Specifically, two sets of institutions have attracted scholars' interests: candidate selection methods and the electoral system. As for the former, O'Brien and Shomer argue that deputies are less likely to switch when their party has an exclusive or closed method of candidate selection because their nomination and electability is a direct function of their loyalty to the party organization.[18] In contrast, open candidate selection methods encourage prospective legislators to cultivate a personal following, which in turn weakens their party's control over them. The expected effect of the electoral system on party switching is more ambiguous. According to conventional wisdom, party-centric electoral systems, such as closed-list proportional representation, are more likely to encourage deputies to remain loyal to the party label that got them elected than are candidate-centered electoral systems.[19] More recent scholarship, however, has challenged this view by arguing precisely the opposite. In this vein Mershon and Shvetsova expect that in a party-centered electoral system parliamentarians are not held directly accountable to the electorate which, *ceteris paribus*, reduces the electoral cost of their disloyalty.[20]

Speaking to the case of Denmark, Nielsen, Andersen, and Pedersen find that legislators with many personal votes will be more likely to switch; however, their decision to do so will be more likely if decision making in the party is in the hands of party leaders and activists rather than the legislators.[21] Similarly, Klein finds that the effect of the electoral system on party switching is indirect: electorally losing parties are more likely to suffer defection under electoral systems that encourage the cultivation of candidates' and legislators' personal reputation as opposed to that of the party label.[22] It has been noted that patterns of party switching underwent considerable change in the aftermath of electoral reform in both Italy and Japan. In the former, the introduction of single-member districts led to the formation of electoral cartels that proved unable to hold onto legislators' loyalty after the election was over.[23] In Japan, the replacement of the single nontransferable vote with a mixed-member electoral system changed the motivation for party switching from pork seeking to policy seeking.[24]

In contrast to candidate selection methods and the electoral system, anti-defection laws have a much more direct effect on party switching because, by definition, they impose a direct cost on party exit. Yet, in spite of the growing interest in anti-defection rules, very few studies have investigated their effects. This lack of scholarly attention to studying what anti-defection laws are meant to achieve—namely, to compel and sanction legislative party unity—is unfortunate because the application of such laws can actually help us re-evaluate some existing claims about party cohesion and party unity. As mentioned earlier, there is a fairly well-adopted view in the literature suggesting that cohesion precedes discipline.[25] The implication of this argument is that the level of cohesion determines how much and what kind of disciplinary measure party leaders may need to invoke and when. In the presence of an anti-defection law, however, this relationship may no longer hold quite the same way. Since an anti-defection law penalizes party exit *ex ante*, political parties enter at the legislature not only with an internally defined level of cohesion, which arises from the party's internal norms, practices and tradition, but also in a state of being institutionally and externally predisciplined by the provisions of the anti-defection law. In other words, the anti-defection law automatically sanctions party unity without having the party leadership intervene and apply disciplinary measures of their own against their dissenting, or potentially dissenting, legislators.

Anti-Defection Laws and The Regulation of Political Parties: The Scholarly Context

The extant study of anti-defection laws grows out of the burgeoning literature on party laws.[26] It has been noted that the number of states, mostly new or fragile democracies, that are adopting such measures is steadily increasing.[27] However, apart from a few studies on individual cases such as South Africa,[28] India, Israel,[29] and Papua New Guinea,[30] as well as a couple of broader regional[31] and global[32] overviews, scholarship on the politics of anti-defection laws remains sparse at best.

The regulation of political parties by state law has had a long history in Western democracies. However, until recently such regulation was mostly indirect in nature. As such, party law used to be understood as "the total body of law that affects political parties,"[33] including electoral law and political finance legislation but also court decisions and administrative rulings.[34] As the modern state has increased its regulatory presence in the life of political parties,[35] a new type of party law defined as "legislation specifically designed to regulate the life of party organizations"[36] has emerged. Accordingly, scholars also started to devote increasing attention to the politics of these direct party laws. However, this literature remains relatively small.[37]

The purpose of party laws tends to vary across different types of political regimes: authoritarian regimes may use party laws to limit political competition; new democracies may adopt them to contain the rise of anti-democratic tendencies, specifically anti-democratic parties,[38] while stable democracies resort to the use of party laws either to safeguard the democratic fundamentals of political parties,[39] reflecting the legacy of historical concern with earlier instances of democratic breakdown (e.g., Austria, Germany), or to create the framework for the public financing and subsidy of political parties.[40]

Janda (2005) notes that one of the key areas where party law differs significantly in old and new democracies is the regulation of party switching and defections.[41] In the former, such regulation is normally left to the political parties themselves. In the latter, however, since the "stateness of the party" in general is much more pervasive, it is not surprising to find that the state plays a stronger role in regulating party cohesion and discipline. In support of this claim, Janda finds that only 14 percent of the forty-one states that report laws, constitutional or not, against party defections and switching were established democracies, while 24 percent were new democracies, the rest being semi- or nondemocratic regimes.[42] Miskin also points out that "dictatorships and fragile democracies"[43] use anti-defection measures more often than established democracies, while Booysen argues that the institutionalization of the party system and the age of democracy can account well for the presence of anti-defection laws, both constitutional and not.[44] According to Miskin, advanced democracies that suffer from high rates of party defection, such as France and Italy, are more likely to use party statues rather than formal laws as a way to keep legislators in check.[45] However, instances of such practice are also reported from new democracies, such as Spain.[46] In what remains the single most comprehensive cross-national overview of anti-defection laws, Malhotra reports that the use of anti-defection laws tends to be particularly common amongst the member states of the British Commonwealth.[47]

A particularly significant area of the growing literature on party laws is the study of the constitutionalization of political parties, an increasingly prevalent practice in newer democracies around the world. The constitutional recognition of political parties entails three principal forms: (1) the definition of democracy in terms of political parties; (2) the definition of key political institutions in terms of political parties; and (3) the constitutional prescription or prohibition of particular "activities or organizational characteristics" of political parties.[48] This phenomenon started in Europe and Latin America during the Second Wave of global democratization, after the Second World,[49] and has continued in Eastern and Southern Europe in the Third Wave.[50] Biezen and Kopecky note that while all but one of the thirty-three Third Wave democracies of Eastern Europe, Latin America, and Africa have given political parties some form of constitutional recognition (the exception being Latvia), only about half of the established democracies have done so.[51] Clearly, significant differences exist across new and old democracies with respect to the patterns of party law in general, and the constitutionalization of political parties in particular. With regard to anti-defection and anti-switching laws, Janda finds that most states that constitutionalize such measures can be found in the developing world. His list of examples includes Belize, Namibia, Nepal, Nigeria, Seychelles, Sierra Leone, Singapore, and Zimbabwe.[52]

Anti-Defection Laws in National Constitutions: A Global Overview

There are currently forty national constitutions around the world that include some form of an anti-defection provision.[53] Table 1.1 provides an overview of the distribution of the forty states according to the following categories: region, Commonwealth status, democracy status in 1973 and in 2015, and type of electoral system. The table leads to a number of important observations. First, the largest concentration of states with constitutionally enshrined anti-defection laws is found in Africa (23), followed by Asia (10). Second, of the forty states, twenty-five have, or had, membership in the Commonwealth of Nations.[54] Third, only seven states had a free political system at the onset of the Third Wave of democratization, in 1973, and of these only four remained a free polity in 2015: India, Israel, Guyana, and Trinidad and Tobago. Finally, in terms of the type of their electoral system, as of 2015, constitutionalized anti-defection laws were equally common among states that used either list-proportional representation (14) or the first-past-the-post (14) electoral rules.

The regional distribution of the cases shows a complete absence of Western Europe, save for Portugal, and North America, two regions that have had the greatest concentration of stable and enduring democracies in the world. A number of studies have shown that the development of representative government in Europe has been coterminous with the gradual disappearance of the imperative mandate and other forms of restrictions on deputies' freedom of action.[55] This European norm was summarized in the 1990 Copenhagen Document of the Conference on Security and Cooperation in Europe, which stated that

> To ensure that the will of the people serves as the basis of authority of government, the participating States will . . . ensure

Table 1.1. States with Constitutionalized Anti-defection Laws

State	Region	Commonwealth	Freedom in 1973	Freedom in 2015	Electoral system
Angola	Africa	No	NA	NF	LIST PR
Antigua and Barbuda	Caribbean	Yes	NA	F	FPTP
Bangladesh	Asia	Yes	PF	PF	FPTP
Belize	Americas	Yes	NA	F	LIST PR
Bhutan	Asia	No	PF	PF	LIST PR
Burkina Faso	Africa	No	PF	PF	LIST PR
Cape Verde	Africa	No	NA	F	LIST PR
Congo-Brazzaville	Africa	No	NF	NF	FPTP TW
DRC	Africa	No	NF	NF	MIXED
Fiji	Asia	Yes	F	PF	LIST PR
Gabon	Africa	No	NF	NF	FPTP
Gambia	Africa	Yes (former)	F	NF	FPTP
Ghana	Africa	Yes	NF	F	FPTP
Guyana	Americas	Yes	F	F	LIST PR
India	Asia	Yes	F	F	FPTP
Israel	Middle East	No	F	F	LIST PR
Kenya	Africa	Yes	PF	PF	FPTP
Malawi	Africa	Yes	NF	PF	FPTP
Mozambique	Africa	Yes	NA	PF	LIST PR
Namibia	Africa	Yes	NF	F	LIST PR
Nepal	Asia	No	NF	PF	MIXED
Niger	Africa	No	NF	PF	MIXED
Nigeria	Africa	Yes	PF	PF	FPTP
Pakistan	Asia	Yes	PF	PF	MIXED
Panama	Americas	No	NF	F	MIXED
Papua New Guinea	Asia	Yes	NA	PF	AV
Portugal	Europe	No	NF	F	LIST PR

State	Region	Commonwealth	Freedom in 1973	Freedom in 2015	Electoral system
Rwanda	Africa	Yes	NF	NF	LIST PR
Senegal	Africa	No	NF	F	MIXED
Seychelles	Africa	Yes	NA	PF	FPTP
Sierra Leone	Africa	Yes	PF	PF	FPTP
Singapore	Asia	Yes	PF	PF	MIXED
South Africa	Africa	Yes	NF	F	LIST PR
Sri Lanka	Asia	Yes	F	PF	LIST PR
Tanzania	Africa	Yes	NF	PF	MIXED
Thailand	Asia	No	NF	NF	MIXED
Trinidad and Tobago	Caribbean	Yes	F	F	FPTP
Uganda	Africa	Yes	NF	NF	FPTP
Zambia	Africa	Yes	PF	PF	FPTP TW
Zimbabwe	Africa	Yes (former)	NF	NF	FPTP

Notes: Freedom scores are obtained from the historical data provided by Freedom House. Electoral system data are obtained from ACE: The Electoral Knowledge Network (http://aceproject.org/epic-en/CDTable?question=ES005) accessed on October 7, 2015. Information about present Commonwealth membership is available at http://thecommonwealth.org/member-countries accessed on October 7, 2015. Abbreviations: F = free polity; PF = party-free polity; NF = not free polity; FPTP = first past the post; AV = alternative vote; TW = two round.

that candidates who obtain the necessary number of votes required by law and duly installed in office and are permitted to *remain in office until their term expires* or is otherwise brought to an end in a manner that is regulate by law in conformity with democratic parliamentary and constitutional procedures.[56]

Similarly, the European Commission of Democracy through Law (Venice Commission) also emphasized this same point when it rendered its opinion on the Ukrainian anti-defection legislation:

Without underestimating the importance of parliamentary groups for a stable and fruitful work, membership of a

parliamentary group or bloc does not have the same status as
that of deputy elected by the people. This distinction is decisive for a parliament representing the people where deputies
comply with their conditions and oath.[57]

The report goes on to emphasize that the practice of representative democracy in the contemporary European legal space is normatively opposed to
any legal restriction on the mandate of the individual deputies in parliament. Instead of legal measures, political parties have used internal means
to keep their parliamentarians loyal.[58] The almost complete absence of
durable democracies among the forty states reinforces the same point. Of
the four states that had a free polity at the start of the Third Wave, two
had only recently become independent polities: Guyana gained independence in 1966 and Trinidad and Tobago in 1962. Therefore, India and
Israel are the only two longer-lasting democracies where anti-defection
measures have become legislated and constitutionalized.

The numbers in table 1.1 also suggest a strong Commonwealth connection: almost half of the fifty-three-member Commonwealth members
have a constitutional anti-defection law. This relationship is not surprising given that almost all members of the Commonwealth were former
British colonies whose institutional design was significantly informed by
the formal practices and structures of Westminster parliamentary democracy. Since Westminster democracy rests on strong party government,
it is understandable that anti-defection laws would be implemented in
order to make and keep parties "parliamentary fit" in the more recently
democratizing states of the Commonwealth. It is important to mention
here that New Zealand, another well-established Westminster democracy
with an anti-defection law, is not indicated in table 1.1 because of the
absence of a formal written constitution. However, given the significance
of the case, it will be discussed in detail in chapter 8.

Finally, the type of electoral system does not seem to be related
to the absence or presence of anti-defection laws. This is a surprising
and counter-intuitive finding because one might expect greater preponderance of anti-defection clauses in states with list-proportional electoral
rules where the design of the electoral system already makes parties
more central to the electoral process than individual candidates. Rampant
defections may severely distort the outcome of the elections and bring
about a parliamentary composition that is disconnected from the voters'
mandate. As such, one might have also expected that parliaments with

candidate-based electoral systems would legislate against defections less frequently because legislators in such states can always claim to represent either the changing political mood of their particular constituency or the growing distance between the political preferences between their party and their constituents. However, this does not seem to be the case.

There is considerable cross-national variation in the content and severity of these laws. With the sole exception of Israel, constitutional anti-defection clauses punish defectors by requiring them to give up their seat in the national legislature.[59] In all of the remaining thirty-nine cases, the constitution calls for the defector's loss of current parliamentary mandate. Anti-defection provisions also vary in terms of how they distinguish and deal with defections, depending on the reason for their occurrence. In almost half of the cases the constitution penalizes only voluntary resignation, while in approximately the same number of instances the constitution also penalizes defection caused by the deputy's expulsion from the party. In the case of India, the initial version of the 1985 constitutional amendment bill covered cases of expulsion; however, it was eventually dropped from the final version passed by both houses of parliament.[60] Where expulsion is treated as defection, constitutions often impose strict conditions that parties must abide by.[61] In most cases where the constitution imposes a penalty for defection, deputies can still exercise their right to a free vote, which means they can vote against their party line without incurring a legal penalty.[62]

Defections in Israel: Kalanterism, Trustees, and Delegates

According to the website of the Israeli legislature, the Knesset, *kalanterism* is

> the phenomenon of politicians changing political parties in return for benefits. This term was named after the politician, Rahamim Kalanter, who was elected in 1955 to the Jerusalem Local Council as a representative of the National Religious Party. The NRP was a member of the coalition on the Council. After the NRP left the coalition, Rahamim Kalanter remained in the coalition as an independent in exchange for the appointment as deputy mayor in charge of religious affairs and sanitation.

Although Israel has had no shortage of outstanding political leaders, it is surprising that the only Israeli politician who left behind the legacy of an *-ism* is not one of the giants of the nation's political history but, instead, one of its much-less-known characters, Rahamim Kalanter, who was a local politician in Jerusalem serving one short term in the city's municipal council in the early 1950s. Yet, his name and legacy have been memorialized in the term *kalanterism*, a pejorative marker of political opportunism.

Conceptually, *kalanterism* stands for the Israeli version and manifestation of office-seeking parliamentary party switching. The very fact that term would find its way onto the webpage of the national legislature suggests and proves its importance and significance. Although historically the number of Knesset members who have remained loyal to their party groups far exceeds the number of those who defected from the party that got them elected in the first place, *kalanterism* has nonetheless played an important role in the nation's political life, not by virtue of their frequency but rather by virtue of the major political changes that they brought about or, alternatively, succeeded to prevent. Some of the major decisions that depended on defectors included the establishment of the campus of the Hebrew Union College in the nation's capital; the passage of the Oslo-2 peace agreements; and the unilateral Israeli Disengagement from Gaza in 2005. Indeed, as the succeeding chapters will show, none of these major events and changes would have been possible had some politicians in a particularly pivotal position not changed their political affiliation at a critical moment in time by abandoning their party and either joining another or starting a new formation that would then support and implement new policies in opposition to the defector's original home party.

Of course, not every kind of change in the partisan affiliation of an elected Knesset member falls into the category of *kalanterism*. In fact, the freedom of individual legislators to express their views, opinions, and vote according to what they deem to be the best interest of the electorate is at the heart of what is called the *trustee* model of representative democracy. According to the *trustee* theory of representation, members of parliament ought to be free from constraints on their legislative work so that the interest of no other political group or association, including the legislator's own political parties, would compromise the paramount objective of the parliamentarian's work, which is to represent the collective. As mentioned in the Introduction, this tradition is rooted in eighteenth-century political thought and can be identified in the famous statements by Sir Edmund

Burke as well as the Marquis de Condorcet, who similarly argued that "as a representative of the people, I shall do what I believe best serves their interest. They appointed me to expound my ideas, not theirs; the absolute independence of my opinions is my primary duty towards them,"[63] among others.

In modern Israeli jurisprudence, the trustee model of representation has been most unequivocally supported by former President of the Supreme Court of Israel Justice Aharon Barak, who stated that "a Member of Knesset . . . is not a 'representative' of the party. He is an organ of the State. He undertook to maintain allegiance to the State of Israel . . . He does not undertake to maintain allegiance to his party. . . . Every member of Knesset is a 'representative' of the entire nation."[64] Viewed from the perspective of the trustee model of representation, the right of an elected legislator to change his or her partisan affiliation should not be necessarily seen in pejorative terms since such an act may be in accordance with what the legislator thinks to be in the best interest of the electorate. For instance, radical changes in the ideological makeup or the senior leadership of his political party may prompt the legislator to realize that jumping ship and join another party would better represent the voters' mandate than staying with his original party group.

The trustee model, however, is not the only theory that informs the organization and institution of representative government. Its main alternative is the *delegate* model, which is rooted in the much older tradition of the imperative mandate according to which members of assembly are merely ambassadors of their constituents with very little scope and room left to exercise independent judgment discretion and action. The delegate model is certainly no longer in vogue among contemporary democratic governments and, in fact, a number of national constitutions expressly forbid the practice of an imperative mandate or placing any restriction on the freedom of parliamentary deputies. Yet, when it comes to the question of allowing parliamentarians to change their party groups between two elections, a small number of democratic states have instituted legislation to restrict or forbid or outright forbid it.

A key defining element of *kalanterism* is that the defecting politician receives tangible benefit in exchange for his or her move. Be it a ministerial or deputy ministerial appointment to the national government, or a safe position on the receiving party's candidate list in the next election, some significant bureaucratic appointment, or in the worst and most appalling cases cash and monetary incentives, *kalanterism* is fundamentally about the transfer of an electoral mandate from one party to another in return for a concrete personal benefit to the defecting politician. That some of the aforementioned monumental decisions in Israeli political history would be the result of such defections and the trading of personal benefits and favors certainly provides cause for alarm and concern about the quality of Israeli political culture, the prevailing standards of political morality, and the meaning of public decency and the civic duty of the legislator. At the same time, the history of *kalanterism* also demonstrates and testifies to the remarkable capacity of the Israeli political system to regulate itself by responding to the political, ethical, and moral preferences of the electorate in a flexible and progressive manner.

A Rational Choice Approach to Anti-Defection Laws

The legal regulation of *kalanterism*, and party switching, poses an important theoretical puzzle: why would a critical number of individual legislators agree that it is in their better interest to pass legislation that curtails their own political freedom by imposing costs on party switching? To answer this question, it is helpful to consider the fundamentally conflicting preferences that party leaders and individual legislators in their legislative party groups have with regard to legislators' autonomy. Party leaders are inherently interested in discouraging party switching: they want members of the legislative party group to behave and vote in a coordinated fashion, which in turn allows the leader to bring the party to realize its collective goals so that the party group could become "parliamentary fit." Leaders have at their disposal a range of disciplinary tools to use in order to sanction the behavior of their legislators. These can include both positive incentives such as the promise of appointment to senior party, legislative, or government positions, and negative ones such as denial of such appointments, removal from current offices that the party group controls, and denial of access to the legislative floor and general legislative perks. Of course, the more cohesive a legislative party group is, the stronger the normative and ideational glue that holds members together, the less it will be necessary for party leaders to invoke the application of such disciplinary measures. Furthermore, there are institutional mechanisms, such as Israel's strong party-centered electoral system and a clearly party-centered organization of the legislature, that can help incentivize individual legislators to behave as dependable and loyal partisans. After all, if their re-nomination on a realistic spot of the party's candidate list or the appointment to prestigious legislative committees depend on the will of the party leadership, legislators' voluntary compliance with the leaders' goals can be expected to be the norm.

However, individual legislators may find that the benefit of loyalty may be smaller than the benefit of exiting from the party. For example, intraparty factional feuding may result in the alienation of some legislators from the party leadership making their appointment to legislative and executive offices or their re-nomination to an electable spot on the party list less likely. Alternatively, the party leadership may have made unpopular decision and choices, either in government or in opposition, leading to the party's imminent electoral decline that makes the position of legislators who were ranked lower in the party's candidate list particularly perilous. In other words, legislators may find that the electoral value of the party label that got them elected is less than what it was in the previous election, prompting them to recalculate the expected benefits of loyalty versus switching. The most important political asset that a legislator has vis-à-vis her party leader is the threat of exit. Of course, a defecting legislator will still incur whatever transactions costs there might be for exit; however, the party group will also suffer as the size of the party group shrinks, causing important political loss for the party leader. To protect party unity, leaders must thus ensure that their use of disciplinary sanctions will not cause legislators to conclude that the benefits of belonging to the party group are outweighed by the net benefits of exit.

In short, under regular circumstances, legislators will want to protect their own freedom to switch as much as possible since the credible threat of exit is the ultimate guarantee of their autonomy, while party leaders want to discourage defection as much as possible without invoking disciplinary measures that may be so harsh as to be counterproductive. Under what conditions, however, would legislators agree that it is in their better interest to limit their own freedom to move and change their party label? It is reasonable to expect that legislators' assessment of the value of the exit option will change when defections by *a few* impose significant losses and costs on the loyal *many*. In other words, when defections constitute a collective action problem, there can emerge a growing number of legislators who realize the need for a solution that can correct it. An obvious situation of this kind is when defections lead to government termination and government instability.[65]

When defections effect changes in government, all loyal legislators suffer losing the benefits that being part of the government or the government coalition provides: a few defectors realize immediate office gains by bringing a new government to power, while the loyal many pay the price of losing office. Similarly, defectors can frustrate their parties' plan to unseat the current government and replace it with an alternative, or move to new elections where they expect to gain increased votes and seats, by exiting and saving the incumbent in office. Defectors can also increase the cost of incumbency without the formal termination of the government if they extract a high price for their return to the government fold. Defecting legislators, who bring down or hold a government to ransom, essentially free-ride and frustrate the delivery of the common good of government stability. The above scenarios depict situations in which existing party-level sanctions and disciplinary mechanisms do not constitute sufficiently strong deterrents against defections. Party leaders and their loyal legislators thus require another collective, credible, and enforceable mechanism to ensure that the defecting "few" will not impose the loss of office on the loyal "many." The adoption of legally enforceable rules against party exit, in the form of an anti-defection law, is precisely such a solution to protect parties against the harmful effects of free-riding.

Electoral accountability provides an additional important reason why legislators may move collectively to pass an anti-defection law. Legislators who change their party labels midterm must always consider the electoral consequences of their own action, which can vary depending on the electoral system and the timing of the switch. However, when defections interfere with the dynamics of government termination and formation, there is a far more severe consequence for electoral accountability that legislators must reckon with. Under the Israeli electoral system of proportional representation, this argument holds special validity because Israeli voters explicitly delegate political parties to form governments on the basis of the number of seats they won in the election and the reconcilability of their policy programs and platforms with ideological programs and platforms. Legislative defections, no matter how widespread, undermine this chain of delegation because they alter the composition of the legislature against the will of the electorate. As long as there are no collective power- or policy-related consequences of such defections, their electoral costs will be limited to the legislators involved. However, once defections lead to changes in government, the voters' mandate will be severely disconnected from the legislative balance of power, the governments, and the policies they produce. If the electorate finds such developments distasteful or unacceptable and in breach of popular representation, legislators will then find it in their interest to pass anti-defection legislation that responds to such public demand.

Once adopted, an anti-defection law is subject to legislative changes and amendment, like any other piece of legislation. Of course, in those states where such a law is constitutionalized, they should be more difficult to amend. But, as we shall see in chapter 2, the key provisions of the Israeli anti-defection law were contained in the Basic Law: The Knesset—which should have given it a special status; the absence of a formal constitution with an entrenchment clause in Israel rendered the anti-defection law liable to relatively easy changes at the hands of the governing majority. Indeed, the history of the subsequent changes to Israel's anti-defection law will reveal that this was precisely the case on every occasion when the incumbent government found itself in need to lure party switchers from the ranks of the opposition or to prevent some of its members from leaving.

Conclusion

Most contemporary democracies do not resort to an institutional regulation of legislative party stability. In Israel, however, the national legislature ended up passing an anti-defection law despite the fact that the trustee model of representation has become the established norm in the political system of the states. As such, the Israeli cases offers a fascinating and unique laboratory to study the conditions under which such legislation emerges and the ways in which such legislation interacts with the norm and practice of legislators' political freedoms. The next several chapters provide the historical evidence about the making and the consequences of the anti-defection law on Israeli party government and legislative representation.

Chapter 2

Kalanterism, the "Stinking Trick," and the Evolution of Israel's Anti-Defection Law

This chapter chronicles the evolution of Israel's anti-defection legislation in three sections. The first section focuses on early attempts and arguments made in the Knesset about taking formal measures against defections and party switching. Prior to the episode of the "stinking trick" in 1990, all these efforts had failed and the Knesset maintained its position to respect the freedom of Knesset members to change their party labels. In and of itself, this is a puzzle given that both the electoral system and the Knesset are strongly party-centered institutions. Yet, when it comes to the question of party switching, the Israeli legislature was consistent in refraining to impose any restrictions, let alone penalties, on its members. In the second section, I review the coalition crisis of 1990 that paved the way to the adoption of the anti-defection law the following year as well as the provision of the legislation in detail. In the third section, I discuss changes made to the anti-defection legislation over the years. Although the anti-defection law has remained an important part of the institutional architecture of the Israeli parliamentary system, this seeming continuity conceals its gradual transformed from an efficient institution, which promotes the collective welfare of all members in a community, to redistributive institution, which promotes the welfare of some at the expense of others.[1] While the anti-defection law was supposed to strengthen party unity and restore public confidence in the integrity of Israel's political institutions, it has actually become an instrument in the hands of the governing coalition to manipulate divisions and engineer further defections among the opposition in order to shore up its legislative base of support.

Early Attempts at Regulating Defections in Knesset

The origin of formal deliberations about the need to regulate party switching in the Knesset can be traced to a letter that Shmuel Mikunis, the General Secretary the Communist party (Maki), sent to Yosef Sprinzak, the Speaker of the Constituent Assembly, three weeks after the first legislative elections held on January 25, 1949. In his letter, Mikunis asked the Speaker to annul the mandate of one Eliezer Preminger, a newly minted MK who was elected to the Assembly from the Maki list.[2] Mikunis explained that the Hebrew Communist Party, which Preminger had originally belonged to, merged with Maki shortly before the elections. However, on February 13, the Maki central committee purged all former Hebrew Communists[3] and, therefore, Preminger should be replaced by Emil Habibi, the next candidate on the Maki list and a well-known and active member of the Palestine Communist Party. Sprinzak argued that the Speaker had no authority to change a duly elected member's mandate but decided to refer the matter to the Assembly's Credentials Committee.

The Committee reported back to the Assembly's plenary on February 16 with a clear decision in favor of Preminger's right to take up his seat and start serving his mandate. Rabbi Mordecai Nurok (United Religious Front) reported on the committee's behalf that their task was to determine whether Preminger's election was legal.[4] After having consulted with the Attorney General, Y. Sapiro, and the chair of the Central Elections Committee, David Bar Rav-Hai (Mapai), the committee resolved there was nothing there to cast any doubt on the legality of Preminger's election. Nurok further noted that the committee was not going to be concerned with the internal matters of the Communist Party.

The battle for Preminger's mandate continued over the next several months. The MK himself submitted a request to the newly renamed Knesset Committee on April 4, 1949, seeking formal recognition as a separate parliamentary faction called the Hebrew Communist Party. He argued that since he was duly elected to the Assembly but the party that had nominated him as a candidate no longer recognized his membership either in the party organization or in the Knesset faction, and since three other parties in the Knesset were represented by a single deputy each, he should be allowed to form a new single-MK faction and receive the same benefits and rights as these other three factions.[5] In opposition to this argument, Tawfik Toubi, an MK for Maki, proposed that the Knesset should rather adopt a legal instrument to ensure that no party would suffer a mandate loss as a result of the departure, or expulsion, of an MK from the parliamentary party faction.[6]

The Knesset Committee took up the matter at its meeting on May 31, 1949, and after some discussion it decided once again in Preminger's favor on both counts: it allowed him to form a single-member new Knesset faction to be called the Hebrew Communist Party, and also allowed him to enjoy the same parliamentary rights and privileges as the other single-MK party groups at the time. The final decision notwithstanding, it is worth noting that there were dissenting voices on the committee. In particular, Israel Bar-Yehuda from Mapam argued the Committee should establish a minimum size for the formation of new factions—at least three MKs, in his view. The first stage of the Preminger episode clearly showed that in the absence of any legislative or regulatory guidelines, the Knesset Committee's behavior was in accordance with the free mandate theory. In the absence of issues regarding the legality of the deputy's election, which may bring into question the legality of his mandate, the Committee found no reason to deny Preminger's request to form a new party group. Of course, this decision was predicated on the fact that the Communist Party had actually removed Preminger from the party in the first place. Thus, it was not clear at this point whether the Knesset Committee would have taken a similar position in the deputy's favor had he been the one initiating the process of leaving the party that got him elected.

This challenge would soon present itself before the Committee when Preminger submitted another request to allow him to formally join the parliamentary faction of Mapam (United Workers' Party), the second largest party in the Knesset at the time. Preminger's request followed the decision by the Hebrew Communists to formally dissolve their organization and call upon all of their members to desert the Communist Party and sign up as individual members of Mapam.[7] The dissolution of the Hebrew Communist meant that Preminger would be left without a party to represent in the Knesset, unless he would follow the party's recommendation and join the Knesset faction of Mapam. The Knesset Committee allowed him to do so, although Maki continued to challenge the decision on the grounds that such a move was a clear violation of the Israeli voters' electoral mandate because it effectively transferred one seat from Maki to Mapam.[8]

The event that gave birth to the term *kalanterism*, which came to define amoral and unethical political defections, took place a few years later on August 26, 1956, in the Municipal Council of Jerusalem on the occasion of the incumbent mayor of the capital, Gershon Agron, facing a vote of no-confidence submitted by the orthodox religious bloc, which until recently had been a part of his local governing coalition. The specific issue that prompted the orthodox parties to bolt from Agron's coalition, and their desire to oust him from office, was the issuance of a construction permit to build a local campus of the Hebrew Union College, the foremost institution of higher learning in the American movement of Reform Judaism. Had party unity prevailed, Agron would have lost the vote. However, thanks to the last-minute defection by Rahamim Kalanter from the Mizrachi party, a constituent of the orthodox bloc, the vote failed by a margin of one.[9]

Kalanterism did not remain a singular event but became an important source of political instability in local government. In 1967, Deputy Interior Minister Shlomo-Israel Ben Meir noted that *kalanterism* had caused the expulsion of at least fifteen mayors since 1955; in 1969, MK M. Porush reported to the Knesset that *kalanterism* in local government was becoming uncontrollable: he cited forty-four cases over the past twenty years, with no fewer than sixteen instances since the 1965 elections alone! The recurrence of municipal *kalanterism* forced the Knesset and the national government to look at the issue of how to strengthen both parties and governments in local politics. In the aftermath of the Kalanter case, Justice Minister Pinhas Rosen proposed a solution by decoupling national and local elections and introducing the direct election of the mayors. Although the bill was passed in the first reading, it lapsed at the committee stage and would not return to the Knesset's agenda until February 1964, when Rosen, this time a member of the opposition, submitted a nearly identical piece of draft legislation. Demonstrating still no interest in the formal regulation of *kalanterism*, the government majority easily defeated Rosen's bill.[10]

The Sixth Knesset witnessed a very unusual but important case of defection that occurred in the aftermath of the merger of three left-wing parties to create the Israel Labor Party. In response to this event, the whip of the Independent Liberal Party (ILP) Knesset faction, Yizhar Harari, submitted a motion to the party executive in December 1967 recommending that the ILP should also join the merger of labor parties that was gaining momentum.[11] Although Harari was badly outvoted on this issue within the party, he remained steadfast in advocating for the merger. He argued that the merger was imperative because Alignment was going to try to increase the electoral threshold to 4 percent, as per a proposal floated by Alignment MK Israel Kargman, which in turn would make it extremely difficult for a smaller party such as the ILP to be re-elected to the Knesset. Moreover, Harari also argued that with the end of the Six-Day War, the nature of Israeli politics would change in ways that rendered the differences between the Alignment and the ILP negligible. The party leadership, however, flatly disagreed. Moshe Kol, Minster of Development and Tourism in the government, argued that while it was very important to work together with the Alignment as a coalition partner, the ILP was far more effective as an independent force than it could ever be as part of a large center-left party federation. The question about the future direction of the party was eventually resolved at its convention in May 1968. In the final vote, Harari's motion that the ILP unite with the Alignment was once again defeated, having gained only eight votes in favor among the 600+ delegates.[12] As soon as the convention ended, Harari informed his party caucus as well as the Speaker of the Knesset, Kadish Luz, that he was quitting the ILP and was seeking admission to the Labor party and the Alignment party group.[13]

Compared to previous defections, Harari's switch from the ILP to the newly formed Labor Party had two novel characteristics. The first was that Harari was not only a senior and experienced parliamentarian who had served in all previous Knessets, he was also the leader of his party's parliamentary group at the time: on no previous occasion had a party whip defected. This was indeed an unusual turn of events, although hardly unexpected given Harari's growing alienation from the party leadership on the issue of the merger, since party whips are normally mandated to hold a party group together and disciplined. The second novelty was that Harari crossed the floor directly from one party group to another, whereas on earlier occasions, Knesset members who were leaving their party groups would either become independents or form a new party group before entering an already existing one.

In all other aspects, however, the Harari case followed earlier patterns. Harari's original party, the ILP, demanded that he should resign and return his mandate to the party. The party also sought his removal from the Foreign Affairs and Defense Committee as well as the sub-committee of the Constitution, Law and Justice Committee responsible for the drafting of the Basic Laws. The latter move was particularly ironic because Harari himself had proposed his famous resolution in 1950 to entrust this particular subcommittee with the gradual drafting of what might become the future Israeli constitution. The Labor Party received Harari with open arms, and the party's Knesset faction immediately approved his application to join. Not surprisingly, the Knesset Committee also approved Harari's switch, thus maintaining its traditional position in favor of respecting the independence and freedom of the individual parliamentarian.[14]

Although the number of party switches in the Sixth Knesset was not dramatically different from earlier legislatures, there were three coordinated private member bills submitted to the Knesset with the objective of amending the Basic Law: The Knesset to disallow this practice in the future. The three bills were submitted by Gahal MKs Yosef Shofman and Yosef Tamir, as well as NRP MK Yitzhak Raphael. In response to the bills, Justice Minister Yaacov Shapiro argued that it was wrong to promote legislation that would only result in the creation of "Knesset Marranos"; he maintained the Knesset's prevailing norm that Knesset members were entitled to change their minds over the course of their term in office.[15] He specifically noted that floor-crossing was as old as the Knesset itself and that he was unaware of any country in the world that would legislate against such practice. Whereas the parties that had suffered defection in the recent past supported these private member bills, the Labor Party was joined in its opposition by the Free Center, the Haolam Hazeh, and Cohen-Tsiddon, whose own switch from Gahal was awaiting formal approval by the Knesset Committee at the time.[16]

Yizhar Harari's defection was not a case of opportunistic *kalanterism*. His original home party was already part of the governing coalition, and there was no discussion whatsoever that the ILP would want to exit from it. Further, Harari received no executive compensation for his defection. Although the Labor Party did put Harari on the Alignment candidates list for the 1969 elections, his position was anything but safe and secure: he was placed in the marginal fifty-sixth rank on the election list and was thus the last candidate to be elected.

The issue of regulating parliamentary defection resurfaced on the national political agenda in the aftermath of the historic 1977 general elections, which marked the first time that the plurality of Knesset seats was not won by the Labor/Alignment Party but, instead, by the opposition Likud.

One week after the polls, on May 26, Israeli newspapers reported that the leader of Likud, Menachem Begin had offered the position of Foreign Minister to Moshe Dayan, a veteran of Israeli Labor politics who had served as Minister of Defense in the preceding Labor-led coalition governments since 1967.[17]

Outraged by the defection of one of its most senior leaders, the Labor Party demanded that Dayan ought to relinquish his Knesset mandate and return his seat to the party. Since according to Israeli law a cabinet minister was not required to be a member of the legislature, Dayan would still have been able to serve as a non-partisan Foreign Minister in the new government even he had quit the Knesset. However, neither Dayan nor Begin were interested in this scenario. Ever since the news of his nomination had surfaced, Dayan had consistently stressed he would not return his Knesset mandate until after the new government was formed and invested in office. Similarly, Begin never asked Dayan to give up his legislative mandate, arguably because he had seen no precedent for such a move. The week before the government's investiture vote, on June 14, Dayan formally submitted his request to the Knesset Committee to approve his formation of an independent single-member group.[18] Although the Labor Party was resolved to contest his request, the Knesset Committee eventually approved, and Dayan formally became a single MK faction in the Knesset on July 12, 1977.[19]

The government's investiture vote took place on June 20, 1977, and resulted in a narrow majority victory for Begin, with sixty-three MKs voting in favor and fifty-three against.[20] Given the tight balance between government and opposition, it proved to be extremely important that Dayan had not given up his Knesset seat. Moreover, by forming his independent party group in the Knesset, he allowed Begin not to have to run his nomination by the Likud channels since Begin could argue that every party in the coalition was entitled to nominate its own candidates to the portfolios to which they were allocated.

The Knesset Committee had its initial discussion regarding Dayan's request to secede from the Alignment faction and set himself up as a single MK party group on July 5, 1977.[21] The committee's chairman, Likud MK Yitzhak Berman, informed the other members that Dayan had originally submitted a letter dated June 12 informing the Committee of his decision to leave Alignment and request recognition as a separate single-MK party group. The chair further cited past precedents of MKs who were granted similar recognition as such single-MK groups.[22] Speaking for the Alignment, however, MK Moshe Shahal countered that Dayan's case was *sui generis* and could not be compared to these precedents since his defection was not based on ideological considerations but was, instead, clearly and evidently motivated by becoming a minister in the new government. In other words, this was a pure case of *kalanterism*, which needed to be contained. Another complication regarding Dayan's request concerned its timing. Since his letter was dated June 12, his defection actually preceded the first meeting of the newly elected Knesset, when party groups were technically established and MKs took their oaths. A procedural problem was thus raised in that Dayan was asking to leave a legislative party group not yet formally established in the Ninth Knesset. This, Shahal noted, was also an act without precedent. He further argued that Dayan neither provided any justification for his action nor was he present at the meeting of the Knesset Committee to present his case. Shahal concluded that the Committee should defer its decision until the Alignment faction was consulted on the matter. The Committee agreed, and the matter was taken up again in its next meeting, exactly one week later, on July 12.

Although the Committee ended up granting Dayan his request at the next meeting, drama and tension persisted. To maintain his argument about the singularity of the Dayan case, Shahal provided a detailed list of all earlier requests for splits and defection.[23] In a sudden turn of events, Likud MK Amnon Linn, who had only recently left the Labor Party, procured a message from Dayan in which the Foreign Minister claimed, "I did not resign from the Alignment. I was expelled from it by means of a letter from (former Alignment secretary-general) Meir Zarmi following my agreement to Prime Minister Begin's request to serve the nation in this most crucial hour, considering it to be my duty to serve."[24] Effectively, this note meant that the Committee could now consider the Dayan case as it had all previous instances of expulsions, which meant the protection of the individual MK's mandate. The chairman thus called for a vote, which was roundly boycotted by the Alignment members of the committee, who promptly left the meeting.[25] Later that afternoon, when the Knesset plenary convened for its regular session, Shahal requested the Deputy Speaker, his fellow Alignment MK Shoshana Arbeli-Almozlino, to amend the order of the day and allow him to bring the House Committee's handling of the Dayan case before the plenum.[26] Although the Deputy Speaker eventually ruled against the request, she did so after a heated exchange over the issue between Likud and Alignment MKs. With this, the Dayan affair, the first instance of *kalanterism* in national party politics, was over, with the Knesset Committee once again deciding in favor of the legislator's freedom of movement.

Attempts at *kalanterism* quickly resurfaced in the next Knesset. Following the 1981 elections, Menachem Begin was able to put together another narrow Likud-led coalition government with the support of sixty-one MKs, which was subject to incessant no-confidence motions submitted by the opposition. Although the government successfully defeated the no-confidence motions, it often came very close to losing office.[27] Eventually, the balance appeared to turn in the opposition's favor when two members of Likud's Knesset faction, Amnon Linn and Yitzhak Peretz, announced their defection and crossed over directly to the Alignment on the eve of a vote of no-confidence on May 19, 1982. Given the two MK's past roots in Labor politics, Alignment leader Shimon Peres emphasized that there was "absolutely nothing in the least distasteful about the way the two gentlemen from the Likud decided to leave the coalition. They very simply came back home."[28] In response to Peres's statement, Prime Minister Begin countered that the two MKs were returning home with a considerable dowry, alluding to the concessions that Linn and Peretz were able to extract for their defection—that is, safe spots on the Alignment's candidate list in the next election and assurance that Peretz would be appointed to government at least at the rank of a deputy minister should the Alignment succeed in toppling the incumbent Likud coalition.

Although the defectors' maneuver failed to effect a change in government, it reignited discussion about the need for legislation to control legislative party switching. Yet, in an address to the meeting of the Engineers Club in Tel Aviv on May 22, Minister of Justice Moshe Nissim noted that while it may be necessary to adopt such legislation in the interest of public life, he personally remained in favor of the free mandate theory of representation and pointed out that he "mourn[ed] the day" when the adoption of such a law would become necessary.[29] A former Liberal colleague of Nissim's, Yitzhak Klinghoffer, went further to prepare a draft recommendation for Nissim's attention in which he suggested that mergers, splits, and even individual MK switches must be approved by a majority of the membership of the party group involved.[30] The proposal further sought to strengthen party unity by allowing a faction to expel and terminate the mandate of an MK who disobeyed party discipline. As such, Klinghoffer clearly favored the party mandate view of legislative representation; however, conditions were not yet ripe for its adoption at the time.

On June 15,1987, Alignment MK and future Speaker of the Knesset Shevach Weiss submitted a private member's bill that followed the spirit of the Klinghoffer proposal. Weiss's bill sought to amend the Basic Law: The Knesset stating that an MK who leaves his or her party group is considered to have given up his or her seat in the Knesset.[31] The bill granted exemptions to MKs who would change parties as a result of the formal split between parties that ran together and formed a joint parliamentary party group after the election or if at least three MKs left their faction to form a new party group. By proposing a precise numerical condition under which a defection would be recognized as an allowable party split, Weiss's proposed bill foreshadowed the logic of the anti-defection bill that would be adopted four years later. The bill further stipulated that a Knesset faction should have the right to declare one of its MKs a defector if such MK voted against the party line without prior permission to do so at least five times. Had it been passed, the bill would have made Israel the first democracy in the Western world to adopt a draconian anti-defection law putting an end to the free mandate of Israeli lawmakers. At the same time, the bill would also have increased the cost of defection so severely that it might very well have prevented the "stinking trick" and the political crises that followed it. In any event, the bill was not supported even by Weiss's party and lapsed on the order sheet of the Knesset without making it even to a preliminary reading.

The "Stinking Trick" and the Adoption of the Anti-Defection Law of 1991

The series of defections that rocked the Israeli political establishment to such an extent that the Knesset was eventually compelled to legislate against *kalanterism* occurred in association with the "stinking trick," a pact between Alignment and Shas to bring down and replace Yitzhak Shamir's National Unity government with a left-religious coalition in the Twelfth Knesset.[32] The first defections were suffered by Likud and Shas on the eve of the no-confidence vote that the Alignment submitted against the government on March 15, 1990. On the very day of the vote, the Knesset Committee formally recognized the formation of a new party, the Party for the Advancement of the Zionist Idea (PAZI), by five dissident Likud MKs: Yitzhak Moda'i, the leader of the group who served as Minister of Economics and Planning in Shamir's government, Pinchas Grupper, Pinchas Goldstein, Yosef Goldberg, and Avraham Sharir.[33] All five defectors were former members of the Liberal Party, which had formally merged with Herut on the eve of the 1988 elections to create the united Likud party.[34] Although PAZI did not formally leave the coalition, their departure from Likud meant that Shamir was no longer in control of the largest party group in the Knesset: the loss of the five members reduced Likud's faction to thirty-five MKs versus the Alignment's thirty-nine, as shown in table 2.1.

The second defection was suffered by Shas, whose leader Yitzhak Haim Peretz left the party in protest against the "stinking trick." After a brief period of sitting as a single-MK, Peretz formed a new party under the name Moriah.[35] Although both PAZI and Peretz had supported the government, the no-confidence motion passed with a margin of sixty to fifty-five, with the five Shas MKs abstaining, and for the first time in Israeli history the incumbent government was voted out of office.[36]

With the government defeated, President Chaim Herzog appointed Shimon Peres, the leader of the opposition Alignment, to form a new government within the next three weeks. Although Peres initially succeeded to enter into a coalition agreement with the ultra-orthodox Aguda party, two of the latter's MKs (Avraham Verdiger and Eliezer Mizrachi) dissented

Table 2.1. The Results of the Twelfth Knesset Elections

Name of list	Number of valid votes	% of total votes	Number of seats
Likud	709,305	31.1	40
Alignment	685,363	30.0	39
Shas	107,709	4.7	6
Agudat Yisrael	102,714	4.5	5
Ratz	97,513	4.3	5
National Religious Party	89,720	3.9	5
Hadash	84,032	3.7	4
Tehiya	70,730	3.1	3
Mapam	56,345	2.5	3
Tzomet	45,489	2.0	2
Moledet	44,174	1.9	2
Shinui	39,538	1.7	2
Degel Hatorah	34,279	1.5	2
Progressive List for Peace (PLP)	33,695	1.5	1
Arab Democratic Party (ADP)	27,012	1.2	1

Source: Knesset website. https://knesset.gov.il/description/eng/eng_mimshal_res12.htm

and publicly indicated their preference for the continuity of a Likud-led government.[37] Simultaneously, Peres opened negotiations with PAZI, which could provide him a cushion in case of an Aguda split. Although PAZI would not formally commit to supporting a government led by Peres, the Prime Minister designate was able to secure the defection of A. Sharir's who went on to explain his reasons for changing sides in an open letter published in a number of Israeli newspapers on April 8. Assuming a united Aguda, Sharir's defection gave Shimon Peres a narrow majority of sixty-one MKs and, therefore, he requested the Speaker of the Knesset, Dov Shilansky, to convene a special session for the morning of April 11, 1990, in order to call a vote of investiture for his new government. However, the vote did not take place: two hours prior to the scheduled start of the session, the news broke that Verdiger was resigning his seat in the Knesset[38] and that Mizrachi was formally splitting from Aguda to form his new political party, Geulat Yisrael. With the defection of these two Aguda MKs, Sharir was no longer pivotal to Peres's coalition, which was reduced to fifty-nine MKs. Since a reasonable chance remained that the four remaining PAZI members might change sides and support Labor, Peres decided that he would request President Herzog to grant him a fifteen-day extension to form a government.

During the next two weeks, PAZI pursued a delicate game of playing the two sides, Labor and Likud, against each other in an effort to get the best deal possible. However, given the prevailing balance of parliamentary arithmetic, the four-MK-strong PAZI could provide only a Labor—but not Likud-led coalition with a parliamentary majority. For the latter to happen, Shamir needed to find and enlist the defection of two more MKs, which he eventually succeeded to do by bringing Sharir back to Likud and having Efraim Gur, a first-time Alignment MK, leave his party. With the support of these two defectors, Likud was in a position to bring PAZI into its coalition, which now reached the size of a parliamentary majority.

On April 26, Peres returned his mandate to President Herzog, who in turn asked Shamir to try to form a government. A little less than two months later, the Knesset voted into office Shamir's second coalition government with a bare majority of sixty-two votes in favor. Shamir had to pay a high price to win back his position as Prime Minister. In order to secure Efraim Gur's pivotal support, Shamir appointed him Deputy Minister of Communications; he further appointed Aguda rebel Eliezer Mizrachi as Deputy Minister of Health. Among the PAZI members, Moda'i received his coveted Finance portfolio, and Pinhas Goldstein became

Deputy Minister of Transportation. Two other former members of PAZI, Sharir and Goldberg,[39] were promised safe seats on the next Likud election list; however, these promises were eventually reneged on, and neither politician ended up contesting the Thirteenth Knesset election. Yitzhak Peretz, the former leader of Shas, who remained loyal to the Shamir government and did not partake in the conspiracy of his co-partisans with the Labor Party, was reappointed to the new government as Minister of Immigration and Absorption.

Although Likud returned to the helm of a new coalition government, the party suffered severe internal discord during the process of its renegotiating and rebuilding. A long line of prominent Likud politicians went on public record to express their disapproval of forming a government that rewarded defections.[40] Former members of the Liberal Party who did not join Moda'i's breakaway PAZI faction were especially adamant that the Moda'i group should not be offered the concessions they demanded.[41] It was thus unsurprising that the initiative to pass legislation to mete out harsh sanctions on future defectors came from one such former Liberal politician, Uriel Lynn.[42]

No sooner had Shamir's second coalition government been sworn in, the Knesset's Constitution, Law and Justice Committee proposed a bill, initially submitted as a private member bill by the committee's chairman Uriel Lynn (Likud), titled "Law for the Prevention of Perfidy (Publicly Elected Persons)." The key provisions in the draft legislation clarified that Lynn specifically sought to ensure that the kinds of perfidious practices in which his former Liberal colleagues had engaged would never arise in the future or, at least, would carry severe sanctions.[43] The sanctions and restrictions that Lynn's bill proposed were (1) an MK who quit his or her party group could not run in the next election; (2) such an MK could not join any other party group in the current Knesset; (3) such an MK could not receive party funding allocation; (4) MKs could not be promised safe seats on election lists; (5) agreements to place an MK on a particular party's election list would be legal only if carried out within ninety days before the next election; (6) there could be no financial or other guarantees to back up promises about appointing or not dismissing particular individuals; and (7) coalition agreements related to the termination or establishment of a government must be submitted to the Speaker of the Knesset within three days of their conclusion and must be brought to the knowledge of all MKs. In addition, the draft legislation also provided that only the person designated by the president to form a government could make promises to appoint ministers and deputy ministers, and that no agreement that promises not to dismiss particular ministers or deputy ministers would be valid if such dismissal were authorized by law. Finally, the Lynn bill also stipulated that none of the sanctions mentioned above apply if the faction breaks up entirely.

The final reading of the bill took place on February 12, 1991, and passed with an overwhelming majority of eighty-two MKs in support, two against, and two abstaining; clearly, the vote indicated a strong consensus in support of regulating defections in the future.[44] The final text of the law departed somewhat from the original bill and was eventually adopted as a package of four legislative amendments to the Basic Law: The Knesset, the Knesset Election Law, the Basic Law: The Government, and the Party Funding Law.[45] The first of these consisted of amending the Basic Law: The Knesset and spelled out a restriction to the candidacy requirements in future Knesset elections. It stated that a Knesset member who leaves his or her faction but does not quit the Knesset soon thereafter cannot be included in the candidate list for the following election of any party represented in the current Knesset. In other words, a disloyal MK would have to join or form a new electoral party if he or she wished to run in the next election. The amendment spoke clearly about individual legislators and explicitly exempted party splits from its provision as long as they followed certain specific conditions. The amendment to the Basic Law: The Knesset further specified that voting against the party line on a question of confidence, or no-confidence, in the government was to be regarded as quitting the party if and only if the MK in question received any direct or indirect benefit or compensation for doing so. As such, the Basic Law continued to allow sincere—that is, non-instrumental—breach of party discipline so long as it could not be demonstrated that a transfer of benefits took place.

The second part of the anti-defection law introduced amendments to the Knesset election law by identifying the precise conditions under which a party split would be recognized as an ideological split, and in which cases; the MKs participating in such splits would thus not incur the sanctions mentioned above. The central provision of these amendments is the one-third rule stating that for a party split to be recognized as such it must involve the secession of at least a third of the total number of the faction's elected members and in any case a minimum of two members. In the case of a faction of six MKs, it would mean a minimum of two MKs leaving together. In the case of an electoral alliance, or a candidate list jointly submitted by multiple parties, factions or organizations, the constituent members could split if they had provided written notice to the central election commission (at the time of submitting their candidate list for the election) of their agreement that marked which parties, factions, or organizations the different candidates belonged to. The amendment designated the Knesset Committee to be in charge of determining splits and establishing the new allocation of seats among party groups as a result of such changes in their ranks. However, the decision of the committee could be appealed and brought before the Jerusalem District Court. If the Knesset Committee determined that a Knesset member had defected from his or her faction, said member could join any other faction during the remainder of the Knesset's term. If a question arose after a split as to which of the new factions would be entitled to represent the original faction, the decision must be based on which of the new parties had the larger number of MKs from the original faction; if these numbers were equal, then the new faction that included the leader of the original factions' Knesset election list was entitled to represent the original group. If a leader has already quit the Knesset, then the MK who was ranked next after the original leader would decide the question, and so on and so forth. Finally, the amended election law forbade the conclusion of agreements and promises with regard to the composition of candidate lists prior to ninety days before the date of the next election.

The third pillar of the anti-defection reform consisted of amending the *Basic Law: The Government* by stipulating that an MK who defected from his or her faction could not be appointed to the government as a minister, or a deputy minister, and that agreements about the allocation of government positions could be carried out only by authorized representatives of factions who were party to the agreement. The amendment further forbade the posting of any direct or indirect monetary or in-kind benefit as a way to guarantee the agreement. The amendment also required that interparty agreements must be made public and transparent; if parties entered into an agreement to present a new government or to seek a no-confidence vote in the current one, then such agreement had to be submitted to the Knesset secretariat within three days of its signing.

The fourth pillar of the anti-defection reform package related to issue of defections to the legislation on party finance. The amendments to the *1973 Party Funding Law* stated that an MK who left his or her faction would not be granted a share of the faction's state-provided funding, a part of which was determined on the basis of the number of Knesset members that a party got elected. Once again, however, recognized splits constituted the exception: according to the new legislation, the factions that resulted from a party split would divide among themselves the amount of state funding that had accrued to the original faction according to the new number of their respective MKs.

The Anti-Defection Law as a Redistributive Institution: Changes and Amendments after 1991

The original anti-defection legislation underwent several changes over the next decades. However, in stark contrast to the dramatic events in the Twelfth Knesset, none of these legislative amendments were actually triggered by a deep political crisis. Quite the contrary, the history of the anti-defection legislation shows that the governing coalition has gained a very strong legal instrument in this legislation to shore up its strategic political need. As such, the stability of the anti-defection law has become extremely vulnerable to the shifting realities of Israeli coalition government. These changes, their key provisions as well as the final vote margin by which it was passed in the Knesset, are summarized table 2.2. The history of the various amendments indicates that governing majorities in the Knesset have frequently altered law to fit their own immediate needs. Thus, it would seem that whereas the anti-defection law may have insulated governments from the negative effects of party instability, the reverse is not true: party unity continues to be vulnerable to the manipulative effects of the governing coalition if and when it is in need of shoring up its legislative support base.

The first amendment occurred soon after the passage of the reform package in the fall of 1994 during the Thirteenth Knesset. In an effort to bolster the legislative base of what had by then become a minority government, Prime Minister Yitzhak Rabin successfully secured the commitment of Yi'ud, a three-member breakaway faction from the opposition Tzomet (Crossroads) party, to join his coalition government. However, while the formation of Yi'ud had satisfied the one-third rule of the recently passed anti-defection law, and as such the split in Tzomet was legal and recognized, the High Court issued a ruling that members of Yi'ud could not be appointed to the government as per the recent change to *Basic Law: The Government*. Although the ruling upset Rabin's agreement with Yi'ud, it also generated a strong pushback from all corners of the political

Table 2.2. Legislative Changes to the Israeli Anti-Defection Law (ADL)

Legislation	Key provision	Final vote
Original ADL, 1992	• One-third rule • Pre-election exemption	82 vs. 2
Yi'ud law, 1994	• Defectors allowed in government	59 vs. 49
Amendment 31 (Knesset Election Law) February 28, 1996	• Definition of party splits includes at least two MKs who leave their party within 90 days before next election	61 vs. 1
Amendment 31 repealed, December 20, 2000	• Above provision repealed	31 vs. 1
The Edelstein amendment, March 15, 2001	• Splinter parties are eligible for funding only two years from last election	25 vs. 0
The Sa'ar amendment, 2004	• Solo defection allowed	42 vs. 22
Mofaz law, 2009	• Seven MK rule • Splinter parties are eligible for funding after three months from last election	60 vs. 43
Governance law, 2014	• Seven MK rule removed • Two-year limit re-imposed	67 vs. 0

spectrum by lawmakers who regarded the Court to have completely mis-understood the original intent of the anti-defection law. With the Court having ruled against the appointment of the two Yi'ud ministers, the only course left available to Rabin was to muster a Knesset majority and pass yet another amendment to the *Basic Law: The Government*, which would make it explicit that MKs who split from their faction to set up a new one under conditions recognized in the legislation would be exempt from the ban on cabinet appointment. In spite of its negative reaction against the Court's ruling, the opposition came out strongly against the Yi'ud law for its alleged motivation to facilitate the resurrection of *kalanterism*.

The second amendment to the anti-defection framework came via the passage of Amendment 31 to the Knesset Election Law on the eve of the 1996 election.[46] This amendment served the purpose of facilitating pre-electoral switches in the last ninety days before the election. The bill initially introduced by the Constitution, Law and Justice Committee on February 21, 1996, aimed at changing the registration of candidate lists for the Knesset elections as well as regulating the financial contributions that parties may receive. During the committee deliberations, however, rebel Likud MK David Magen—a supporter of senior Likud leader David Levy, who had lost the Likud leadership primary to Benjamin Netanyahu in March 1993—insisted on introducing an additional provision that would allow a minimum of two MKs to secede from his or her party group in the last ninety days before the next election without suffering the consequences of the anti-defection law.[47] Ostensibly, Magen sought this reform in order to pave the way for his own and Levy's departure from Likud, which the governing Labor Party was most favorable toward.

Although the chair of the committee, David Zucker (Meretz), agreed with the proposals, the Likud majority on the committee was able to strike them down. Nonetheless, Magen's proposals were re-inserted in the bill when it came up for its second and third readings, which it successfully passed a week later thanks to the support of the governing coalition, which was all too happy to drive a wedge in the ranks of Likud, the largest opposition party at the time. Indeed, Amendment 31 was tailor-made to facilitate the departure of two Likud MKs, Magen and David Levy, who would proceed to set up their new formation, Gesher (Bridge), for the next election. Unexpectedly, however, Amendment 31 also created the opening for a split in the governing Labor Party that would suffer the exit of two of its MKs on the eve of the next general elections. Although the law was passed without significant opposition—not a single MK voting against it—it clearly did not enjoy the kind of wide support in the Knesset as the initial anti-defection law had.

The next amendment to the anti-defection law was sponsored by Yuli Edelstein (Yisrael Be'aliyah) and passed by the Fifteenth Knesset in a move that once again showed the prevailing interest of the governing coalition. Edelstein's bill came up in response to the defection of two MKs from his own party, Yisrael Be'aliyah (*Israel Rising*), Roman Bronfman and Aleksander Tsinker, at the time of the formation and investiture of Prime Minister Ehud Barak's coalition government after the 1999 elections. The details of this event will be discussed in chapter 4. For now, however, it is important to note that while the departure of the two MKs did not prevent Yisrael Be'aliyah from entering the coalition government, it had two concrete and immediate effects: first, the party incurred financial losses because the two MKs took with themselves their proportionate share of the party's state funding, and, second, the chances that Edelstein would become a minister in the Barak government became hopeless because with two fewer seats under its control Yisrael Be'aliyah became the smallest member of the coalition that could no longer entertain the hope of receiving an additional portfolio.

Initially, Edelstein submitted a private member bill to amend the Basic Law: The Knesset disallowing defections and switches in the first two years after a general election. Evidently the bill sought to prevent the recurrence of a scenario that his party had recently suffered, although he pointed out that his amendment was in no way targeting joint electoral lists where it was clear that the different constituent parties' autonomy should be respected. While the bill enjoyed broad support, Yosef Paritzky of the Shinui (*Change*) party noted that the legislation compromised the freedom of the elected deputy and suggested that, while defections should be allowed, the new legislation should remove financial benefits that accrue to the party switchers.[48] The final version of the bill incorporated this suggestion, and the revised bill was passed on March 6, 2001, as an amendment to the 1973 Party Funding Law with no opposition (although with a very low level of support). The Edelstein amendment denied state funding to splinter parties, even if they otherwise met the requirements of a legal split, within the first two years of the newly elected Knesset. As we shall see in chapter 5, the Edelstein amendment, even in its revised form, proved to be very effective in keeping Knesset party groups together in the first two years after a general election.

The Fifteenth Knesset was also responsible for repealing David Magen's Amendment 31 to the Knesset Election Law. The bill to rescind this legislation was put forth by Prime Minister Ehud Barak's government on December 12, 2000, a day before the candidate registration deadline for the special Prime Ministerial election of 2001. The government argued, correctly, that the legislation was financially damaging to existing political parties because it encouraged candidates who did not get a high enough placement on their party's list to exit. All in all, the government claimed that Amendment 31 encouraged party instability and splitting and wanted the legislation repealed altogether. It was not a coincidence that the day after the government submitted this bill, former Likud MK Uriel Lynn, chief architect of the original anti-defection legislation, published an opinion piece in which he identified this Amendment as one of the main obstacles to continued political reform and in no uncertain terms argued that it should be wiped out.[49] A week later, on December 20, with the unanimous passage of the government bill, the Knesset did so.

The next two changes to the anti-defection law triggered noticeably large opposition in the legislature. The first of these was put forward by Gideon Sa'ar, the chairman of Likud Prime Minister Ariel Sharon's coalition, in response to the imminent merger of the small three MK-strong Am Ehad party group with the largest opposition party, Labor-Meimad in the Sixteenth Knesset. The leader of Am Ehad, former Labor MK and Histadrut chief Amir Peretz, indicated following the 2003 Knesset elections that he was interested in merging his party with Labor. Arguably, Peretz was motivated to advance the merger so he could run for the leadership of Labor, while the Labor Party was interested in increasing the number of its MKs in order to be in a stronger position to enter a national unity coalition with Likud.[50] However, one of the three Am Ehad MKs, David Tal, who had been an MK in the ranks of the orthodox religious Shas party in the previous Knesset, was adamantly opposed to the merger and noted that he would rather either split from Am Ehad and seek to form a single-MK party group in the Knesset or resign from his seat and quit parliament altogether. The first of these possible paths that Tal noted was not feasible under the existing anti-defection legislation according to which a single MK could not legally split from his or her party; if Tal were to do so, he would become a formal defector. On the other hand, his resignation would have created a problem for Amir Peretz, since the next candidate from the party's election list who would have replaced Tal was Adisu Messele, who had also opposed the merger and had actually left the Labor Party earlier after having been sidelined in the party's candidate selection process, vowing never to return.[51] Nonetheless, Peretz proceeded with the merger negotiations and, according to the Dalia Itzik, who represented the Labor Party in these talks, he was hoping to get a ministerial portfolio in case the Labor Party would join Sharon's coalition government down the road.[52]

Evidently, it was not in Prime Minister Ariel Sharon's interest to allow the Labor Party to become stronger from the pending merger. Therefore, in early 2004, his coalition chairman Gideon Sa'ar submitted a private member's bill seeking to amend the Knesset Election Law by allowing a single MK to leave his or her party group if said MK opposed the merger of his or her party group with another.[53] In such a case, the draft bill continued, the Knesset Committee would have to give its simultaneous consent both to the merger and the split. The partisan motivation of this bill was blatant, and tailor-made to facilitate David Tal's exit and to weaken the prospects of the merger. The bill quickly progressed through the legislative process and was passed on the third reading in the Knesset on March 1, 2004. Although Amir Peretz questioned the legitimacy of this legislation, which allowed the creation of a single MK faction, when it took a minimum of two MKs for a party list to be elected to the Knesset under the prevailing electoral threshold, and called the amendment a "dirty trick designed to steal money from his party,"[54] the coalition majority secured its safe passage with forty-two votes in favor and twenty-two against.[55] Chapter 6 will discuss in further detail how and why David Tal ended up joining Prime Minister Sharon's new party, Kadima (*Forward*), which he launched at the end of the Sixteenth Knesset.

The Eighteenth Knesset witnessed two important changes to the anti-defection legislation. Both were part of Likud Prime Minister Benjamin Netanyahu's strategy to divide the opposition Kadima Party, which incidentally won one more seat in the 2009 Knesset election than Likud did. Following the elections Netanyahu explored the possibility of having Kadima join his government in a broad national unity coalition, which was also advocated by Shaul Mofaz, the former leader of Kadima who had narrowly lost his party's leadership primary to Tzipi Livni a few months earlier. However, at the meeting of the Kadima caucus on March 2, 2009, Livni's position prevailed and the party decided to stay in opposition rather than join the Likud-led coalition.[56]

Notwithstanding Kadima's decision, the Netanyahu leadership remained adamant in its pursuit of trying to have several senior Kadima politicians split, form a new party, and enter the coalition in exchange for lucrative ministerial appointments. The first step in this strategy was the passage of what became (in)famously called the Mofaz law, which essentially implemented the provision about amending the rules on party splits in the Likud-Yisrael Beitenu (Israel Our Home) coalition agreement.[57] Proposed as a government bill on June 16, 2009, the new draft legislation set out to establish a new condition for a party split that would specifically make it easier to split a larger political party in the Knesset by stating that a legal split did not have to include more than seven MKs. In other words, a party group of more than twenty-one MKs could legally suffer a split if seven of its MKs were to leave, even though this number would be less than the one-third of the party group required of smaller parties. Prior to the second reading of the Mofaz law, the government inserted an additional clause to amend the party funding law according to which a duly recognized and approved splinter party could qualify for state funding if the split took place after the third month of the start of the Knesset's term, rather than after two years, as legislated by the Edelstein amendment eight years earlier. Both amendments passed with a majority of sixty-three votes in favor and forty-three votes against. Although Shaul Mofaz emphatically denied any interest in taking advantage of the new legal circumstances and splitting the Kadima faction in the Knesset,[58] the Mofaz Law clearly created a new institutional framework that encouraged rather than discouraged party splits in the Knesset.

The most recent change to the anti-defection legislation was the eventual rescinding of the Mofaz law as part of the Governance Legislation that the newly Likud-led coalition introduced and passed in the Nineteenth Knesset on March 11, 2014.[59] The main thrust of the Governance Legislation was to provide institutional pillars to protect the stability of the government. To that end, the draft legislation sought to increase the electoral threshold, introduce the constructive vote of no-confidence as the mechanism by which the opposition could replace the incumbent executive, as well as introduce limitations on the frequency of no-confidence motions. The Governance Law also contained two provisions related to defections and party switching.[60] As David Rotem explained during the second reading of the bill on behalf of the Knesset Constitution, Law and Justice committee, it was sensible to re-introduce measures that made party splitting more difficult at the same time that the Knesset was going to legislate an increase in the electoral threshold. Since a higher threshold incentivizes pre-electoral mergers among smaller parties, it was logical to reinforce the same objective of encouraging the formation of larger parties by further limiting legislative defections and party switches. To that end, the Governance Law proposed to rescind the Mofaz Law and reinstate the applicability of the one-third rule to all political parties, regardless of size; it re-introduced the Edelstein amendment that allowed state funding only to those splinter factions formed in the Knesset after more than two years since the last election; it provided that the exemption under the Sa'ar amendment to allow MKs to split from their parent parties at the time of a merger would apply only if all MKs who opposed the merger would move together to form a new party or join an existing one; and it categorically removed state funding from individual MKs who would defect and form a single-MK party group. Since the opposition announced it would boycott the vote on the entire legislative package, and the coalition parties imposed strict discipline, the Governance Law was passed with a comfortable margin of sixty-seven votes in favor with none against on March 11, 2014.

Conclusion

The adoption of the anti-defection law in 1991 was a clear break in the tradition of Israeli legislative politics, which had previously not tolerated any formal legislative restrictions on the freedom of individual parliamentarians. However, the scandalous events of the "stinking trick" and the blatant parliamentary horse-trading that followed required a credible and meaningful response from the political class. The legislation was an integral part of the broader set of measures that the Knesset took to reform the political system, which also included the direct election of the Prime Minister as well as the passage of the Parties Law. Political parties also responded to the reform spirit of the time as more and more of them adopted democratic and inclusive internal leadership and candidate elections.

Although the original passage of the anti-defection law enjoyed broad support from both government and opposition, the history of its later amendments show that governing majorities remained very interested and motivated to altering the law to fit their own immediate needs. Thus, it would seem that whereas the anti-defection law may have insulated governments from the negative effects of party instability, the reverse is not true: party unity continues to be vulnerable to the manipulative effects of the governing coalition if and when it is in need of shoring up its legislative support base. In this, the anti-defection law also shows the limits of institutional reform in Israel's fundamentally majoritarian parliamentary democracy. The consensus, which marked the adoption of the initial law, clearly indicated that the law was regarded by all parties in the Knesset as highly desirable and necessary for the continued functioning of the system. Indeed, it was not the intent of the initial legislation that any particular party or groups of parties would be privileged over others: the law sought to enhance party unity in a universal and undifferentiated manner, and as such it was an efficient institution. However, this efficiency quickly disappeared and subsequent changes to the law were passed to serve the interests of governing majorities.

Chapter 3

The Growing Incidence
of Party Switching in Israel

One of the most intriguing puzzles about the effects of the Israeli anti-defection law has been its seeming failure to discourage party switching and keep legislative defections at bay. Indeed, several indicators show unequivocally that the incidence of party switching in the Knesset has actually increased rather than decreased since the law was introduced. This chapter seeks to document and provide an explanation for why this may be the case. While the previous chapter showed that the passage of the anti-defection law was part of a broader political reform process in the aftermath of the "stinking trick," this chapter argues that key elements of these political reforms had unintended countervailing effects that actually encouraged legislative defections and party splintering. These specific institutional changes were the adoption of the direct election of the Prime Minister, which triggered a sudden increase in the fragmentation of the party system, and the concurrent adoption of democratic candidate and leadership selection methods by a growing number of political parties. Had the Knesset adopted a stricter anti-defection law in the first place, which would have put a categorical ban on party switching, it is plausible that defections might have been kept at bay effectively. However, given the strong tradition of respect for the free mandate of elected legislators in Israel, there was no, and has not been, any support to pass such a strong anti-defection law. As a result, while the anti-defection law has remained consistent with that tradition insofar as it only made party switching costlier but not forbidden, it failed to exert a strong constraint on legislative party switching precisely when other institutional changes actually incentivized it.

After an empirical review of the changes in the number of cases of party switching over time, I take a closer look at the case study of the disintegration of Likud during the Fourteenth Knesset. To date, this was the single largest case of party switching in the Israeli parliament in terms of the total number MKs who left their original party group as well as the most complex in terms of the diversity of ways in which these exits occurred. Following the 1996 election, the joint electoral list of the Likud, Gesher, and Tzomet parties entered the Fourteenth Knesset and formed a united party group with thirty-two seats. However, by the end of the term of the Knesset, three MKs had left to form a new party called Herut; three MKs had left to re-establish Gesher as an independent party; another three MKs had left to re-establish Tzomet, but one of them quickly jumped over to another small party called Moledet; and four MKs had left to partake in the formation of the new Center Party, although one of these switched again to the centrist Shinui party before the next elections. That all of these changes formally took place in the pre-electoral period showed that while the anti-defection law could not prevent massive party switching, the one-third requirement for a legal split could at least contain and delay a large-scale formal split in the Prime Minister's party.

Party Switching in Numbers

Table 3.1 summarizes the number and types of switches occurring in the Knesset between 1949 and the 2019, a seventy-year period that covers the first twenty Israeli legislatures. The first column of the table identifies the Knessets from the First to the Twentieth; the second column shows the actual number of individual MKs who have switched from their party group at least once during a given Knesset; the total number of switches is listed in the third column under "Switch events." The last two columns distinguish between the two principal types of party switches according to their composition, that is, solo and collective ones. The actual events and the names of the MKs and party groups involved are listed in the appendix.

Table 3.1 clearly shows that collective switches have far exceeded solo switches in the Knesset and that their preponderance has been particularly more frequent following the adoption of the anti-defection law. Prior to the Thirteenth Knesset, there were several legislative terms in

Table 3.1. Party Switching in the Knesset, 1949 to 2010

Knesset	No. of switchers	Switch events	Solo switches	Collective switches
1	3	4	4	0
2	12	18	0	18
3	0	0	0	0
4	0	0	0	0
5	18	18	1	17
6	8	8	5	3
7	3	4	4	0
8	11	16	6	10
9	17	24	15	9
10	6	9	3	6
11	11	13	10	3
12	9	12	7	5
13	12	14	5	9
14	20	23	7	16
15	12	13	4	9
16	24	25	5	20
17	3	6	1	5
18	16	16	2	14
19	0	0	0	0
20	4	4	1	3
Total	**189**	**227**	**84**	**143**

which solo switches were more frequent than collective ones, including the First, the Sixth, the Seventh, the Ninth, the Eleventh, and the Twelfth. In stark contrast, solo switches have never outnumbered collective ones subsequent to the passage of the anti-defection law. It is striking to note that while the total number of party switches has slightly decreased since 1992 (101) than before (126), the average number of switches per Knesset has increased from 10.5 to 12.6. In other words, the adoption of the anti-defection legislation has coincided with an actual increase in the frequency of legislative party switching per legislative term.

Another way of measuring the incidence of defections is to treat the legislative party as the unit of analysis and count the number of parties per Knesset that have suffered defections of any size and magnitude.[1]

Figure 3.1 provides a bar chart to illustrate the changing frequency of such party changes in the Israeli legislature. In the period prior to the adoption of the anti-defection legislation, the average number of Knesset party groups that suffered at least one switch was 2.2, compared to 3.6 in the period following the adoption of the legislation. This comparison, however, does not provide adequate information because the number of parties in the Knesset has varied considerably over time. It is thus preferable to look at how the percentage of parties that suffer exits has varied across the two periods. Once again, the difference is striking: prior to the adoption of the anti-defection legislation almost one-fifth (19.8%) of Knesset parties suffered at least one switch, while during the period following the adoption of the law this increased to almost one-third (31.3%).

Patterns of party exit have also changed with regard to the size of the party that MKs deserted. Figure 3.2 shows the distribution of the parties that suffered at least one switch across the two periods and the size of the legislative party group. The latter is organized in three categories: small parties that had fewer than 10 percent of the Knesset seats, intermediate parties that fall between having 10 to 30 percent of the seats, and large parties that had more than 30 percent of the seats. Despite no change in the number of intermediate parties to suffer a

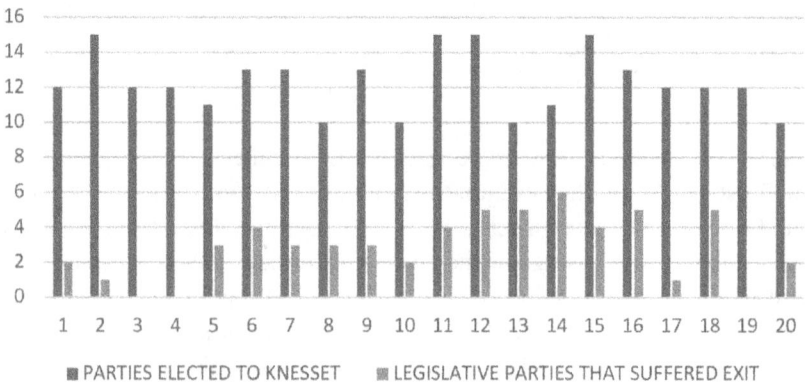

Figure 3.1. Parties that suffered switches in the Knesset 1949 to 2019.

switch, a dramatic drop occurred in the number of large parties to lose at least one MK, along with a corresponding increase in the number of small parties to suffer and exit.

The Anti-Defection Law in the Context of a Changing Israeli Party System

In order to understand why the Israeli anti-defection law and its various amendments have not reduced the overall number of party switches, we need to consider countervailing effects that continue to weaken the cohesion of and encourage the fissiparous tendencies within political parties: the electoral system, the party system, and the growing personalization of Israeli political parties. The Israeli electoral system provides an institutional environment with relatively low barriers of entry, which encourages legislators to experiment with the formation of new political parties that may stand a realistic chance of entering the Knesset and acquiring coalition potential[2] in an already fragmented party system. Three specific features of the electoral system encourage disgruntled legislators to seek to exit rather than stay loyal to the party group: (1) the low threshold of representation; (2) the closed-list nature of the ballot; and (3) a generous state-based funding of political parties. Among Western democracies that use a list-based PR system, Israel continues to stand out as the state with

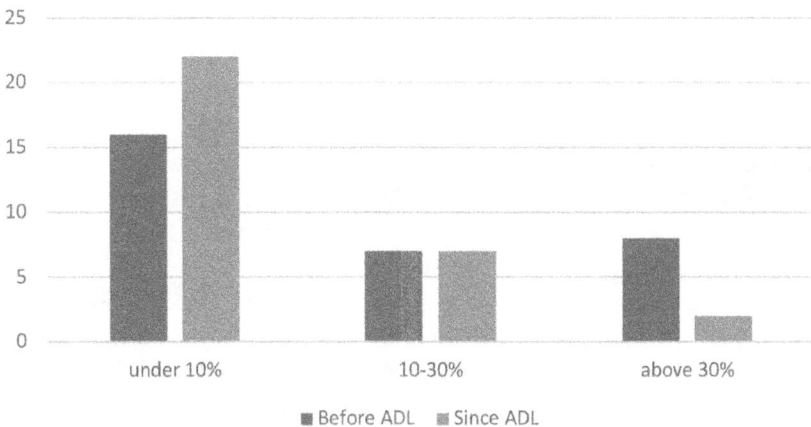

Figure 3.2. Party Switching and Party Size.

one of the lowest electoral threshold. Although the minimum percentage of the popular vote that parties need to win in order to secure representation in the Knesset has increased over time (it was at 1% until 1998, when it was increased to 1.5%, then to 2% in 2006, and to its current level at 3.25%), it remains comparatively quite low, which bodes well for small political parties as well as new political parties that have not yet developed strong roots in the electorate, as it increases their likelihood of winning some seats at least. Since the electoral system does not impose a high barrier on new parties, it fails to act as a deterrent against defections. Similarly, the closed party list also protects defectors because they do not have to face their electorate in a direct contest and defend their decision of abandoning the party they ran for in the previous polls.[3] Finally, Israeli parties receive an important part of their state funding on the basis of a formula that takes into account the number of their Knesset members both in the outgoing and in the newly elected Knesset. Prospective defectors thus have an incentive to exit and set up new parties before the election in order to increase the amount of their share of state subsidies.

The second institutional factor that hinders the effectiveness of the anti-defection law is the steep increase in the level of legislative party system fragmentation. The steep increase that occurred in the effective number of parties in the 1990s—see figure I.2 in the Introduction—can be directly attributed to the consequences of the direct election of the Prime Minister introduced in 1996. As discussed by scholars such as Reuven Hazan and Gideon Rahat, the reform encouraged Israeli voters to engage in split-ticket voting, which benefitted the two large parties in the prime ministerial election but had a very strong positive effect on the vote shares of the small parties in the Knesset election.[4] Figure I.2 also shows that high levels of party system fragmentation have remained in effect long after the direct election of the prime minister was rescinded. In short, precisely at the time when the anti-defection law became operational, another institutional reform shifted the format of the Israeli party system to a new equilibrium, marked by a significantly higher number of effective parties.

An increasingly more fragmented legislative party system can encourage legislative party switching by increasing the number of entry options, that is, the number of other parties that potential defectors can choose to join. However, the sudden proliferation of smaller parties and the concomitant weakening of the large parties in the Knesset also meant that the anti-defection law was making it easier, rather than more difficult, for prospective defectors to meet the conditions of the numerical loophole that allowed them to split from their parties without the penalty: the condition that exempted a collective exit by one-third of a party's MKs from the penalty under the law became much easier to meet when the size of the party groups was becoming smaller. Indeed, figure 3.2 shows precisely such an increase in the number of relatively smaller parties to suffer switches.

The third source that counteracts the effects of the anti-defection law in Israel is the growing personalization of Israeli politics, which in good part has been accelerated by the proliferation of increasingly more inclusive, or democratic, candidate selection processes adopted by several political parties in anticipation of the direct prime ministerial elections.[5] Open and inclusive candidate selection methods ensure a regular supply of political entrepreneurs seeking to cultivate their own political following and agenda and, in the process, making the internal politics of political parties increasingly more competitive. In the aftermath of the adoption of open candidate selection methods, the legislative cohesion of Israeli political parties has suffered a marked decline, as evinced by the steep increase in the number of private members bills, particularly bills geared toward the interests of the constituencies to whom MKs owe their election in the internal party primaries.[6] Moreover, on more than one occasion, disgruntled candidates could use the electoral base that they built up through the party primaries to leverage their position vis-a-vis the party leadership. Thanks to Israel's low-threshold electoral system, they could (a) make a credible threat to run in the election with the potential to enter the Knesset on their own, or (b) spoil and harm the electoral prospects of their original party even if they were to fall below the threshold and cause the wasting of votes that the party could have otherwise had, or (c) bargain their way back and form a joint electoral list with the party they had deserted.

Finally, under the terms of the Parties Law, also adopted in 1992, political parties must be properly registered with the Parties Registry in order to be eligible to participate in the elections as well as to receive state funding to cover their election and current expenses. Often, a new party formed within the ninety-day period before the next election lacks sufficient time to go through the arduous process of party registration. In such cases, they can go to the Party Registry and pick off the "shelf," as it were, a party that had once been registered but has since gone inactive. The shelf party (*miflagat madaf*), an intriguing Israeli invention, effectively provides the organizational skeleton or shell, and importantly the legal right, that allows the new party to become a formal entity. Clearly, the shelf party phenomenon shows yet another way in which existing institutions make it easier rather than more difficult to set up new parties but in the process also contribute to the destabilization of the party system and weaken the bite of the anti-defection law.

A Case Study: The Disintegration of Likud in the Knesset and the Effects of the Anti-Defection Law in the Fourteenth Knesset (1996–99)

In addition to the increase in the number of party switches, the aftermath of the adoption of the anti-defection law was also associated with the single largest volume of exits suffered by any party group in the history of the Knesset. This was the case of Prime Minister Benjamin Netanyahu's Likud faction, which entered the Knesset as a united party group of the three parties that ran a joint list of candidates in the election (Likud, Gesher, and Tzomet) with thirty-two seats. By the end of the term of the Knesset, however, the party group had lost 40 percent of its MKs. The dynamics through which the disintegration of the Prime Minister's party group unfolded provides important insight into the way the effects of the anti-defection law are hindered by the effects of the electoral system, the fragmentation of the party system, and the adoption of internal leadership primaries.

The background to this case study starts with the 1992 Knesset election in which Likud not only suffered a significant electoral loss but for the first time since 1977 the party was not able to participate in the formation of a new government. Outgoing Prime Minister Yitzhak Shamir tendered his resignation from the leadership of the party, paving the way for a leadership primary, the second such election ever held by a major political party in Israel, in March 1993.[7] The initial lineup of contenders for the Likud party leadership included David Levy and Moshe Katsav, both senior members of the party with past legislative and executive experience, relative newcomers Benjamin Netanyahu and Benny Begin, son of former Prime Minister Menachem Begin, and Meir Shetreet. The leadership primary was won by Netanyahu, a still relatively inexperienced parliamentarian who started his legislative service only in 1988, having served as Israel's ambassador to the United Nations the four previous years. As per the recently adopted party rules, the newly elected party chairman was also going to be the Likud candidate for Prime Minister in the first direct elections to that post in 1996.[8]

The runner-up to Netanyahu was David Levy, a former Deputy Prime Minister and Foreign Minister in Shamir's previous government, who refused to rally around the new leadership and, instead, started a long, drawn-out, and bitter feud against Netanyahu who, in turn, marginalized him within the party.[9] For the duration of the Thirteenth Knesset (1992–1996), Levy thus acted effectively as an internal opposition against the party's leadership, never failing to attack and criticize Netanyahu. The last straw in this feud was the decision by the Likud leadership to elect the party's candidate list for the next Knesset at a national rather than local basis by the regional party branches.[10] Levy, who claimed to have strong support in several of the local branches, favored the latter option and feared that a nationwide candidate primary would completely wipe out his supporters from the next Knesset. When he failed to get his way, Levy announced that he would soon leave the party. The announcement of the formation of his new party, Gesher ("Bridge") was expected in June 1995; however, it was postponed until February 1996, when another MK, David Magen, joined him once Amendment 31 was securely in effect.[11] The departure of the two MKs from Likud was formally recognized by the Knesset Committee at its March 11, 1996, meeting after virtually no discussion on the issue.[12]

Levy's strategy worked. Fearing the fragmentation of the rightwing vote in the 1996 election, Likud entered into an electoral agreement with two smaller parties, Gesher and Tzomet, guaranteeing them realistic positions on a joint candidate list. By running together with his former party, Levy secured the spectacular return of five Gesher candidates to the Fourteenth Knesset: himself and David Magen; Maxim Levy, his brother; Michael Kleiner; and Yehuda Lancry. In addition to increasing his new party's Knesset representation from two to five seats, Levy's position was further strengthened in that while Netanyahu won the 1996 prime ministerial election, the joint list of Likud, Gesher, and Tzomet failed to make any electoral gains and actually won fewer seats than did the Labor Party, whose leader, Shimon Peres, Netanyahu had defeated in the prime ministerial contest. In fact, the joint list included only twenty-two Likud MKs and five each from the party's two electoral partners. Therefore, in the new coalition government, which had a combined strength of sixty-six MKs, the Prime Minister's position was extremely weak: his own party had only one-third, and even the combined strength of his party's joint list with Gesher and Tzomet commanded less than half of all the coalition seats. With five MKs under his control, David Levy was in a powerful position to make a credible exit threat—which he eventually realized—and bring the government to the brink of losing its majority.

The first major policy challenge that confronted the Netanyahu government was the re-deployment of Israeli troops from Hebron, located in Area A under the Oslo Agreements, but also home to one of the most ancient Jewish communities, to Area C. Despite fierce opposition from his own party, as well as key coalition partners, Netanyahu was determined to carry out the evacuation of IDF troops. The two most outspoken internal critics of this policy were Likud ministers Benny Begin and Ariel Sharon, but three other ministers (Likud's Lior Livnat, Tzomet's Rafael Eitan, and Yisrael Be'aliyah's Yuli Edelstein) also voted against the move in the cabinet prior to the final vote in the Knesset plenum. When the Hebron Agreement was eventually passed on January 16, 1997, it did so with a very wide margin of parliamentary support (eighty seven to seventeen) but it lacked solid coalition backing. Members of the coalition who either voted against the Agreement or abstained from the vote included the entire NRP faction; Likud MKs Benny Begin, Hayim Dayan, Reuven Rivlin, Uzi Landau, David Re'em, and Ariel Sharon; Moshe Peled from Tzomet; Michael Nudelman and Yuri Shtern from Yisrael Be'aliyah; and Michael Kleiner from Gesher. Most significantly, in the immediate aftermath of the vote, Science Minister Benny Begin quit the Netanyahu government,[13] and the seventeen MKs who did not support the Agreement formed a cross-party alliance called the "Land of Israel Front" under the leadership of Gesher's Michael Kleiner, also a former MK of Likud.[14] Subsequent to the vote on the Hebron protocol, Kleiner petitioned the High Court against the Prime Minister, arguing that Netanyahu had no authority to sign the Hebron Agreement until it was voted on in the Knesset.[15] Although the Court rejected Kleiner's petition, it was extremely unusual for a coalition MK to go so far as to seek judicial intervention against the head of government.

The Prime Minister's relations with Gesher were tested over both budgetary issues and the allocation of responsibilities between Netanyahu and Foreign Minister David Levy in handling the peace process. Having threatened to resign over the latter issue, Levy eventually forced the Prime Minister to issue a memorandum on dividing the tasks between the Prime Ministers' and the Foreign Minister's Offices and to create a new steering committee consisting of Netanyahu, Levy, and Defense Minister Yitzhak Mordechai. On the issue of the budget, a fundamental conflict existed between the Prime Minister's pro-market vision of economic liberalization and Gesher's commitment to social justice and helping the needy, among many of the party's Oriental supporters. In December 1996, the Gesher MKs successfully threatened to exit the coalition unless some of the austere provisions were removed from the budget.[16] Had the government failed to pass the budget, new special elections would have had to be held both to the Knesset and to the office of the Prime Minister.

Notwithstanding the highly public nature of Levy's and Kleiner's confrontation with the Prime Minister, the first casualty of the growing tension between Likud and Gesher was Deputy Finance Minister David Magen, author of Amendment 31 of the Knesset Election Law discussed in the previous chapter, and Gesher's second-in-command. In May 1997, Magen quit his position in the government and called on the Gesher leadership to sever its ties with Likud and follow his lead.[17] He argued that the party should run independently in the next Knesset election, focus on its socioeconomic platform, and position itself at the center as a prospective coalition partner to either Labor or Likud, depending on which party's candidate won the next prime ministerial race. A month after Magen's departure, the Netanyahu government suffered another exit by a senior Likud member of the cabinet, Finance Minister Dan Meridor, over an internal cabinet dispute regarding the management of the Israeli currency' exchange rate.[18]

The departure of the two senior Likud politicians from the cabinet, Begin in January and Meridor in June 1997, indicated deeper structural changes in Likud, as both former ministers came from the line of the so-called Likud princes, with family lineage that intimately tied them to the history of the Herut party, as well as the pre-State Irgun militia.[19] Both Begin and Meridor were widely touted as likely successors to Yitzhak Shamir's leadership of Likud, and had actually formed an alliance in support of the former in the Likud leadership primaries of March 1993. The consolidation of Netanyahu's grip on power within the Likud was sealed with Begin's and Meridor' open resignation from the government and, eventually, from the party itself.

The confrontation between the Prime Minister and his opponents inside the Likud Party reached its climax at the November 1997 party convention. A central issue meant to be decided on at this meeting was the method of choosing the party's candidates in the next Knesset election.

Netanyahu favored a closed candidate selection method, which angered most of his cabinet ministers, who stood to gain from running in candidate nomination primaries where their access to executive office would prove to be an asset. Yet, the convention turned into an unruly revolt among the rank-and-file against the party leadership. In the immediate aftermath of the convention, Likud's mayor of Tel Aviv, Roni Milo, publicly unveiled his plan to unseat Netanyahu by effectively taking Likud from him. To do so, Milo claimed, he would need to line up twelve Likud MKs on his side since, according to the anti-defection legislation, the majority faction would hold onto the party's name, assets, and institutions in case of a split.[20] Milo's calculation was based on the fact that the thirty-two-MK-strong joint list of Likud, Gesher, and Tzomet contained twenty-two Likud MKs. If twelve of them were to join his plot, then not only would the one-third provision of the anti-defection law be satisfied, but the rebel faction would also clearly have a majority on its side. Although the announcement of Milo's plan threatened to encourage a cascading of Likud rebels to come forth, the legal advisor of the Knesset Committee, Zvi Inbar, made a crucial announcement on November 19 that put a temporary stop to internal rebellion and prevented an open split.[21]

Inbar had been asked by Gesher MK Michael Kleiner to re-examine and rule on the question of how many Likud MKs were required to split the party and take its resources with them. Kleiner contended that the Likud-Gesher-Tzomet list was one electoral party for the purposes of electoral administration as well as the allocation of party funds. Since this was the case, noted Kleiner, it should take seventeen MKs, and not twelve, to carry out Milo's plot. Inbar agreed, and with this revised ruling it was now impossible that Milo would have the numbers he had hoped to rally initially.[22] A few days later, Livnat also made peace with Netanyahu and decided to stay on in the cabinet while Milo's supporters proceeded to register the formation of a new centrist political party called Atid ("Future").

The discontent in the rank of both Likud and the coalition came to a boiling point after the Prime Minister had signed the Wye River Agreement in October 1998 without having secured the support of his cabinet and the coalition. The Agreement, which formalized the continuation of the redeployment of Israeli forces from 13 percent of the West Bank as designated by the Oslo Accords, re-ignited the same cleavages within the party, cabinet, and the coalition that had already surfaced at the time of the Hebron vote. When the Prime Minister presented the Wye Agreement to his cabinet, he was able to secure the support of only eight of his ministers, with four voting against and five abstaining.[23] While this was sufficient to secure cabinet ratification, Netanyahu had to rely on the opposition parties to ensure that the Agreement would also pass in the Knesset, which it did with a large margin of seventy-five in favor and nineteen against. The deep divisions within the coalition over the Wye Agreement were manifest in that only a minority of twenty-nine of the sixty-two coalition MKs voted in favor of the government's motion, with the rest either voting against or abstaining.[24] In an effort to mend these divisions, Netanyahu tried to delay the implementation of the newly signed agreement; however, his efforts were to no avail, and the Knesset passed a vote for its early dissolution with new elections to take place on May 17, 1999.[25]

The splintering of Likud in the Fourteenth Knesset was finalized and formalized by the Knesset Committee in the pre-electoral period. The re-establishment of David Levy's Gesher and the establishment of Benny Begin's Herut were uncontroversial since both groups satisfied the requirement for a legal split under Amendment 31. The three MKs who wanted to reconstitute Gesher as an independent party group (David Levy, Maxim Levy, and Yehuda Lancry) insisted the name of their party be removed from the official name of the Likud-Gesher-Tzomet faction, which the Committee also approved.[26] Michael Kleiner, a fourth member of the erstwhile Gesher party did not participate in the re-creation of the party but followed instead Likud MKs Benny Begin and David Reem in setting up Herut.[27]

The most interesting case of new party formation that resulted from the splintering of Likud was that of the Center Party by two groups of MKs from the Likud-Gesher-Tzomet faction (Dan Meridor and Itzhak Mordechai from Likud, David Magen from Gesher, and Eliezer Sandberg from Tzomet) and the Labor Party (Nissim Zvili and Hagai Merom). In addition to these MKs, the Center Party brought together a wide variety of politicians from across the Left–Right divide of the Israeli party spectrum in a genuine attempt to present a centrist alternative to the voters.[28] Formally, the Knesset Committee had to establish the two separate splinter groups according to Amendment 31 as "Israel in the Center A" and "Israel in the Center B" before it would authorize their merger, which completed the formation of the new legislative party group. By this time, the Center Party had also formally registered with the Party Registry, which meant it could obtain the full benefits of public funding as a party with a legislative faction.

With these changes, the disintegration of the Likud-Gesher-Tzomet party group was complete. Prime Minister Netanyahu's job to put together and manage a coalition government under conditions when his own party group did not command the largest number of seats in the Knesset was difficult in the first place. By the time the Fourteenth Knesset was dissolved, the Prime Minister's party had lost both members of his three-party alliance, and his own party was reduced to a mere nineteen seats. The complexity of party switches was further demonstrated by the fact that neither Gesher nor Tzomet remained intact after having split off from the three-party alliance with Likud, and several of their MKs continued to switch parties further.

Conclusion

The central argument of this chapter is that the anti-defection law was hindered in its ability to reduce, or at least contain, party switching by countervailing tendencies that stemmed from other features of the Israeli party and electoral systems. Through the case study of the Likud party in the Fourteenth Knesset, the chapter has shown that the adoption of democratic leadership primaries, which was in response to the direct election of the Prime Minister, intensified intraparty factionalism. Although the anti-defection law, and its careful interpretation by the legal advisor of the Knesset Committee helped Prime Minister Netanyahu contain a large-scale internal revolt, it was only a matter of time before the intense factionalism would tear the party apart. The disintegration of Likud at the end of the term of the Fourteenth Knesset also bears evidence to the important consequences of Amendment 31, which effectively reduced the cost of splitting the party in the last ninety days before the next election. By replacing the one-third rule with a "minimum of two MKs" rule in the pre-electoral period, Amendment 31 reduced the coordination costs involved in organizing a party split. Although this also eliminated the asymmetry that previously made the splitting of larger parties more difficult than that of smaller ones, Amendment 31 severely inflated party switching and made even large parties vulnerable to disintegration by a number of separate uncoordinated splinter groups.

These findings reinforce the proverbial wisdom that institutions matter: politicians evidently made their decisions about whether and when to switch from their parties according to the incentives of the existing rules of the game. Therefore, a full account of both the frequency and the timing of party switching should always be done with full accounting for such institutional effects. Since different institutions may at times give rise to conflicting incentives, they should be carefully discerned in order to get an accurate explanation for the mode and timing of party exit.

Chapter 4

"Acquire a Friend for Yourself!"

The Rise of Collective Defections in the Knesset

On July 17, 1994, the Israeli High Court of Justice issued a show-cause order instructing Prime Minister Yitzhak Rabin's government to explain why it should not refrain from appointing two new ministers to his cabinet: Gonen Segev and Alex Goldfarb of the Yi'ud party.[1] The Court's intervention in the process of government expansion was surprising because it was a purely political issue that would normally pertain to the competence of the legislature. However, much was at stake in this instance not only from a political but also from a legal point of view. Specifically, the central legal question had to do with the correct interpretation of a particular provision of the recently adopted anti-defection legislation: given that Yi'ud was formed as a breakaway faction by three MKs who had been originally elected on the Tzomet party list to the Thirteenth Knesset, were its members allowed to be appointed as ministers to the government or, like other defectors, were they barred? From a political point of view, Prime Minister Rabin was in dire straits to ensure that the former was the case since his coalition government, recently reduced to a parliamentary minority, badly needed to shore up its base of legislative support as it was getting ready to sign Israel's historic peace treaty with the Hashemite Kingdom of Jordan.

During a preliminary hearing, the petitioner, the B'tzedek civic organization, argued that according to the recently adopted anti-defection passage of the Basic Law: The Government, no MK who had left his or her party group could be appointed to the government even if they belonged to a break-away faction that otherwise qualified as a legal split. The petitioner's argument was based on the point that the legislation was specific and explicit about which of the penalties such MKs were exempted from, yet eligibility for appointment to the government was not mentioned. In contrast, the government's attorney, Nili Arad, argued that MKs of such a legal breakaway faction ought to be treated as MKs of any other party group that were elected to the Knesset. Invoking a famous line from chapter 1 of the *Ethics of the Fathers* (*Pirkei Avot*), a foundational text of Jewish ethical literature in the Mishna, a collection of Jewish legal precepts, two members of the judicial panel—Meir Shamgar, the President of the Israeli Supreme Court, and Justice Zvi Tal—noted that the government's position would lend new meaning to what the mishnaic Rabbi Yehoshua ben Prachya meant by saying, "acquire a friend for yourself"! The justices argued that the government's interpretation would incentivize an MK to defect from his or her party and avoid the penalties under the anti-defection law by "acquiring" and dragging their friends and associates along.

Eventually, as we saw in chapter 2, the government reconciled to pass an amendment to the Basic Law: The Knesset, the so-called Yi'ud Law, in order to circumvent the Court's final decision that forbade the Segev's and Goldfarb's appointment to the government. As such, the story of Yi'ud played an extremely important role in the historical and legal evolution of the anti-defection law. However, the story of Yi'ud also exemplified an important and key characteristic of the new pattern of party switching in the Knesset which, as Justices Shamgar and Tal noted, had to do with finding and securing the cooperation of the requisite number of "friends" and associates, one-third of the party group, that would allow a defector to break away from his or her party group with no penalty. As such, the anti-defection not merely incentivized the organization of collective switches but in so doing both inflated the number of MKs exiting and prolonged the internal divisions within a party group.

In chapter 3, we established that the anti-defection law accelerated collective party switches in the Knesset by making the formation of new party groups the single most frequent type of party exit. In this chapter I further argue that the one-third provision of the anti-defection law has made "one-third" an important focal point in the politics of party switching in the Knesset such that not a single instance of a new party formation involved any more, or any fewer, MKs than what was minimally necessary for the split to be legally recognized. This suggests that while the one-third provision may have been instituted as a legal operationalization for what could be considered an ideologically grounded party split, it often created more harm both by incentivizing the creation of new party groups that were extremely unstable and lacked any real sense of cohesion and by undermining the unity of larger parties where finding the "one-third" was more challenging and took longer. Taken together, these effects meant that the anti-defection law actually made several Israeli parties even less "parliamentary fit" than they were in the first place. I explore these processes through the case studies of three party groups that split in the middle of the legislative term: Tzomet in the Thirteenth Knesset, the Pensioners' Party in the Seventeenth Knesset, and the Labor Party Led by Ehud Barak in the Eighteenth Knesset.

Case 1: The Rise and Fall of Yi'ud

Tzomet was a relatively new party in the Israeli party system, having been founded by former IDF Chief of Staff Rafi Eitan ("Raful") in 1983.[2] In the election to the Twelfth Knesset, the party had only two MKs, Raful and Yoash Tziddon, but four years later, in 1992, the party performed remarkably well by winning eight seats, becoming the fourth largest party in the Knesset and, even more importantly, the second largest party in the rightwing opposition. Characteristic of his iron-fisted management of the party's affairs, Raful replaced Tziddon as the party's second-placed candidate with a rookie politician, Gonen Segev, who was also his neighbor in the moshav Tel Adashim.[3] In fact, apart from Eitan, all other members of the Tzomet faction were rookie legislators, which earned the party the popular nickname "Raful and the seven dwarfs," suggesting that the leader was in complete dominance over his peers and the party in general.

During the first year and a half of the Thirteenth Knesset, Gonen Segev made a name for himself for being one of the most outspoken opposition critics of the Rabin government. Some of his charges included the demand that Ambassador Itamar Rabinovitch be dismissed for alleged violations of income tax and foreign currency rules during his posting in the United States[4]—an unsuccessful petition to the High Court of Justice seeking to force the government to present to the Knesset any document it was negotiating over with the PLO before such documents would be signed.[5] In early 1994, however, Segev started to mobilize other Tzomet MKs who were incensed by Raful's alleged mismanagement of party funds.[6] Together with Deputy Speaker Ester Salmovitz and Alex Goldfarb, who respectively occupied the last successful spots on the party's electoral list, Segev demanded to hold the party leader and his secretary, Doron Shmueli, accountable for the proper use of party funds.[7] Apart from concern for the management of the party's affairs, Segev's challenge may have been also triggered by reports that Raful was considering to replace him as the party's second-ranked candidate in the next elections with Doron Shmueli himself. Whatever the exact cause may have been, Segev's attacks against his party's leadership in the Fall of 1993 coincided with Prime Minister Yitzhak Rabin's Labor-led coalition government losing its majority in the Knesset, which gave rise to the speculation that the government might have been behind the mobilization of dissent in the ranks of Tzomet in order to woo defectors who would help it shore up its weakened legislative base. Although Prime Minister Rabin emphatically denied his own involvement in any such overtures, he did not exclude the possibility that some members of his party may have done so.[8]

On February 3, 1994, Israeli newspapers reported that Tzomet had officially split and the three dissidents (Segev, Salmovitz, and Goldfarb) would form a new parliamentary party group under the name Yi'ud.[9] The following day, the Tzomet central committee expelled the three defectors and called on them to resign from the Knesset and return their mandates to the party, which, arguably, they had pledged to do when they accepted to run on the party's Knesset list in 1992. Four days after the announcement of the split, the Knesset Committee met and ruled to accept the formation of Yi'ud as a new parliamentary party whose formation was exempt from the penalties of the anti-defection law because the three MKs accounted for at least one-third of Tzomet's eight mandates.[10] With this decision, Yi'ud became a "parliamentary party without a party organization"; the Party Registrar thus issued a statement that no operating funds would be processed to the new party until it had been officially registered and incorporated as such. The founding assembly of the Yi'ud party organization took place in June 1994, and soon thereafter the party entered into negotiations to join the Labor-led coalition government.[11]

Rabin's invitation for Yi'ud to join the government immediately brought to the surface the deep internal divisions among the three MKs. Whereas Segev and Goldfarb were in principle open to the idea, Salmovitz remained firmly opposed on the grounds that the government's position on the peace and territorial issue fundamentally conflicted with the Tzomet platform on which all three MKs had run.[12] It is impossible to say if Salmovitz's position would have been different if the Prime

Minister had offered all three Yi'ud MKs a ministerial appointment each. What remains known, however, is that Salmovitz's position never changed during the term of the Knesset and she would consistently vote with the opposition on all major bills even though technically her new party belonged to the government.

The formation of the breakaway Yi'ud group created a complicated political and legal situation exposing some of the inherent contradictions and problems in the recently passed anti-defection legislation. At the heart of the legal issue was the question whether any member of Yi'ud was actually allowed under the law to take up ministerial position in the government, while at the heart of the political issue was the complication that only two of the three MKs, Segev and Goldfarb, were interested in switching from being in opposition to joining the government, with the third member, Salmovitz, adamant not to change her ideological position and stay with the rightwing opposition. The rift among the three MKs put Salmovitz in a particularly difficult bind: as a single MK, she was no longer able to change her partisan affiliation in the Knesset and return to Tzomet, which she contemplated to do, without incurring the penalty of the anti-defection law, which required a minimum of two MKs for a legal split. As long as she received no direct benefit for breaking party discipline, she would be able to vote against her two colleagues, who were set on joining the coalition, which essentially meant that she was not going to be able to realize any gains from having left Tzomet in the first place.[13]

The Labor Party signed a coalition agreement with Yi'ud in early July, and Prime Minister Rabin was making preparations to induct Segev and Goldfarb as Ministers of Energy Infrastructure and Deputy Minister of Construction and Housing, respectively. Under Knesset rules, only Segev's appointment as minister required a formal Knesset vote, while Goldfarb could be appointed a deputy minister without such a vote. Both appointments, however, were blocked by the High Court of Justice, which issued a temporary injunction in response to two petitions it received trying to block the appointment of the two Yi'ud ministers.[14] The petitioners argued that the anti-defection legislation explicitly exempted legal party switchers from the penalty of the law in specific enumerated cases such as inclusion of the MK in the candidate list of a party that was represented in the Knesset at the time of the switch or the receipt of party funding provided by the state. With regard to the issue of government appointment, however, or so the argument went, the legislation was silent. The petitioners thus argued that "legal defectors" should not be allowed to join the government because the legislation did not explicitly allow for it, whereas the legislation was explicit regarding all other exemptions. In other words, if the makers of the legislation had wanted to allow "legal defectors" to enter the government, then it would have said so explicitly. The government's counterargument was that once a new legally constituted parliamentary group was formed, there was no reason it should not be treated as any other parliamentary party, including the possibility of entering and existing governments.

In an extremely controversial decision, a panel of five High Court justices ruled on July 25, the same day that the landmark peace treaty between Israel and Jordan was signed in Washington, DC, that Yi'ud was *not* allowed to enter the government because the legislation indeed did not explicitly allow for it.[15] The decision was reached with a narrow three-to-two split on the panel and led to an almost immediate wide-scale criticism in the Knesset from both the government and the opposition sides.[16] Several MKs who had participated in the initial drafting of the anti-defection legislation in the previous Knesset argued that the Court clearly misinterpreted the intent of the law, which was not to sanction legally constituted new factions. The ruling of the Court left the government with two options as far as the entry of Yi'ud into the coalition was concerned. The first was to fast-track legislation that would circumvent the Court's ruling and explicitly authorize members of a new parliamentary party formed as a result of a legal split to take up a ministerial appointment. The second option was to have Segev resign from the Knesset and be inducted as a minister without a Knesset seat. The main drawback of the former option was the time it might take to legislate a new "Yi'ud law," during which the Rabin government may not be able to take its new coalition partner's support for granted. As for the second option, Segev's resignation from the Knesset would have allowed his original party, Tzomet, to nominate another person from the party's last candidate list to the Knesset, which effectively would have reduced the coalition's legislative gain from the Yi'ud defection to a single vote—Goldfarb's.

The government decided to pursue the first option and brought its draft bill to the Knesset Constitution, Law and Justice Committee. In the first instance, the government's version of the draft legislation was torpedoed in the committee by MK Yosef Azran, himself a renegade MK in the Shas party, who managed to get a committee majority to support his amendment that would postpone the application of the new law to the next Knesset. However, once the governing coalition asserted its control over its legislators in the Committee, it was able to secure a re-vote and have its own version advance through the three required plenary readings. Although the opposition Tzomet and National Religious Parties tried to delay these votes by submitting concurrent no-confidence motions against the government on both the first and the final readings, the coalition managed to defeat them every time. In the end, the "Yi'ud law" that expressly authorized legally constituted breakaway factions, and their members, to enter the government was passed on December 19, 1994, with a fifty-nine to forty-nine margin as the Eighth Amendment to the Basic Law: The Government.[17]

The episode of the "Yi'ud law" showed that the anti-defection law failed to survive its first major political and legal test. In order to ensure that the governing coalition would fully benefit from the split in the Tzomet party and that the defectors would be compensated for their action, the government had to resort to passing yet another legislative amendment in the face of a judiciary that erred on the side of a strict reading of the anti-defection law. Several opposition MKs noted that they were not opposed to the Yi'ud law on substantive grounds; in fact, the only party that did so was Tzomet for obvious reasons, but only on political ones, meaning that they resented the government's blatant use of its majority to fix a piece of legislation in order to serve a very concrete and narrow political objective. As we saw in chapter 2, this became a recurring trope that revealed a key institutional weakness of the anti-defection law. The previous Knesset had passed the anti-defection law with a very strong consensus between government and opposition since both sides suffered the cost of unregulated defection during the cabinet crises that were triggered by the "stinking trick." However, since the legislation was not protected with a super-majority amendment clause, three years later it quickly become the subject of manipulation by a government desperately seeking to shore up its shrinking legislative support base.

Once the legal and legislative hurdles that prevented the induction of the two Yi'ud MKs to the government were removed, the party officially joined the governing coalition on January 9, 1995, with Segev becoming Minister of Energy and Goldfarb assuming the role of Deputy Minister of Construction and Housing. The party's third MK, Ester Salmovitz, remained trapped for a while, however; she assumed a pivotal role in the internal drama of Yi'ud when the relationship between Segev and Goldfarb hit rock bottom during their battle to assume control over the embryonic institutions and the membership of the new party.[18] In May

1995, Salmovitz and Goldfarb met in their capacity as the new party's central secretariat and resolved to sack Segev as the leader of the party. [19] Although the two MKs remained firmly opposed to each other's policy positions, they eventually agreed to coordinate and leave Yi'ud together in order to form a new political party called Atid (Future).[20] The formation of this new party was not at all driven by ideological convergence between Salmovitz and Goldfarb: the two MKs took radically different positions on the two major bills that came before the Knesset in the second half of 1995: the Golan bill and the Oslo-2 Accords. On both of these bills, Goldfarb cast the pivotal vote to help the government win, whereas Salmovitz voted for the Golan Special Majority Law[21] and against the Oslo-2 Agreement.[22] Instead of policy agreement, what united the two MKs in their effort to form the new party was their common objective to circumvent the punitive provisions of the anti-defection law that otherwise would have compromised their political futures: Salmovitz was planning to enter the Likud candidate primaries, while Goldfarb received permission from the Labor Party to contest its southern regional primaries for the next Knesset election.[23] By leaving Yi'ud together, the two MKs avoided the penalties of the anti-defection law and were in a position to run in the Knesset election. As fate would have it, however, they both failed in their respective primary contests.

In sum, Yi'ud underwent considerable change in its composition during the short period of the party's existence. At first, the three MKs coordinated to split from Tzomet, which was soon followed by the marginalization of Salmovitz, the only MK who did not realize any office gain or policy gain from the collective defection. Next, Salmovitz and Goldfarb coordinated in order to unseat Segev, and finally, in an effort to secure their political future against the provisions of the anti-defection law, they ended up splitting from the party by forming Atid (Future). The electoral fate of the three defectors was miserable: whereas all five Tzomet MKs who remained loyal to the party (Raful, Pini Badash, Haim Dayan, Moshe Peled, and Eliezer Sandberg) were re-elected in the 1996 election, the three Tzomet defectors were not.

Case 2: The Disintegration of Gil (Pensioners' Party)

Gil (Pensioners' Party) stormed onto the Israeli political scene with an unexpected first-time electoral victory of seven Knesset seats in the 2006 election and its subsequent entry to the governing coalition. Yet, in the summer of 2008 the Pensioners' Party suffered the collective defection of three of its legislators, only to see two of them return four months later. All members of the Pensioners' Party, both the defectors and those who remained loyal to the party label, paid a very high electoral price for this instability as none of these seven politicians ever returned to the Knesset. The story of the Pensioners' Party demonstrated that whereas the anti-defection law was clearly effective in terms of incentivizing the size and the timing of the split, it failed to encourage legislators to try to overcome their differences and work toward rebuilding party unity. Moreover, the episode also brought to light a thereto unexpected possibility under the anti-defection law: a newly formed extra-parliamentary party, Social Justice, merged with the renegade splinter Pensioners and in so doing sought to use the splinters' presence in the Knesset to advance the political agenda of a new party that never even contested the last election. It was exactly this move that the Knesset Committee's majority so passionately regarded as anathema and violation of the voters' mandate.

The Pensioners' Party was formed in 1996 on the eve of the Fourteenth Knesset elections with Nava Arad, the MK who entered the Knesset as Prime Minister Yitzhak Rabin's replacement following the latter's assassination, at the head of the list and Moshe Sharoni as its second-ranked candidate. At that time, the party was able to run a list of sixty-nine candidates, but having secured only half a percent of the popular vote, it failed to enter the Knesset. In the 1999 election, another Pensioners' party, Power for Pensioners, ran with a list of forty-two candidates, but this party also failed to get a Knesset seat. In 2006, Gil re-entered the electoral scene with a modest list of eighteen candidates but managed to have seven of them elected, including Moshe Sharoni.

The unexpected performance of Gil was attributed to two main factors: protest voting in the aftermath of the political turbulence of the Sixteenth Knesset and the choice of Rafi Eitan as party leader to head the list.[24] Indicative of the non-institutionalized nature of the party, Eitan was confirmed in his position only two weeks before the party filed its candidate list with the Electoral Commission after he had accepted the invitation of pensioners' associations that were represented by the party. Moreover, according to his own admission, Eitan had at first attempted to explore the possibility of running on the Kadima list instead of forming and leading a new political party.[25] While he may have been a novice to party politics, Eitan was certainly well known in Israel for his accomplishments as a security agent in several high-profile cases, including the capture of Nazi leader Adolf Eichmann in Argentina as well as his involvement in the well-known Jonathan Pollard case.[26] The latter incident became an actual legal and political issue that threatened to disturb the coalition formation process. Upon the revelation of the coalition agreement between Kadima and Gil, signed on April 26, which specifically provided that Eitan would be appointed a cabinet minister, Pollard and his wife petitioned the High Court of Justice seeking to have this agreement annulled on the basis of their claim that Eitan purposefully withheld documents the release of which to the American authorities would have allowed Pollard to be released from his long captivity.[27] In the end, nothing came of the petition and Eitan was duly inducted to the new cabinet.

The difficulty of keeping together the party group that was entirely comprised of first-time MKs was manifest very early on when the faction had to decide about allocating the two ministerial portfolios it received under its coalition agreement. The agreement specified that Gil's leader Rafi Eitan would receive one of the portfolios (Ministry for Senior Citizens); however, the second portfolio (Health) was left up to the party to decide later on.[28] Sharoni, the only member of the party group with a claim to long-standing membership, announced that he would compete for the portfolio against the party's second-ranked candidate Yaacov Ben Yizri. Eventually, Sharoni was appointed as chairman of both the Gil parliamentary group as well as the Knesset Labor, Welfare and Health Committee, whereas Ben Yizri received the Health portfolio. Sharoni's frustration, however, remained a constant source of irritation and conflict within the party. For example, Sharoni and another Gil MK, Yitzhak Galante, defied coalition discipline and voted against the expansion of the government when Prime Minister Olmert secured the addition of the secular nationalist Yisrael Beitenu Party. [29] The continued tense relationship between Sharoni and party leadership eventually led to a decision by the Gil parliamentary party in October 2007, in a tight vote of four to three, to dismiss Sharoni both as faction chair as well as chair of the Knesset's Labor, Welfare and Health Committee and to replace him with Galante in both roles. The two MKs who sided with Sharoni were Elhanan Glazer and Sara Marom Shalev, ranked sixth and seventh on the party's candidate list in the previous election.

Six months later, the three MKs, Sharoni, Glazer, and Shalev, announced they were formally leaving the Gil party group. The timing of the announcement was directly and explicitly related to the 2001 Edelstein amendment of the Party Finance Law, discussed in chapter 2, which ruled that state funding would be provided to new factions only if they were formed after the first two years of the Knesset's term, which in this case meant any time after April 17, 2008. Furthermore, to ensure that the new party would not remain merely a "parliamentary faction without a party organization," which would not have allowed it to collect state funds for operating expenses, Sharoni entered into negotiations with Arkady Gaydamak, a millionaire businessman with political aspirations, who had floated a new political organization called Social Justice in 2007, but who had no Knesset mandates.[30] While Gaydamak's political aspiration were initially focused on competing in the 2008 mayoral elections in Jerusalem, the alliance with the three Gil rebels would have also allowed him to have representation in the Knesset, which in turn might have opened a way for him to enter the government as a cabinet minister. Reportedly, Gaydamak was specifically interested in the portfolio of Diaspora Affairs, and since the Basic Law: The Government, did not require ministers to be members of the Knesset, Gaydamak's putative arrangement with Gil seemed to create a win-win situation: in exchange for supporting Gaydamak's political aspirations, the three dissident MKs would handsomely benefit from the enhanced state funding they would be entitled given their connection to Gaydamak's newly registered party.

Although the three rebels vehemently denied that any such deal was pending with Gaydamak, a formal merger eventually took place.[31] As a result of this development, the Knesset Committee ruled against approving the split of the Gil party group, with a decisive majority of thirteen members voting against, seven in favor, and one abstention at its meeting on May 28, 2018.[32] Opponents of the split argued that the Gaydamak deal was tantamount to open political bribery and a blatant abuse of the voters' mandate. Thus, in an unprecedented move, the Committee voted to disallow the formation of the new party group, even though it met the technical requirements of the one-third split, and relented only when the three MKs pledged not to enter into their putative agreement with Gaydamak. A month later, Sharoni negotiated a similar agreement with Tzomet, a party that had not won seats in the Knesset since the 1996 election, which the Committee had no reservation against.

The final chapter in the life of the Pensioners' Party was intimately connected with the leadership change at the helm of Kadima and resignation of Prime Minister Ehud Olmert. In the light of mounting evidence against him in a series of corruption cases, Olmert announced he would step down as party leader and head of government as soon as Kadima chose a new leader. In the leadership primary held in September, Foreign Minister Tzipi Livni defeated Deputy Prime Minister Shaul Mofaz by a very narrow margin. In an effort to build a new government, Livni prevailed upon Sharoni and Eitan to close ranks so she could count on the participation of all seven Pensioners in her new coalition. The sole dissension came from Elhanan Glazer, who opted not to return to Gil but form instead his new party, the Right Way, and contest the next election in alliance with Tzomet. Eventually, Livni failed to put together a new government, which paved the way for early elections to the Eighteenth Knesset in February 2009. The Gil Pensioner's Party failed to cross the threshold.

Similar to the case of Yi'ud, the story of the split in the Pensioners' Party shows that the anti-defection law had a very strong effect both on the size and the timing of the defection: the number of switchers, three, was exactly the minimum number that the legislation requires in order to avoid the penalties associated with midterm party switching. Further, the split occurred exactly after the expiry of the two-year window during which party funding provisions were denied to party switchers as per the Edelstein amendment. These institutionally induced effects, however, harmed rather than strengthened party cohesion and unity: the one-third provision of the law meant that the number of defectors was greater than what would have been the likely case in the absence of such a requirement; and the time that it took for the split to meet the two-year limit was spent on deepening the division rather than seeking to rectify the internal discord in the party. In short, these provisions of the law appeared to have resulted in a larger split and a prolonged discord.

This case study also shows that the Knesset Committee could become a very important actor in managing the politics of party splits and defections. In all prior cases that came before the Committee under the anti-defection legislation, its role was limited to a simple registration of approval. While there were contentious cases before the Committee in earlier legislatures as well, the committee's default position would be to delay a decision and have the parties resolve their disagreement over the interpretation of the legislation rather than take a position, let alone vote against a request outright. However, this is not what happened in 2008. The merger of the three rebels with Gaydamak's Social Justice Party significantly increased the stakes of approving the split in Gil because it *de facto* allowed an extra-parliamentary party, which itself had been formed only very recently to help promote Gaydamak's campaign in the upcoming mayoral election in Jerusalem, to gain a foothold in the Knesset.

Case 3: The Labor Party Split of 2011

The split of the Labor Party in 2011 offers another important case to study the effects of the anti-defection law on the mobilization of collective party exits. Unlike the previous two cases, which involved small and new political parties, this one involved one of the oldest parties in the Israeli party system, the Labor Party, which was considerably larger than either Tzomet or the Pensioners' Party, even if paling in comparison with its former legislative dominance. However, as this case study will demonstrate, the anti-defection law had a similarly destabilizing effect on the party both by increasing the number of MKs involved in the split as well as prolonging the deep and divisive factional infighting.

The context for the split in the Labor Party was provided by its extremely poor electoral performance in the elections to the Eighteenth Knesset and its subsequent participation in the new coalition government under the leadership of Likud Prime Minister Benjamin Netanyahu. As for the former, the Labor Party scored its worst-ever electoral performance in the 2009 national polls, winning only thirteen seats and, for the first time ever, failing to return as one of the two largest parties in the Knesset. Labor was led in these elections by Ehud Barak, a former leader of the party between 1997 and 2001 and prime minister between 1999 and 2001, who had recently recaptured the party leadership from Amir Peretz in the internal elections of 2007. With regard to government participation, great differences of opinion were already detectable during the election campaign. Several prominent Labor candidates—such as Yuli Tamir, who served as Minister of Education in the outgoing Olmert government, and Shelly Yachimovich—demanded that the party leadership should make it absolutely clear that Labor would have no share in a government that included Yisrael Beitenu, which they regarded as a dangerous and racist organization.[33]

Two days after the election, Barak met with his new caucus and polled them about their preferences regrading coalition talks with Likud. In addition to Tamir and Yachimovich, four former Labor ministers from the Olmert government (Amir Peretz, Ophir Pines-Paz, Eitan Cabel, and Benyamin Ben-Eliezer) also took the view that the party should go into opposition. Peretz formally demanded that Barak should resign and allow new leadership primaries to take place immediately if he wanted to participate in the government.[34] Over the next several weeks, MKs Daniel Ben-Simon and Avishay Braverman also joined this group, which came to constitute a majority (seven of thirteen) of the party's legislative contingent. In spite of the sizable opposition to joining a Likud-led coalition, Barak appointed a negotiating team and started to explore the conditions under which Labor might enter the new government.

The collision between the two camps in the Labor Party came to a head at the meeting of the Labor Central Committee on March 24, 2009. Although the Committee vote was in Barak's favor, with 680 delegates supporting his position and 507 voting against, the meeting showed how divided the Labor Party had become. Ben-Simon and Braverman announced they would respect the decision of the Central Committee and vote in support of the formation of a new coalition government, including the Labor Party. The other five rebel MKs, however, did not do so and maintained their adamant opposition to joining the government until the investiture vote, and beyond. Indeed, although the Netanyahu government was voted into office with a comfortable majority of sixty-nine votes in favor and forty-five against, the five Labor Party rebel MKs (Amir Peretz, Opher Pines-Paz, Eitan Cabel, Shelly Yachimovic, and Yuli Tamir) defied their party and the coalition by abstaining from the vote.[35] The Labor MKs who supported Barak were handsomely rewarded as the party received five cabinet portfolios and two deputy ministerships.[36] In addition to these appointments, the coalition agreement between Labor and Likud also specified that the Labor Party would have the right to appoint the chairs of important Knesset committees in a rotating fashion: during the first third of the Knesset' term Labor would provide the chair of the Foreign Affairs and Defense Committee, followed by Immigration Absorption and Aliyah in the second, and the Education committee in the last third of the term.[37]

Over the course of the next year and a half, the relationship between Barak and the Labor rebels gradually worsened, although it appeared that by late 2010 Barak was gaining the upper hand. Following the investiture of the new government, the same five Rebels also voted against the new budget, which the government sought to have approved for a two-year period. In a terse statement, Ben-Eliezer told them in no uncertain terms that if the Rebels could not support the government then it was best if they resigned their Knesset seats altogether and left the Labor Party.

In order to weaken the unity among the Rebels, Barak moved quickly to punish their leaders while also making changes to the constitutional structure of the Labor Party that would give him more time to consolidate his position and authority. As a first decisive move, Barak dismissed Eitan Cabel as the party's Secretary-General and replaced him with his trusted confidante, Weizmann Shiri. Soon thereafter, the first crack appeared in the Rebels' group when Shelly Yachimovich voiced her public disapproval of the idea of splitting the party while remaining also critical of having the Labor Party support and be a fig-leaf to the rightwing government. Next, Barak secured a change to the Labor Party constitution, which would have required the call for a leadership primary within fourteen months after an election debacle. It was in Barak's interest to make sure that this timeline was extended so that he could shore up his position in the party against the Rebels. To this end, he called a special party convention in August 2009, where he was able to move the leadership primary to October 2012 just before the next legislative elections were scheduled. Barak was able to bring about this important change by entering into an agreement with Isaac Herzog, Ophir Pines-Paz, and Avishay Braverman, who all held leadership aspirations and regarded themselves as likely candidates against Barak.[38]

In November 2009, the Rebels organized a public meeting in which they launched a formal organization, the Democratic Forum, that would act as the extra-parliamentary platform for their activities, and possibly become the nucleus of a future new political party. In addition to the four Rebels, the chairman of the party's Knesset faction, Daniel Ben-Simon, attended the meeting and expressed his support. However, he stayed short of joining the group as the pivotal fifth member. The new Democratic Forum initiative did not take off, and the Rebels started to lose steam. The death blow to their efforts was struck by Ophir Pines-Paz's sudden decision to quit the Knesset, and political life altogether, in January 2010, soon to be followed by Yuli Tamir in April. The two incoming MKs who replaced them took very different positions on the division within the Labor parliamentary faction. On the one hand, Einat Wilf, who replaced Pines-Paz, was cautiously critical of the party's performance in the government but remained squarely opposed to any possibility of splitting and formally dividing the party.[39] On the other hand, Raleb Majadele, who had been a minister in the Olmert government, decidedly followed Tamir's position and joined the Rebels as soon as he took up his seat.[40]

Barak's control over the Labor Party organization started to slip when Hilik Bar, a political protégé of Benyamin Ben-Eliezer, succeeded Shiri as the party's Secretary-General in the fall of 2010.[41] This transition reinvigorated the latent opposition to Barak's leadership, and both Herzog and Braverman started to demand a revision in the timing of the next party convention. Ben-Eliezer, whose relations with Barak soured after the latter's unsuccessful moves to try and prevent him from becoming the point person of mediating with Turkey amidst the quickly worsening diplomatic relations between the two states, also went on the offensive and made a public demand that the party should get rid of Barak and its leadership should be assumed by an outside candidate.[42]

The faction chair, Daniel Ben Simon, also became an outspoken critic of the party leader when Barak failed to intercede on his behalf to be appointed as chair of the Knesset's Immigrant Absorption and Diaspora Affairs Committee. As per the coalition agreement with Likud, the Labor Party was supposed to receive the rotating chair of this committee. However, prior to allowing Ben-Simon's appointment, the coalition chairman, Zev Elkin of the Likud, demanded that Ben-Simon ought to sign a pledge to support coalition policies in his new role, which he refused to do. Since Barak let this go and did not stand up for Ben-Simon, Likud filled the committee chair with one of its own MKs, Danny Danon, on a temporary basis.[43] Ben-Simon's hostility against Barak and the government proved irreversible, and in early January 2011 he was the single coalition MK to vote against the government's new budget.[44]

Barak's solution to dealing with the looming crisis was to seize the initiative, and by rallying his remaining allies he split the party under the provisions of the anti-defection law. On the morning of January 17, he held a press conference announcing the formation of a new party called Haatzmaut (Independence) together with four other Labor MKs (Matan Vilnai, Einat Wilf, Orit Noked, and Shalom Simhon), which thus amounted to one-third of the party's Knesset faction. Although Barak could comfortably rely on the support of Simhon, Wilf, and Vilnai, he could not at first take Orit Noked's support for granted given the latter's close ties with Ben-Eliezer. Barak thus resorted to a trick that ultimately paid off.[45] Before approaching Noked, Barak reached out to Ben-Simon with an offer to allow him to secede from the Labor Party and form his own single-MK party group. Since Ben-Simon accepted, and made his decision public very quickly, Barak could approach Noked and inform her that the splinter faction already had four MKs, which was one-third of the twelve MKs who would remain in Labor after Ben-Simon's exit. When Noked agreed to join Barak's group, the offer to Ben-Simon was rescinded, leaving the faction chair not only humiliated but also stuck between the two rival camps.[46]

The request to recognize the new Haatzmaut faction as a Knesset party group was brought before the Knesset Committee by Einat Wilf. Since the formal requirements for a legal party split were met, the Committee's legal advisor pointed out that that there was no scope to exercise discretion, and following a lengthy debate the split was duly approved with a large majority of eleven in favor and three against. In a rare move, the Committee chair called for a roll-call vote, and the records show that three Kadima MKs (Yohanan Plesner, Shlomo Mollah, and Rachel Adatto) voted against allowing the split.[47] The new faction benefitted from the revised rules on party funding passed the previous year together with the Mofaz Law. Therefore, although Haatzmaut split from the Labor Party within the first two years after the previous Knesset election, the new party was able to collect the proportional share of the Labor Party state funding for its five MKs. Following protracted negotiations between Labor and Haatzmaut over the next months, the two parties eventually agreed that Barak's group would give up half of its funding in exchange for the Labor Party desisting that Haatzmaut should pay its share of the Labor Party's debts.

The formation of the new party had immediate consequences for the composition of the government because the three Labor ministers who were not part of Barak's new party (Herzog, Braverman, and Ben-Eliezer) immediately tendered their resignations. In a surprising move, however, Prime Minister Netanyahu did not reduce the number of portfolios that he was willing to allocate to Barak's party, even though the Defense Minister was left to lead a rump party of only five MKs. Thus, four of the five Haatzmaut MKs became ministers, with Einat Wilf remaining the only one without a portfolio; Shalom Simhon replaced Ben-Eliezer as Minister of Industry, Trade and Labor, Orit Noked replaced Shalom Simhon as Minister of Agriculture and Rural Development, Matan Vilnai was appointed to the newly created portfolio of Minister of Home Front Defense, and Ehud Barak retained his position as Minister of Defense. Although the appointment of the new ministers was easily approved in the Knesset plenum with a vote of fifty-three in favor and forty against[48], the process was not without excitement. Immediately after the vote, a number of Kadima MKs jumped to their feet and started spraying air fresheners in the air of the plenum, crying to clean up Israeli political life. The widely reported incident brought home the point to the Israeli public that while *kalanterism* in its classic form may have been phased out, it was back in the political game in a new form couched as a legal party split. Indeed, on the face of it, Barak's move was reminiscent of *kalanterism* in the sense that four of the five Haatzmaut MKs were rewarded with executive appointments in exchange for staying in the coalition. At the same time, since the Labor Party was not a pivotal member of the coalition to start with, the government's survival did not depend on holding onto the new faction.

In spite of its quick rise to power, the new party proved to be quite short-lived. Four months after its formation in the Knesset, Barak secured an agreement with Avigdor Kahalani according to which Haatzmaut would use Kahalani's defunct but still registered party, the Third Way, as its shelf party, a platform on which to build the organization of this new party.[49] Technically, there was no formal requirement for this step. However, it allowed Haatzmaut to avoid having to go through the laborious process of setting up a new party, collecting the necessary signatures, and formally registering with the Party Registry. Instead of starting this process afresh, the agreement with Kahalani simply led to the Third Way changing its name to Haatzmaut and then letting Barak use and control the party as if it had been created anew. In Kahalani's words, the Third Way was already on the "shelf" and since he was not interested in returning to active political life, he agreed to Barak lifting it to facilitate the establishment of his new party in exchange for a promise that the Third Way's raison d'etre of never returning the Golan Heights would be honored.

A few days after the agreement with Kahalani was sealed, Barak convened the first meeting of his new party's eighty-strong governing council to a lavish meeting in Tel Aviv.[50] The rules that the new party adopted gave the party leader immense powers over both the organization and the Knesset faction. The party resolved that it would not elect its Knesset candidates through internal primary elections and gave Barak great clout over filling the top spots on the new list. In spite of these early effervescent signs of a new party coming to life, the enthusiasm quickly vanished. Following polls reporting that Barak's new party would not cross the electoral threshold in the upcoming elections, the Defense Minister announced his retirement from political life eight weeks before the elections to the Nineteenth Knesset, which Haatzmaut, now leaderless, did not contest.[51]

Conclusion

The three case studies bring to light two important consequences of the anti-defection law. First, by creating a numerical condition for a legally recognized party split, the anti-defection law incentivized rebel MKs to "acquire friends for themselves" in order to ensure they would avoid the punitive provisions of the legislation. The instrumental motivation to increase the size of a rebel group until it would reach the one-third threshold meant the lack of ideational convergence and commonality among the defectors, leading to further lack of cohesion and unity in the ranks of the new parties formed. In other words, while the one-third rule was established to be a proxy for ideological splits, it actually created an institutional framework and incentive for instrumental splits and defections. Second, the one-third provision also meant that MKs in the larger parties, such as Labor in the Eighteenth Knesset, would find it more difficult to reach that critical threshold than would MKs of smaller parties. Indeed, had it not been for the effects of the Edelstein amendment, Sharoni and his associates in the Pensioners' Party would have been unlikely to wait two years to split and form a new party. In the case of the Labor Party, however, the divisions were genuinely prolonged because neither the party leader nor his opposing faction had the number of MK on their sides to satisfy the one-third rule. In both cases, however, party unity completely broke down and neither the Pensioners' Party nor Labor functioned as unified party groups until the divisions could be eventually formalized.

The findings of this chapter offer two significant implications for the comparative study of anti-defection laws. The first has to do with the introduction of additional veto players in the game of party switching beyond legislators and their parties. Once adopted, an anti-defection law, like any legislation, may give rise to litigation over conflicting interpretations of its provisions. As such, the judicial system may be dragged into the political drama, further complicating an already tense political situation, prolonging it and potentially leading to inter-branch conflict between the legislature and the judiciary. The legal case brought against the appointment of Yi'ud ministers to the Rabin government was a clear case in point. Similarly, the Knesset Committee is another veto player in the formal recognition of party switches whose decisions may at times impede the timely resolution of a party split.

The second important finding has to do with the counter-intuitive relationship between the anti-defection law, which is supposed to keep party groups together, and party cohesion. While weak party cohesion may lead legislators to contemplate switching in the first place, the terms of the anti-defection law may actually inflict further damage on party cohesion: the case studies of this chapter show that the "one-third" rule of the anti-defection law was indeed responsible for further destabilizing already unstable party groups.

Chapter 5

The Preponderance of Pre-Electoral Party Switching

On February 27, 1999, the *Jerusalem Post*, Israel's largest English-language daily newspaper, reported an unusual story under the title "Mass divorce, Knesset style." The reporter of the story, Liat Collins, informed readers that on the previous day the Knesset House Committee was taken over by a storm of requests to approve MKs' changing their party affiliations. In a single meeting, the Committee set a new, and still unsurpassed, record by approving the requests of seventeen MKs, most of them, as we saw in chapter 3, from the Likud party. As we have seen in the previous chapters, the large number of MKs exiting their parties was not particularly surprising given that the anti-defection law incentivized collective party switches. However, as I argue in this chapter, the more important aspect of the story was not *how many* MKs changed party groups but rather *when* they did so. According to the theory of party switching put forth by Mershon and Shvetsova, legislators should avoid changing their party labels right before a general election lest they incur the wrath of the electorate and suffer accordingly for their perfidy.[1] As such, the above-mentioned "mass divorce" was extremely puzzling because it took place precisely at the start of the official electoral period, that is, ninety days before the elections to the Fifteenth Knesset. Moreover, the story also became emblematic of a major characteristic feature of Israeli party switching since the adoption of the anti-defection law, namely, the steep increase in the number of pre-electoral party exits. This chapter will describe and explain how and why pre-electoral label change has become a prevalent feature of the politics of Israeli party switching since the adoption of the anti-defection law.

The central argument presented in this chapter claims that pre-electoral switches have increased dramatically in their number and frequency because specific provisions, and amendments, of the anti-defection legislation encouraged MKs to delay their exit from their party until the pre-electoral period. The number of pre-electoral switches was particularly high in the Thirteenth and Fourteenth Knessets when Amendment 31, passed with the precise intention to facilitate pre-electoral switches by MKs who otherwise did not satisfy the one-third rule, was in effect. The Eighteenth Knesset also saw a steep increase in the pre-electoral switches; however, this was the result of the effects of the Mofaz Law, which eased the conditions for a legal party split. After an empirical overview of the increase in the number of pre-electoral switches, I will demonstrate the effects of these provisions through case studies of pre-electoral switches in the Thirteenth and Fourteenth Knessets as well as the formation of the new party Hatnua (Movement) Tzipi Livni by a group of renegade Kadima MKs toward the end of the term of the Eighteenth Knesset.

The Temporal Dimension of Party Exits in the Knesset

Figure 5.1 provides a striking visual illustration of the steep increase that has taken place in the pre-electoral party exits. The bar chart divides party switches in two categories according to their timing: those that took place during the official pre-electoral period, that is, ninety days before the actual election, and those that took place prior to that. The numbers along the vertical axis indicate the number of MKs involved in the various exits. Figure 5.1 shows that overall pre-electoral exits increased by more than two and a half times since the original anti-defection legislation was introduced, and over the entire 1992–2019 period they have constituted almost half (47%) of all party exits compared to only 14 percent over the 1949–1992 period.

Figure 5.2 provides further nuance by showing the relative frequencies of the two types of party exits in each Knesset since 1949. The figure shows that prior to 1992, pre-electoral exists involved far fewer MKs in every Knesset, with the exception of the Tenth, whereas in three of the eight legislatures since 1992 (the Thirteenth, Fourteenth, and Eighteenth), pre-electoral exits outnumbered those that took place during midterm.

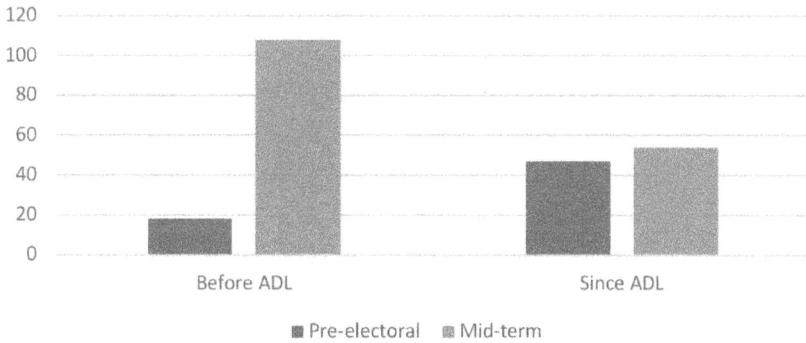

Figure 5.1. Pre-electoral versus midterm party switches in the Knesset.

The cases of the Fifteenth and Sixteenth Knessets are worth special mention because they do not appear to conform to this pattern due to specific confounding factors. In the case of the Fifteenth Knesset, the confounding factor that interrupted the regular pattern of legislative life, as well as the pattern of party exits, was the holding of a special prime ministerial election in 2001, right in the middle of the term of the Knesset, which led to the formation of a new coalition government. Eight of the ten midterm exits in the Fifteenth Knesset took place around the time and in connection with this special election and the new government it led to.

The Sixteenth Knesset not only had the highest total number of MKs exiting from their party since 1992 but also had more midterm than pre-electoral party switches. The large increase in party exits in this Knesset was due to the desertion by fourteen Likud MKs who formed a new party group called Kadima (Forward) led by the incumbent Prime Likud Minister Ariel Sharon. The details of this event will be discussed in chapter 6, but for now it is important to stress that this collective exit occurred right before the start of the pre-electoral period: as soon as Kadima was formed, the Prime Minister announced his decision to ask the Knesset to vote for fresh legislative election. In other words, the formation of Kadima occurred on the very cusp of the start of the pre-election period. A similar event would take place in late 2018 in the Twentieth Knesset when three MKs from the Jewish Home party group (Naftali Bennett, Ayelet Shaked, and Shuli Moalem-Rafaeli) quit to set up their new party called The New Right also on the very cusp of the start of the pre-electoral period.[2]

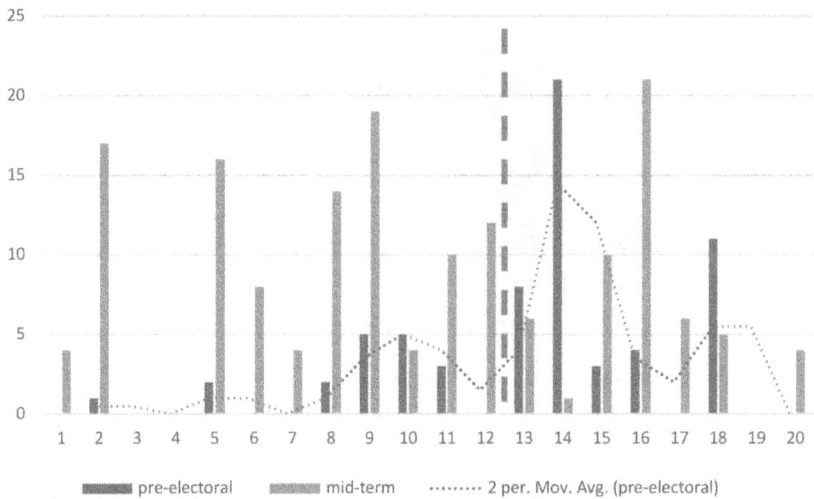

Note: The vertical dashed line separates the time series between the years before and after the adoption of the anti-defection law.

Figure 5.2. Pre-electoral versis midterm party switches per Knesset, by type, 1949 to 2019.

The overall numbers in figures 5.1 and 5.2 are not only consistent with the institutional incentive of the anti-defection law to encourage pre-electoral exits but also show the effects of two amendments made to the original legislation: Amendment 31 of the Knesset Election Law and the Mofaz Law. The former was in effect during the Thirteenth and Fourteenth Knessets, which accordingly witnessed steep increases in pre-electoral exits. Moreover, the pre-electoral frenzy of party exits at the end of the Fourteenth Knesset also showed how the proliferation of inclusive candidate selection processes in more and more political parties interacted with the easing of the anti-defection rules to produce a further increase in the number of exits. Likewise, the Mofaz Law, in effect during the Eighteenth Knesset, facilitated the split of the largest legislative party group, Kadima, that occurred in the pre-electoral period. The next sections will provide illustrative case studies that bring to life the effects of these institutional rules on the strategies and calculations of MKs with regard to the timing of their exit.

Strategic Delay of Party Exits

On the same day that Amendment 31 was passed by the Thirteenth Knesset, the Knesset Committee made a ruling in the protracted case of MK Yosef Azran's defection from his Shas faction. Azran's exit was the culmination of a long, drawn-out internal conflict that originated at the time of the formation of Prime Minister Yitzhak Rabin's (Labor) coalition government that included the ultra-orthodox Shas and the radical left Meretz parties, after the 1992 elections. Azran was vehemently opposed to his party's decision to join the coalition government that also included the Meretz Party, although he obeyed party discipline and voted for its formation. Although he had been Deputy Minister of Finance in the previous government, Azran did not receive an executive appointment but was made instead Deputy Knesset Speaker and his party's representative on the Knesset presidium.[3]

During the next fourteen months that Shas spent in the coalition, Azran maintained an independent position and frequently clashed with the leader of his party group, Minister of Interior Aryeh Deri. For example, early on in its term the new government sought to amend existing legislation that banned Israeli politicians and civil servants from engaging in contact with the Palestinian Liberation Organization. Although the amendment was eventually passed, Azran tried to block it both in the Knesset Law Committee as well as in the plenum despite the fact that Deri had already given his consent in the Ministerial Security Committee.[4] On another occasion, Azran played an instrumental role in mobilizing support against and eventually defeating the coalition's efforts to pass a human rights bill and a new Basic Law.[5] The final clash, however, happened when Azran was overlooked for a possible government appointment. Although he was barred from taking up a portfolio, party leader Aryeh Deri insisted that the Interior Ministry, which he had vacated due to the court order against him, should not be filled even though Prime Minister Rabin offered the party two portfolios an as enticement to have Shas return to the coalition. Since Deri's argument was a clear and direct blow against Azran, who was expecting a government appointment, the latter formally announced that even if Shas returned to the coalition, he would not do so.[6]

The battle between Azran and the Shas party came before the Knesset Committee when Shas proceeded to strip him of his parliamentary privileges, including his committee membership and, most importantly, sought to remove him from his position as Deputy Speaker.[7] Technically, this latter move was not possible under existing House rules because the Speaker and Deputy Speakers of the Knesset were elected for a full legislative term. Azran sought to exploit this provision and offered Shas a compromise whereby he would relinquish his role in exchange for Shas supporting his request to obtain recognition as a single-MK parliamentary party. The party refused to budge and asked the governing coalition to terminate Azran's appointment and force him to give up his seat in the Knesset so that the party could appoint another MK in his place. Since neither side was able to prevail, Azran waited until exactly ninety days before the next election, set to be held on May 29, 1996, to make his defection from Shas formal. At its meeting on February 28, 1996, the Knesset Committee quickly approved of his exit and soon thereafter Azran formed and registered his new political party, Telem Emunah, which ran in the next Knesset election, albeit with no success.[8]

The debate that took place in the Knesset Committee about the Azran case revealed the importance of party funding rules in shaping the political dynamics of party exits and defections. The Knesset Committee's legal advisor noted that it was not clear in the legislation whether the parties that suffered a defection would lose the share of their party funding that they had previously received before the renegade MKs exited. This was an important question since the calculation of the election advances that parties received from the State were related to the number of their MKs. To prevent potential losses to the parties, the Knesset Finance Committee thus introduced an amendment to the 1973 Party Funding Law on May 1, four weeks before the election itself, according to which all parties that suffered an exit would receive their election financing as if they had not lost an MK, that is, on the basis of the number of MKs they had elected in the last election.[9] Although two Hebrew University professors and a graduate student famously petitioned the High Court of Justice alleging to annul the amendment, the Court did not render a decision before the polls.[10] As a result, the petitioners pointed out, the Israeli taxpayer was burdened twice by having to foot the bill for the election advances of the defectors, whose defection was legal and recognized, as well as those of the parties they had left.

The formation of the Third Way party in the Thirteenth Knesset further illustrates the point that the anti-defection law prolongs rather than helps resolve intraparty conflict. The Third Way was formed in May 1994 as a nonpartisan movement to bring together political figures and activists concerned about the Rabin government's approach to territorial compromises during the Oslo peace process.[11] A particularly important point in the Third Way's aims was to ensure that the government would not return any part of the Golan Heights to Syria. The name of the movement suggested that its organizers were trying to find a middle ground between the increasingly more dovish attitude of the Rabin government and the hawkish noncompromising position of the national-religious camp. At first, it seemed that the Third Way might command a significant presence in the Knesset because the fourteen Labor MKs who took part in the formation of the movement constituted a group that came extremely close to one-third of the forty-four-MK-strong Labor Party Knesset faction. This group also included, at least initially, prominent Laborites such as Agriculture Minister Yaacov Tzur[12] and Yehuda Harel, who had served as Rabin's personal aid; however, the two MKs who had been actively involved in the movement from the start were Avigdor Kahalani and Emanuel Zisman. Kahalani was a first-time Labor MK in the Thirteenth Knesset and was elected from the relatively safe thirty-first spot on the Labor list, while Zisman, who had already served in the Twelfth Knesset, was elected from the much more marginal thirty-ninth spot on the list. In spite of its promising start, the movement did not succeed in establishing a broad reach beyond a small group of Labor MKs and politicians.

As the Oslo peace process was unfolding, Kahalani and Zisman solidified their opposition to the government by submitting draft legislation about the Golan Heights that directly contravened the direction of the Labor Party. Further, the two MKs consistently voted against the government on issues that concerned security and territory.[13] On the famous Oslo-2 vote where the *kalanterism* of Yi'ud played such a critical role, the two renegade Labor MKs actually cast their vote against the government, which prompted Prime Minister Rabin to try to remove them from their Knesset committee positions.[14] From that point on, although the two rebels remained formal members of the Labor Party Knesset faction, they faced mounting pressure to resign their seats and return their mandates to the Labor Party. As Labor Secretary-General Nissim Zvili noted, it was unacceptable that the Labor-led coalition government was being held ransom by two mandates in the Knesset that were actually won by the party.[15] Nonetheless, both Kahalani and Zisman remained as Labor MKs until the arrival of the pre-electoral period when the Third Way became formally registered as a separate political party, collecting the appropriate state funds and contesting the 1996 elections under the leadership of Kahalani as its chairman.[16]

Three years later, the Third Way provided yet another illustration of the unexpected consequences of the anti-defection law. Zisman, a co-founder of the party, requested to be formally and officially designated a defector—something that MKs normally tried to avoid at any cost because of the penalties associated with it—in the pre-electoral period leading to the 1999 Knesset elections.[17] Zisman's decision to leave the party was prompted by the party's denial to grant him the second spot on its candidate list, which went to Yehuda Harel, the party whip. At the Knesset Committee meeting, which took up the issue ten days later, the discussion focused on what consequences Zisman's defection would have for the Third Way party group. The Committee's legal advisor explained that since Zisman was requesting to be a formal defector, as opposed to seeking a legal split, there were no financial implications of his request, since the anti-defection provision of the *1973 Party Finance Law* forbids the payment of current expenses to defectors, other than the calculation of television and radio time that parties receive during the campaign according to the number of their MKs.

The Committee thus had to rule on whether the Third Way would be considered a reduced three-MK party group after Zisman's defection or if it would still be considered a four-MK party group given that the anti-defection amendments to the *1973 Party Finance Law* specified that defections should not result in financial losses for the party that suffers them. By the time the Committee chair called the vote, the only two members left in the room were split. A few minutes later a re-vote was requested, which passed with a majority of three votes in favor and one vote against after the return of two more MKs to the meeting. With this decision, the Committee formally approved Zisman as a defector, at his own request, and at the same time determined that the number of MKs in the Third Way was reduced to three MKs, meaning less advertising time for the party in the upcoming election. Yehuda Harel, who represented the Third Way at the meeting, protested that the Committee's decision was against the law.[18] In contrast to other cases when solo MKs exited from their parties in the pre-electoral period in order to set up a new party for the next elections, and benefit from the public funds that they could collect for such a purpose, Zisman did not do so. A few days after the Knesset Committee approved his defection, it was reported that he was joining Ehud Barak's One Israel alliance. Although he could not run as a candidate, he asked that his TV time be transferred to his new party.[19]

On a few occasions, the pre-electoral period witnessed multiple switches by individual MKs seeking out the most advantageous position they could secure on a candidate list in the coming election. The case of Eliezer Sandberg provides a particularly helpful illustration of the dynamics of party switching under the rules of the the anti-defection law. Sandberg was elected to the Knesset from the Tzomet component of the joint Likud-Gesher-Tzomet list in 1996. Toward the end of the Fourteenth Knesset he was one of four MKs who exited from the joint party group to help form the new Center Party. However, when he failed to secure a realistic spot on the Center's candidate list for the upcoming 1999 election,[20] he exited and formed a new political party called Hatzei-rim (The Young Ones). Technically, he would not have been able to do so without penalty since by that time the Center Party already had six MKs, of which he would have been only one. His departure from the Center Party was thus made possible by a maneuver that would be used only on very limited occasions in the future: on March 22, 1999, the Center Party submitted a request to the Knesset Committee to recognize a split in its ranks, with five MKs departing and taking with themselves the party's name. Under the original anti-defection legislation, in the case of a split, the segment with the majority of MKs would be entitled to keeping the original party name, and this is exactly what the five Center MKs did. Moreover, since five of the six MKs more than satisfied the one-third requirement, the approval of the request was automatic and effectively allowed Sandberg to remain a free agent and keep his share of public funding.[21] The Committee further approved of Sandberg's request to be recognized in the Knesset under the new name Hatzeirim, which one week later merged with Avraham Poraz's Shinui, which agreed to reserve the fifth spot on its candidate list for Sandberg.[22]

The Effect of the Mofaz Law on the Kadima Split in 2012

Although the Mofaz Law was arguably passed by Prime Minister Benjamin Netanyahu's coalition in 2009 in order to make it easier for Shaul Mofaz and other Kadima MKs to leave their party and join the Likud-led coalition government in the Eighteenth Knesset, three years later this legislation actually ended up facilitating the splitting of the party against Mofaz, who had become its leader by then. The split in the ranks of the Kadima Party took place in December 2012 on the eve of the elections to the Nineteenth Knesset, and was orchestrated by the party's former leader, Tzipi Livni.

The disintegration of Kadima in the Eighteenth Knesset took place over a period of eight months, spanning from late March to November 2012. Following Likud's decision to hold internal leadership elections in January 2012—well in advance of the next election, which were widely expected to take place only in late 2013[23]—Kadima also held a leadership contest on March 27, 2012. In what appeared to be a rerun of the last Kadima leadership fight in 2008, the two leading contenders were once again Tzipi Livni and Shaul Mofaz. However, whereas Livni had defeated Mofaz four years earlier by a narrow margin of a few hundred votes, this time Mofaz scored a resounding victory by securing 62 percent of the votes cast. The result clearly showed that Mofaz commanded far greater support among the Kadima rank-and-file than did Livni, yet the party's MKs were far more evenly divided: twelve MKs were reported to support Mofaz, and twelve MKs were reported to support Livni, while veteran politician and former Speaker of the Knesset Dalia Itzhik as well as Avi Dichter stayed on the fence.[24] After his newly gained victory, Mofaz went on the offensive in the Knesset against the Netanyahu government while at the same time appealing to Tzipi Livni to stay in the party and work together toward this shared goal.[25] Given that just about half of the Kadima caucus consisted of Livni's allies, it was imperative for Mofaz to find reconciliation with her predecessor. His appeal, however, was to no avail, and Livni resigned from the Knesset at the end of April.

A month after the Kadima primaries, the coalition government was facing imminent defeat over the issue of the Tal Law in the Knesset.[26] In order to avoid it, Prime Minister Netanyahu decided to call early elections and initiated a bill asking for the early dissolution of the Knesset. In a surprising move, as legislators were making arrangement to bring the dissolution bill for its second and third reading to the plenum, Netanyahu and Mofaz struck a last-minute deal that brought Kadima into the coalition, with Mofaz becoming Vice Prime Minister. While the addition of Kadima seemed to stabilize the government temporarily, Mofaz came under severe criticism by several Kadima MKs in Livni's camp who preferred staying in opposition and prepare for the next elections from a position of critiquing the government. Indeed, three of Livni's solid supporters (Orit Zuaretz,

Shlomo Molla, and Robert Tiviaev) neither voted in favor of Kadima entering the coalition nor for the appointment of Mofaz as a minister in the government. According to the coalition agreement between Likud and Kadima, the latter agreed to support the government and its budget until the end of the term of the Knesset and Likud committed itself to work toward electoral reform and a solution to reforming the Tal Law.[27] To the latter end, the Prime Minister proceeded to strike a committee under the leadership of Kadima MK Yohanan Plesner, tasked to provide recommendations.

Immediately after Kadima entered the governing coalition, one of its rookie MKs, Yuval Zellner, who had replaced Tzipi Livni upon her retirement from the Knesset, prepared a private members' bill, dubbed the "Confinement Law," to reverse the provisions of the Mofaz Law of 2009.[28] The draft legislation proposed to eliminate the new rule according to which seven MKs could legally split from a party even if they did not constitute one-third of the party's Knesset faction, as well as restore the Edelstein amendment that denied public funding to splinter parties formed within the first two years of a newly elected Knesset. Zellner's bill was evidently an attempt to contain the fallout from the division among the Kadima MKs over the issue of joining the coalition, not unlike what tore apart Ehud Barak's Labor Party the year before. If passed, Zellner's legislation would have required a group of ten Kadima MKs to bolt and form a new party. Facing strong opposition against the bill, Mofaz decided not to press ahead with it, and the bill lapsed. It is worth noting, however, that two years later both of the bill's provisions would be passed as part of the comprehensive 2014 Governance Laws.

Kadima's membership in the coalition lasted only seventy days. On July 1, the Prime Minister disbanded the Plesner Committee, citing its inability to work toward a workable formula to replace the Tal Law after several religious MKs had resigned from the committee.[29] Although Netanyahu invited Mofaz to work together and resolve the issue, the dissolution of the Plesner Committee was seen to damage Kadima's electoral prospects. Therefore, Mofaz called a meeting of his MKs and suggested that the party should leave the coalition immediately. The vote in favor of exiting was nearly unanimous, with only Avi Dichter, Otniel Schneller, and Yulia Shalamov-Berkovich voting against it.[30] Two days later, on July 19, Kadima formally left the coalition, but in the process the Prime Minister was reported to have had personal meetings with a number of the party's MKs (Arie Bibi, Avraham Duan, and Yulia Shalamov-Berkovich) and offer them government appointments in exchange for staying with the coalition.[31]

The number of MKs who were considering to quit the party steadily grew and came to include Otniel Schneler, Nino Abesadze, Jabod Edery, Rachel Adato, and Nachman Shai as well. To prevent the split, Mofaz decided to seize the initiative and the Kadima party group formally requested the Knesset Committee to designate four of its MKs (Arie Bibi, Avraham Duan, Yulia Shalamov-Berkovich, and Otniel Schneller) as defectors and mete out to them the appropriate penalties under the anti-defection law. Maintaining its tradition to protect the individual MK's mandate in case of doubt, the Committee voted overwhelmingly against Kadima's request and with a large majority of eleven votes to two, the Committee denied the party's request.[32]

Having suffered Kadima's exit from the coalition, the Prime Minister continued to struggle passing key pieces of legislation, most importantly his government's next budget. As the unity of the coalition was crumbling, Netanyahu finally announced on October 9, 2012, that early elections would be held; the date was eventually set for January 22, 2013. In the context of preparing for the elections, Tzipi Livni was approached both by the Labor Party and a new political party called Yesh Atid, led by former television show host Yair Lapid, to join their ranks and run as the second-placed candidate on the respective lists.[33] Livni declined both offers and on November 27 re-entered the political game by announcing the formation of her own new party, Hatnua (Movement). Immediately following her announcement, three Kadima MKs (Rachal Adatto, Yoel Hasson, and Shlomo Molla) resigned from their party and declared they would run with Livni.[34] While the announcement by the three MKs lent immediate credibility to Livni's new initiative, she needed four more Kadima MKs to join Hatnua so that the party could claim a share of Kadima's public funds. In an unexpected turn of events, the reduced threshold for a legal split that the Mofaz Law introduced at the start of the Eighteenth Knesset actually came to threaten Kadima itself because seven MKs were now sufficient to constitute a legal split. Had Zellner's "Confinement Law" been passed, it is not at all clear that Livni would have been able to recruit the ten MKs it would have taken to form a new splinter party. Under the Mofaz Law, however, she needed only four more.

Within a week of its formation, Hatnua managed to recruit the seven MKs that it needed to have its own Knesset faction. A few days after the first three Kadima MKs had left their party, another three followed their suit: Robert Tiviaev, Majale Whbee, and Orit Zuaretz. With the exception of Whbee, who was serving his third Knesset term, these MKs were junior legislators serving their first (Adatto, Tiviaev, Zuaretz) or second (Hasson, Molla) terms in the Knesset. What the new party was still lacking, however, was not only the crucial seventh member from Kadima but someone with the credentials of a senior politician whose name would lend clout and credibility to the new party. On December 2, veteran member MK Meir Shetreet finally delivered on both counts. With Shetreet's switch, the seven MKs were now in a position to approach the Knesset Committee and request the recognition of the formal split of Kadima and the establishment of their new party.

The Committee met the evening of December 3, 2012, to discuss the case. After a stormy debate that lasted over two hours, it approved the split and recognized Hatnua as a new faction now entitled to collect its funds from Kadima. The Committee arrived at its decision with a close margin, as all four Kadima members voted against authorizing the split, and the coalition had only five members present at the time of the vote. In addition to the close vote, another important feature of the discussion was the presence and the active involvement of former MK Avraham Poraz, who was the head of the defunct Hetz (Arrow) party. Poraz explained to the Committee that he had made an agreement with Livni according to which Hatnua would use the "skeleton" of Hetz for the purposes of setting up the new party and its candidate list. The agreement was essentially the same as the one that Barak had concluded with Kahalani allowing a new Knesset party group to become the formal representative of a "shelved party."[35] In this case, however, not only did the use of the "shelf party" allow Livni to bypass the time-consuming process of organizing the formal registration of her new party,[36] a process that would have taken more time than was left before the deadline to register Knesset candidates, it also resulted in the transfer of all the funds remaining in the party coffers of Hetz since the 2006 elections, the last one the party had contested.

The status of these funds in the possession of Hetz was questionable according to some.[37] Prior to the 2006 elections, the party had duly received an advance from the state to defray the costs of its campaign. However, since the party received only 0.3 percent of the votes, it was required under the terms of the Party Funding Law to return the balance in its account. Poraz had taken the state to court over the issue on grounds that no other party in the history of Israel had ever been required to return such funds. As a result of this unresolved legal issue, Hetz still had about two million shekels, which it agreed to sign over to Livni's new party under their agreement. Technically, these funds could not be used for election purposes, but they were made available to fund Hatnua's current expenses. The agreement between Livni and Poraz raised another issue ethical in nature. At the time of their deal, Poraz was a registered lobbyist of the Knesset, which suggested that Hatnua may become unduly influenced by the interest and agendas he represented. In the end, the Committee majority approved of the formal recognition of Hatnua as a Knesset party group, which put these concerns to rest.[38] In the days remaining before the candidate registration deadline, Tzipi Livni managed to have former leaders of the Labor party Amram Mitzna and Amir Peretz agree to join her list on the second and third spots of the party's candidate list. From among the seven Kadima defectors, however, only Meir Shetreet was ranked sufficiently high, on the fifth spot, to win a seat in the next election to the Nineteenth Knesset.

Conclusion

This chapter has argued that two amendments of the Israeli anti-defection law—Amendment 31 and the Mofaz Law—were responsible for the nearly threefold increase in the number of pre-electoral party switches that have taken place in the Knesset since 1992. Amendment 31 facilitated switches at the end of the Thirteenth and Fourteenth Knessets, and the Mofaz Law was responsible for easing the split of the Kadima party group, which might not have happened under the one-third rule of the original anti-defection law. These case studies also offer an important contribution to the comparative study of party switching and anti-defection laws. As mentioned at the start of the chapter, legislators may be reluctant to change parties on the eve of a general election lest they incur an electoral penalty for their disloyalty. Institutions, however, may provide very powerful incentives for them to do so, especially, as is the case in Israel, there are financial gains at stake. Anti-defection laws that incentivize pre-electoral party switching also affect the nature of party competition in an indirect way. As the number of legislators who form new party groups before the election increases, so does the fragmentation of the party system.

Moreover, by keeping up the supply of new parties in the party system, the anti-defection law may counterintuitively also weaken the institutionalization of the party system, which is precisely what it was meant to strengthen in the first place.

Chapter 6

Between Government and Opposition

The Directionality of Exit

On January 10, 2005, Prime Minister Ariel Sharon presented members of his new government for their investiture in the Knesset. Sharon's previous coalition, which was formed after the 2003 Knesset elections and comprised center, right, and religious parties, gradually disintegrated due to interparty tensions within the coalition and a deep schism that developed within his own party, Likud, over the issue of Israel's unilateral disengagement from the Gaza Strip. The Prime Minister's second government was a National Unity coalition including ministers from his own Likud and the Labor Party, which had previously been leading the parliamentary opposition. Although the new government passed the investiture with fifty-eight votes in favor to fifty-six against, it could do so only with the help of the opposition Yahad and Am Ehad party groups, abstentions by six Arab MKs, and two other MKs, Yosef Paritzky of Shinui (Change) and Michael Nudelman of the National Union, whose parties had left Sharon's previous coalition government and were now in the opposition. Above all, the formation of the new government was extremely unusual because thirteen Likud MKs, just one fewer than what would have been required to satisfy the one-third rule of the anti-defection law's condition for a legal split, voted against the new government, prompting veteran Likud MK Reuven Rivlin to note that for all intents and purposes, if not formally and legally, Likud was split and fresh elections were inevitable.[1]

The formation of Sharon's governments in the Sixteenth Knesset bore witness to the fact that the anti-defection law did not provide panacea against defections and exits upsetting the stability of incumbent governments. While we saw in chapter 2 that the original motivation to pass the anti-defection law in the aftermath of the "stinking trick" was precisely to ensure that defections would not interfere with, let alone undermine, the stability of future governments, in this chapter I will show that this intended effect of the new law was only partly achieved. On the one hand, no incumbent prime minister lost and regained office, as Yitzhak Shamir did in 1990. On the other hand, defections, splits, and exits continued to play an important and, on occasion pivotal, role in helping incumbent governments remain in office. Following an overview of how the directionality of party switching between government and opposition has changed after the introduction of the anti-defection law, the present chapter will use the case study of the Sixteenth Knesset to illustrate the strategies that political actors employed to circumvent the application of the anti-defection law.

The Sixteenth Knesset is an important legislature to study because it saw not only the alternation of three different coalition governments in office, each led by Prime Minister Sharon, but also the eventual breakup of his own party as the Prime Minister led one-third of his loyal Likud MKs to form a new party, Kadima. Similar to what we saw about the history of changes and amendments to the anti-defection law, the case of the Sixteenth Knesset also shows that the anti-defection law favors the incumbent government, which can use creative means to divide the opposition and prolong its stay in power.

The Directionality of Party Switching in Numbers

Figure 6.1 provides a comparison between the directionality of party switches in the Knesset before and after the adoption of the anti-defection law. The figure identifies four types of party switches in terms of their direction: those that take place within the parliamentary opposition, those that occur within the governing coalition, those that see MKs move from an opposition party to a coalition member, and vice versa. The numbers along the vertical axis indicate the percentage of switches observed per type in each of the two time periods. Prior to the adoption of the anti-defection law, almost half of all switches took place within the opposition, followed by one-fifth of all cases within the coalition. The remaining two types of switches are particularly important because they directly affect the balance of power between the coalition and the opposition and can therefore lead to the termination and replacement of the government. Before 1992, more than twice as many switches were moving from the coalition to the opposition (22.2%) than the other way around (9.52%), suggesting that MKs who changed a party group with the intention to have an impact on the government–opposition balance very motivated more to weaken rather than to strengthen the size coalition.

The adoption of the anti-defection law in 1992 resulted in minimal changes in these distributions. While within-opposition switches remained the most prevalent, a large percentage of switches took place within the coalition, which has amounted to one-quarter of all switches in this period. Also, movement from the opposition to the coalition remained the least frequent type, and the percentage of switches that weakened the coalition slightly decreased. These aggregate numbers suggest that the anti-defection law might not have had a strong measurable effect on the legislative strength and base of governing coalitions. However, the next

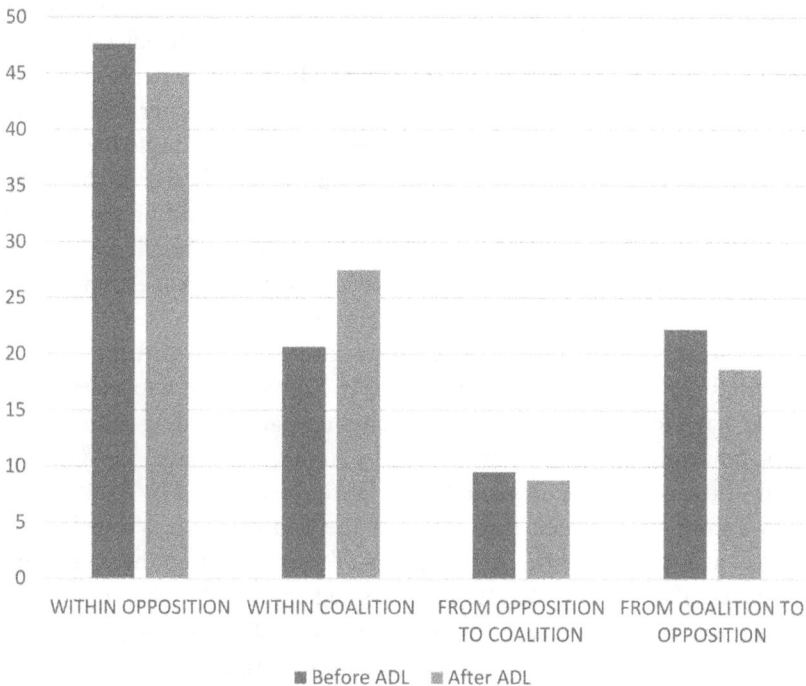

Figure 6.1. Direction of party switching in the Knesset.

section will provide several examples of how the anti-defection legislation influenced the dynamic changes of the parliamentary balance between government and opposition in ways that may not be adequately reflected in these numbers.

Party Switching and Ariel Sharon's
First Coalition Government in the Sixteenth Knesset

The general elections to the Sixteenth Knesset took place on January 28, 2003, and led to the formation of a narrow majority government comprising Prime Minister Ariel Sharon's Likud party (thirty-eight MKs), the centrist Shinui (fifteen MKs), and the right-religious National Union (seven MKs) a month later. The National Religious Party also joined the government five days after its formation. The coalition formation process was completed with an act of party switching when the two MKs of the Yisrael Be'aliyah party, Marina Solodkin and Yuli Edelstein, decided to merge with Likud. Although the technical merger of the two party groups did not seem to pose any legal and political challenges, the Knesset Committee discussion showed otherwise.[2] On behalf of the two parties, Gideon Sa'ar and Yuli Edelstein informed the committee that as per their agreement the two party groups should be considered as one united entity for all purposes except for party funding. Citing Article Twelve of the Party Funding Law, the parties had requested that they should be considered as separate entities and that, accordingly, the Knesset should forward to each party their respective amounts for election and current expenses that they were entitled to according to the election results.

The legal advisor to the Knesset Committee noted that the law did not allow for such a practice and that if two factions were to merge, this would have to be for all purposes, including party funding. This objection, however, was quickly overruled by Likud MK Ronni Bar-On, the chair of the committee. A second complication was raised by Amir Peretz (Am Ehad), who argued that although the two groups requested to be treated as separate entities for purposes of party funding, the legislation stipulated that if several factions came together under the framework of one parliamentary party group, then one additional party financing unit would be given to this joint entity. According to Peretz, this meant that in addition to receiving their due shares on the basis of having won thirty-eight and two seats, respectively, the merged Likud-Yisrael Bealiyah party would also be entitled to one additional party-funding unit. Interestingly, the Likud representatives on the committee were caught unaware of this provision, which was brought to their attention, quite paradoxically by an opposition MK, who, as we shall later, was to benefit from precisely the same provision. Yet a third point was raised by Shas MK Yitzhak Cohen, who argued that the merger de facto provided a transfer of fourteen million shekels from one party to another to cover their election-related debts, which is something that should normally be watched and regulated by the office of the State Comptroller.[3] In the end, the Committee ruled with a majority vote, Yitzhak Cohen being the only MK voting against, to allow the merger and accept the agreement between two parties. In addition to the implication for party funding, the merger also meant that the number of Likud MKs in the government increased from thirty-eight to forty. In other words, the position of the coalition was strengthened and Marina Solodkin was appointed to the government as Deputy Minister of Aliyah and Integration.

The dramatic move that rocked the foundations of Ariel Sharon's first coalition government was the declaration of his government's commitment to a unilateral withdrawal of Israeli presence from the Gaza Strip.[4] Sharon's decision to remove the Israeli settlements was a direct and frontal attack on the interests of the key constituency of the National Union and a number of supporters of the NRP. It was especially significant that the recently chosen new leader of the NRP, Effie Eitam, represented the same religious settler sector that made up the bulk of the National Union's support base. In order to acquire a majority support for his plan within the coalition cabinet, Sharon fired two of his National Union ministers, Benny Elon and Avigdor Lieberman, which in turn reduced the parliamentary base of his coalition to a bare majority of sixty-one seats.[5]

Nonetheless, for a number of institutional and political reasons, Sharon's leadership was not under immediate threat. In terms of the former, the Basic Law: The Government provided for a constructive vote of no-confidence meaning that the incumbent prime minister could be replaced only if the opposition were to agree on an alternative MK to form a government, which was extremely unlikely given the ideological dispersion among the opposition parties. Furthermore, Sharon was still able to bank on the legislative support of renegade MKs Michael Nudelman (National Union) and David Tal (Am Ehad). Although due to the prohibition of the anti-defection law neither of these politicians would actually break away from their parent parties until later in the term of the Knesset, they indicated their commitment to supporting Sharon's leadership and Gaza disengagement program. In sum, Nudelman's and Tal's support lent the government a legislative base of sixty-three seats.[6]

The cabinet approval of the Gaza Disengagement Plan caught the NRP faction in a very difficult situation.[7] Whereas the entire NRP caucus was opposed to disengagement, there was a major difference of opinion as to how best to represent this point. Two of the party's three ministers in the government, party leader Effie Eitam and Yitzhak Levy, broke their party's rules and decided to follow the example of the National Union by quitting the government, leaving Zevulun Orlev as the sole NRP minister.[8] Orlev's position, supported by two other NRP MKs, Gila Finkelstein and Shaul Yahalom, was that quitting the government required prior authorization by the central party organs and that it was more effective to exert pressure on Prime Minister Sharon and to torpedo the Disengagement Plan from the inside. Both arguments had strong political logic. By quitting their executive positions and noting they would vote against the government, Eitam and Levy caused the Sharon government to lose its majority and drop to a minority of fifty-nine seats which, they claimed, should force the government to change direction or face imminent defeat. On the other hand, Orlev argued that it was important to remain in government and hold onto ministerial position in order to bear stronger influence on the process. Indeed, Orlev's fear was justified when Sharon refused to replace the departing NRP ministers with NRP MKs loyal to the government. In place of Eitam, Sharon appointed Likud MK Tzipi Livni, who quickly moved to cancel mortgage projects held by Israeli settlers in Gaza.[9]

The summer of 2004 brought another latent division to the fore when it was revealed on national television that Yosef Paritzky, MK of the Shinui party and Minister of National Infrastructure in the government, sought to frame Avraham Poraz, a founding member of his own party, with the help of a private investigator.[10] Although no police charges were brought against Paritzky, his party effectively ousted him both from the party organization as well as the caucus and called on Prime Minster Sharon to fire him. Sharon complied with the request and replaced Paritzky with Eliezer Sandberg. Although removing Paritzky from the executive was a relatively simple matter, his status as an MK was much more difficult to change.[11] Since he was only one of fifteen MKs in the Shinui faction, Paritzky clearly was not able to secede without penalty under the one-third rule of the anti-defection law. Although the party called on Paritzky to resign his seat and allow the next candidate from the Shinui list to enter the Knesset, he flatly refused to do so. In an effort to resolve the matter, Shinui even offered Paritzky one million shekels in exchange for his seat, but even this offer was to no effect.[12] Thus, Paritzky effectively became a single-MK faction, voting as he pleased, although formally he would remain part of the Shinui faction. Technically, this move did not yet alter the parliamentary balance between government and opposition; however, this would change dramatically when Shinui left the coalition at the end of the 2004.

The final vote on the Disengagement Plan was held in the Knesset on October 26, 2004, and passed with a comfortable majority of sixty-seven to forty-five.[13] In spite of the strong margin, the vote brought to the fore latent divisions within both the coalition and the opposition parties: the Likud faction was split with a narrow majority of twenty-three MKs voting in favor and seventeen against the Disengagement Plan; all National Union MKs except for Nudelman voted in favor; and David Tal abstained although his two co-partisans in Am Ehad voted in favor. Although all six NRP MKs voted against the Disengagement Plan, Orlev suggested in the aftermath that the party may still remain in the coalition if Sharon agreed to one of the following conditions: (1) to hold a referendum on the issue; (2) to call early elections before the evacuation of the settlements would start; or (3) to put a freeze on the implementation of the Disengagement Plan altogether.[14] However, once Sharon rejected all of these options, the NRP followed the lead of the National Union and quit the coalition on November 11, 2004. As a result of the departure of the NRP, Prime Minister Sharon's government lost its majority in the Knesset, as it was now reduced to two coalition members: a divided Likud of forty MKs and Shinui of fifteen MKs. In order to beef up his government's support in the crucial months ahead when the disengagement from Gaza would be implemented, Sharon reached out to Labor, and the ultra-orthodox United Torah Judaism (UTJ) and Shas to join in a National Unity government.

Prime Minister Sharon's first coalition government in the Sixteenth Knesset finally collapsed when its budget bill failed on its first reading on December 1, 2004. Since Sharon sought to send the UTJ a credible message of cooperation, the budget allocated a generous sum for the religious educational institutions under the UTJ's tutelage. However, this allocation was not acceptable to the secular Shinui, which therefore voted against the budget of the government that it was still technically a part of. Immediately, the Prime Minister fired the five Shinui ministers from their position, and a week later his party concluded coalition agreements with Labor and UTJ to set up a new government.[15]

Party Switching and the National Unity Government

The formation of the National Unity government brought to the fore the unresolved cases of three MKs—Nudelman, Tal, and Paritzky—who defied their parties on the government's investiture vote. According to the anti-defection law, voting against the party line on a vote of (no) confidence constituted defection and should have incurred all the penalties contained in the law. However, as long as such disobedient MKs received no favor or compensation in exchange for their breach of party discipline, they could technically not be considered defectors. Therefore, since there was no tangible evidence that would have substantiated the charge of defection against these MKs, they remained unaffected by the legislation at this point.

The strict reading of the law notwithstanding, Shinui went before the Knesset Committee and asked for a ruling against Paritzky, arguing that his vote against the party line on the investiture vote was a clear act of defection.[16] Shinui's position was that Paritzky must be formally excluded from the party's parliamentary group and must not receive any party funding, which normally would be at the expense of the parent party. The chairman of the committee, Likud MK Ronnie Bar-On, called on the two sides to find a mutually acceptable compromise or else he threatened to introduce legislation that would allow the Knesset Committee to overrule the one-third rule and permit any single MK to split legally as long as the committee supported it with a two-thirds majority. From the perspective of Likud, it was very important to enable Paritzky's legal exit from Shinui so that the government could always count on his vote in the Knesset. The Paritzky affair eventually ended in May 2005 with all Shinu MKs, save Paritzky, splitting from him, which allowed Paritzky to keep his seat and form a new party under the name Zionism, Liberalism, and Equality.[17] Simultaneously with the settlement of the Paritzky case, the Knesset Committee approved of David Tal's exit from Am Ehad to form a new party group called Noy (Ornament). However, since neither Tal's nor Paritzky's new party had an extra-parliamentary organization, they were not able to benefit fully from the party funding provided by the state. The approval of Tal's exit from Am Ehad was justified according to the terms of the recently passed Sa'ar amendment that made such an exit legal if all other MKs of the same party group merged with another one: indeed, the remaining two MKs of Am Ehad, Amir Peretz and Ilana Cohen, were in the process of completing such a merger with the Labor Party, which eventually enabled Peretz to enter and win the Labor leadership primaries later that year.[18]

Party switching also continued to change the ranks of the parliamentary opposition. Specifically, the conflict within the NRP came to a head in the early months of 2005 when the party's former ministers Effie Eitam and Yitzhak Levy threatened to quit the party group formally unless they collectively agreed to merge with the National Union and sign an agreement to run a joint list in the next election.[19] The two politicians' exit threat was credible given that they met the terms of the one-third rule of the anti-defection law and they had also waited long enough for the two-year waiting period, as per the Edelstein amendment, to qualify for party funding. Accordingly, Eitam proceeded to sign a merger agreement with Zvi Hendel of the National Union in January 2005, to which the NRP legal panel responded by removing him from his position as party leader.[20] The clash between the two renegade NRP politicians and the central party organization reached a point of no return: on February 24, Eitam and Levy announced the formation of the new Religious Zionist Party that would take effect on April 4.[21] Although the Knesset Committee did not reject the formation of the new group, it did disallow the name, which was temporarily changed to Hitchabrut (Connection), and then in May 2005 to Renewed National Religious Zionism.

The largest case of collective party switching in the Sixteenth Knesset, and ever since the introduction of the anti-defection law, was the secession of fourteen Likud MKs, led by Prime Minister Ariel Sharon, who formed, together with David Tal's Noy, a new party, Kadima, that came to dominate the center of Israeli party politics for the next six years.[22] Sharon was not the first prime minister to quit his party; the first prime minister of the State of Israel, David Ben-Gurion, also split from his Labor Party and formed Rafi in 1965. However, Sharon was certainly the first Israeli Prime Minister who quit his party while still an incumbent head of government. Moreover, unlike Rafi, which was returned in the next Knesset election as a minor political party, Kadima was returned to the next Knesset as the largest party that also proceeded to form the next government.

The formation of Kadima was the culmination of the deep factional discord in the Likud between Prime Minister Sharon and his supporters, on the one hand, and the party's more conservative MKs and ministers who opposed both the idea and the implementation of the Disengagement Plan, on the other. The latter MKs maintained their strong and consistent opposition to Sharon's government, which meant that for all intents and purposes Likud ceased to function as a united party group during the term of Sharon's second government in the Sixteenth Knesset. For example, when the Disengagement Implementation Law was voted on in the plenary on February 16, 2005, the government prevailed with a margin of fifty-nine to forty; however, seventeen Likud MKs voted against it and four were absent.[23] In short, the Prime Minister was able to secure the support of only nineteen of his party's forty MKs on this vote, which was crucial for the implementation of his key policy initiative. These nineteen MKs included the thirteen who would later join Sharon in the formation of Kadima, as well as Eli Aflalo, who was ill at the time of the vote. With the help of the opposition parties, Sharon managed to defeat the Likud rebels' initiative to tie the implementation of disengagement to a national referendum and pass the 2005 budget, which gave the ultimate "green light to proceed" with the evacuation of the Gush Katif settlements. When the actual process of the evacuations began, Sharon's Finance Minister Benyamin Netanyahu resigned from government and indicated he would challenge Sharon for party leadership.[24]

The last strategic battle between the two camps took place over the scheduling of the Likud leadership primary. The rebels, led by Netanyahu and Uzi Landau, called for an early primary to be followed by a general election where the party would be led by the newly elected party leader with a fresh mandate. In contrast, Sharon demanded that the Likud central committee should schedule the leadership race only after the general election. Although the committee sided with Sharon, the battle was not settled because the rebel MKs announced that they would become a de facto opposition to Sharon and would vote against the government consistently.[25]

The final clash between the two camps was over the approval of the appointment of four new Likud ministers (Ronnie Bar-on, Zev Boim, Ehud Olmert, and Matan Vilnai), which Sharon sought in order to improve the proportionality of portfolio allocation in favor of his own party. His earlier dismissal of Uzi Landau, along with the voluntary resignations by Netanyahu and Sharansky, left Likud with only eleven portfolios vis-à-vis Labor's eight, even though the united Likud faction was nearly twice the size of Labor (forty to nineteen).[26] Sharon remarked that if his four nominees were not appointed to the government, he would seriously consider leaving Likud and forming a new political party. Indeed, the rebels prevented the appointment of Boim and Bar-On on November 8, and two weeks later Sharon announced the formation of a new political party under the name Achrayut Leumit (National Responsibility), soon to be changed to Kadima. At the same time, Sharon announced that he was asking the Knesset to pass a vote for its early dissolution so that fresh elections could be held to what was by most accounts one of the most tumultuous parliaments in Israeli political history. In splitting from Likud, the Prime Minister was joined by thirteen other Likud MKs, including five other ministers and six deputy ministers, as well as David Tal, who immediately merged his Noy party with the new formation. It is worth noting that once again the size of the splitting faction was the absolute minimum required under the one-third rule.

The formation of Kadima followed in the footsteps of the Labor Party leadership primary, which resulted in Amir Peretz's victory over Shimon Peres on November 10. True to his campaign pledge, Peretz withdrew the Labor party from the coalition so that it could focus on preparing for the next election under his leadership.[27] With Labor's exit, Sharon's second government also came to an early end, leaving his new party Kadima and UTJ, its small coalition partner, in office as a caretaker coalition minority government. The formation of Kadima also generated a wave of exits by several high-profile MKs, including Shimon Peres, Dalia Itzik, and Haim Ramon from the Labor Party, who resigned their Knesset seats in order to run with Sharon's Kadima in the next election.[28]

In contrast to these Labor MKs, National Union MK Michael Nudelman tried to hold onto his mandate while also declaring his intention to run as a Kadima candidate in the upcoming election. Trying to prevent him to do so, the National Union party group submitted a claim to the Knesset Committee, asking it to designate Nudelman as a defector.[29] A number of committee members claimed that Nudelman should be treated in the same way as those Labor MKs who had quit the Knesset. Yet, since Nudelman only declared his intention to run with Kadima without yet formally joining the new party, his situation was more ambiguous. The Knesset's legal advisor, Arbel Astrachan, urged members of the committee to keep in mind the original intent of the anti-defection legislation and measure the merit of the Nudelman case accordingly. She stressed that the anti-defection law was passed with the specific intention to prevent the kinds of defections and horse-trading that became emblematic of the "stinking trick." As such, the question the committee had to answer was whether Nudelman had committed anything of the sort. From a legal standpoint, Astrabel further noted, a mere declaration by an incumbent MK that he or she would like to run on the list of another party, new or existing, did not constitute defection since the Knesset Law clearly allowed parties and candidates to make arrangements for the preparation of candidates lists within ninety days before the next election. Thus, the issue boiled down to assessing whether there was sufficient evidence in Nudelman's legislative behavior to warrant branding him a defector.

The argument against Nudelman was brought by Zvi Hendel, leader of the Tekuma Party within the National Union. Hendel argued that Nudelman had already turned against the faction for over a year and half, as demonstrated by his voting behavior. Moreover, he stopped attending the regular faction meetings, which made it more difficult to work with him. By far the most effective evidence against Nudelman was his vote in favor of the Sharon government's Disengagement Plan on October 26, 2004, even though all the other MKs of the National Union faction voted against it. Moreover, Nudelman had been voting consistently in favor of the government on almost all no-confidence votes ever since his party left the coalition in the summer of 2004. In short, plenty of evidence appeared to favor the faction's argument that Nudelman had left its ranks both de facto and de jure. In this context, Hendel further argued, Nudelman's inclusion in the Kadima list for the next election constituted precisely the kind of compensation, or consideration, that the anti-defection legislation set out to penalize. Thus, the faction argued, Nudelman was a defector who received compensation for his exit and therefore ought not to be allowed to run on the Kadima list, and he should also suffer all other legal consequences associated with defection.

Nudelman's defense stressed two important procedural details. The first had to do with the timing of the case. The anti-defection legislation clearly stated that the Knesset Committee's investigation had to take place in close temporal proximity to the event suspected to constitute a breach of party loyalty. Given that the National Union faction was citing evidence against Nudelman that was a year-and-a-half old and that none of the issues against Nudelman were brought up any time before, although there had been plenty of committee meetings to provide such opportunities, Nudelman should not at this stage be charged with defection. In fact, his recurring votes against the rest of his faction, and the failure of the faction to charge him at the time these supposed infractions took place, seemed to support the fact that there was a tentative agreement between him and the faction to allow him to vote his conscience if ever he wanted to.

The second issue had to do with the complex question of which party Nudelman was actually representing in the Knesset. During the pre-electoral frenzy of splits and mergers that took place before the simultaneous Knesset and prime ministerial elections in 1999, Nudelman and Yuri Shtern had left their party, Yisrael Be'aliyah, and formed a new party called Aliyah—For a Renewed Israel. In the 1999 elections, the two MKs formed an alliance with Avigdor Lieberman's newly formed party Yisrael Beitenu (Our Home Israel). In the 2003 election to the Sixteenth Knesset, however, Yisrael Beitenu ran as a member of a four-party conservative electoral alliance with the National Union, Moledet, and Tekuma parties. Shtern and Nudelman occupied safe spots on the joint list, ranked third and fifth, respectively (the list won seven mandates). Technically, Nudelman argued in the Knesset Committee, he was one of two MKs of the Aliyah Party, whose discipline he never breached. However, the National Union argued that Aliyah was not a separate member of the joint party group and, therefore, Nudelman was bound by its rules and instructions.

The final decision for the Knesset Committee was a clear reflection of the partisan interests involved. Of the ten MKs present at the committee meeting and the final vote, exactly half belonged to Likud, and one each to Shas, Meretz, Aguda, the National Religious Party, and the National Union. With the exception of the Shas and Meretz representatives, all other MKs voted in favor of the proposal to consider Nudelman a defector and to sanction him accordingly. The combined efforts of the rightwing opposition parties (Likud, NRP, and the National Union) had a clear electoral orientation: since Nudelman was considered a respected leader among the immigrant Russian-speaking voting population, having him barred from running on the Kadima list would have weakened the party's appeal to the Russian electorate, leaving ever more of its voters in the camp of Yisrael Beitenu.

In a final move of the dramatic unfolding of the ripple effects of the formation of Kadima, Nudelman used his right under the anti-defection legislation to appeal the decision of the Knesset Committee before the Jerusalem District Court. Interestingly, the Court's decision went against the Knesset Committee and allowed Nudelman to run on the Kadima ticket in the upcoming elections on the condition that he immediately resign his seat in the current Knesset.[30] Complying with this ruling, Nudelman quit the Knesset, a week after the committee's original decision against him, and he was subsequently re-elected to the Knesset from the twenty-seventh spot on the Kadima list.

Conclusion

The central objective for the introduction of the anti-defection law after the "stinking trick" was to ensure that defections and party switching would not undermine government stability. Yet, the anti-defection law could neither prevent individual MKs, groups of MKs, or the government in power to seek and find ways around the technicality of the law and influence the prevailing legislative balance of power between government and opposition. Just as Prime Minister Yitzhak Shamir's incumbent government ultimately proved to have an advantage in luring defectors to its side, this chapter showed that Prime Minister Ariel Sharon's government enjoyed a similar advantage in manipulating the effects of the anti-defection law to its own interest. Although the introduction of what Hazan calls a quasi-constructive vote of no-confidence[31] rendered Sharon's position much safer from termination than Shamir's had been, Sharon's ability to attract the support of key defectors played a very important role in keeping his government in office.

In short, defections and party exits continued to play a key role in shaping the dynamics of government survival even after the anti-defection law took effect. This argument lends an important and interesting interpretation of the finding presented at the start of the chapter according to which most party switches continue to take place within the parliamentary opposition. It appears that a critical portion of these within-opposition switches are carried out with the objective of dividing the opposition and thus advance the interest and stability of the government in office. These findings, therefore, suggest that the anti-defection law may actually have achieved its central objective to keep the incumbent government's tenure safe from the harmful effects of party switching even if the actual means by which it was achieved were unexpected.

The conclusion that the Israeli anti-defection law can help keep governments prolong their term in office has important comparative relevance beyond the literature on party switching. Although extant scholarship on the relationship between legislative institutions and government termination has emphasized the role of the design of the different types of no-confidence vote,[32] this chapter shows that the anti-defection law can also have a strong effect on the relationship and balance between the incumbent government and its parliamentary opposition. By increasing the transaction costs for switching, an anti-defection law can discourage prospective defectors who might otherwise drag incumbent governments into the vortex of cascading exits, splits, and eventual collapse. Thus, even if the Israeli anti-defection laws may not have kept parties more stable overall, it has helped governments remain more durable, which is an important institutional lesson for other comparable cases.

Chapter 7

Does Defection Pay?

The Electoral Consequences of Party Switching

On December 30, 2018, at 11:30 a.m., the Knesset Committee was convened in order to discuss a request submitted by Naftali Bennett, Minister of Education and Diaspora Affairs and leader of the eight-MK-strong Jewish Home party group, to approve his exit from his own party group together with two other members, Minister of Justice Ayelet Shaked and Shuli Moalem-Rafaeli. The three politicians also requested to set up a new Knesset party group under the name "The New Right." Since the number of MKs satisfied the one-third conditions for a legal split, the Knesset Committee did not have to spend much time discussing the request and in a unanimous decision granted its approval. Furthermore, the Committee also approved that the New Right could use Tzalash (Zionism, Liberalism, Equality), Yosef Paritzky's erstwhile registered party that had already stopped functioning effectively for a long while, as its shelf party so that it could be properly set up as a Knesset party group with an extra-parliamentary organization and receive appropriate financial benefits.[1]

The formation of the New Right took place on the very eve of the pre-electoral period leading to the 2019 April legislative elections. In those general elections, the New Right fought a vigorous campaign and came extremely close to entering the Twenty-First Knesset. However, when the final results were tallied, the party remained 1,500 valid votes short to cross the electoral threshold. It appeared that the bet of the two former cabinet ministers—widely touted as the powerful duo on the political scene of the contemporary Israeli Right and who had worked hard to broaden the electoral appeal of their Religious-Zionist political bloc—had not paid off, with their adventure ending in a disappointing defeat and failure.

Yet, thanks to the turbulent electoral politics of 2019 and 2020, which were marked by that fact that three general elections had to be held in quick succession until a National Unity / National Emergency government could be eventually formed, the New Right did not have to remain in the Israeli political wilderness for long. For the next Knesset elections, held five months later in September 2019, the New Right entered into a renewed electoral alliance with the two ministers' former party, the Jewish Home, and under Ayelet Shaked's leadership it contested the elections as Yamina (Rightward). Although Yamina's overall electoral performance was poorer than what most polls had anticipated, both Shaked and Bennett safely regained their Knesset mandates, with Bennett formally becoming Minister of Defense in Prime Minister Netanyahu's caretaker government.

The story of the New Right provides an excellent illustration of one of the key patterns that characterize the electoral consequences of party switching. This chapter will show that leaving the legislative party group that an MK was elected to represent does not provide positive electoral benefits: in fact, considerably more MKs who switch end up not returning to the next Knesset. As such, the first part of the short electoral history of the New Right fits this general pattern. However, as the second part of the story shows, politicians can avoid the negative electoral cost for party switching by entering into an electoral alliance with other parties and bargaining for sufficiently high spots on the joint candidate list. It was exactly this logic of forming an electoral alliance with the former party of Ministers Bennett and Shaked that allowed the two protagonists of this episode to fight, and eventually find, their way back to the Knesset. Moreover, the story also shows that political experience matters: while both Bennett and Shaked were ultimately successful to re-enter the Knesset, the third MK, Shuli Moalem-Rafaeli, who helped them form the New Right, and whose participation was pivotal under the one-third rule, did not do so.

The chapter analyzes the electoral consequences of party switching for both individual MKs and the party groups they form. As we have seen in previous chapters, the anti-defection law encourages the formation of new party groups by incentivizing disgruntled MKs to engage in collective party switching. This chapter will show that the electoral success of such newly formed party groups varies with their origin: new party groups formed as a result of a legal split, either under the one-third or under the pre-electoral conditions, tend to become electorally successful either when they secede from one of the larger parties or when they reactivate an already well-established party label, whereas new party groups that result from the splintering of smaller or mid-sized parties become successful only if they can form a viable multiparty electoral alliance in the next election.

The interconnected logic of the formation and the electoral performance of new parties has direct implications for the electoral consequences of party switching for individual MKs. Since the Israeli electoral system is closed-list PR, MK's re-electability fundamentally depends on whether they secure a realistic spot, high enough placement, on the candidate list of a party that will cross the electoral threshold. In the competition for such placement, political experience matters and those with less experience are less likely to be re-elected. This chapter will describe and illustrate these processes in further depth, following a brief empirical overview of the electoral consequences of party switching both for individual MKs and for party groups.

An Empirical Assessment
of the Electoral Consequences of Party Switching

Figure 7.1 compares the re-election rates of party-switching MKs before and since the adoption of the anti-defection law. For the purposes of this comparison, every individual MK who changes a party group at least once in a Knesset is counted as one observation. If the same MK switches more than once in the same Knesset he or she will still be counted once; however, if the same MKs change party group in different Knesset terms, those are entered as separate observations. For example, MK Eliezer Sandberg switched in both the Fourteenth and Sixteenth Knessets and is thus counted separately for those legislative terms: after the former, he was re-elected to the Fifteenth Knesset; however, following his switch in the Sixteenth Knesset, he was not. Similarly, MK Meir Shetreet, who switched in both the Sixteenth and the Eighteenth Knessets and was re-elected to both legislatures that followed, is also counted twice. However, MK Elhanan Glazer served only one term in the Seventeenth Knesset and, although he switched twice during that short period followed by not being re-elected to the Eighteenth Knesset, he is only counted once.

The percentage of switching MKs who have been re-elected has dropped significantly across the two time periods. Since the adoption of the anti-defection law, only 40.6 percent of MKs who changed their party group have been re-elected to the next legislature, in comparison to 55 percent during the previous period. The institutional incentive of the anti-defection law is evidently related to this difference: by encouraging larger and collective switches, the anti-defection law has resulted in party switching by those MKs as well who did not have a realistic chance to be re-elected and whose participation in the collective switch was motivated by the need to satisfy the condition of a legal split. Prior to the anti-defection law, however, MKs could be, and were, much more circumspect about gauging the probably electoral consequences of their party change and would take that into consideration when deciding to switch or stay put. The contrast between the collective exit by a group of eight Mapai MKs led by former Prime Minister Ben Gurion to form a new party Rafi in 1965 and that by the seven Kadima MKs who proceeded to form the new party Hatnua Tzipi Livni in 2012 is instructive. In both cases the new party groups were re-elected to the following Knesset. However, while six of the eight former Mapai MKs were successfully returned, only one of the seven former Kadima MKs did so.

Figure 7.2 shows significant variation across the Knesset terms with regard to the re-election of switching MKs. At one extreme, the Fourteenth and Sixteenth Knessets stand out with particularly high re-election rates that far exceed the average for the period. In the former, 55 percent of MKs

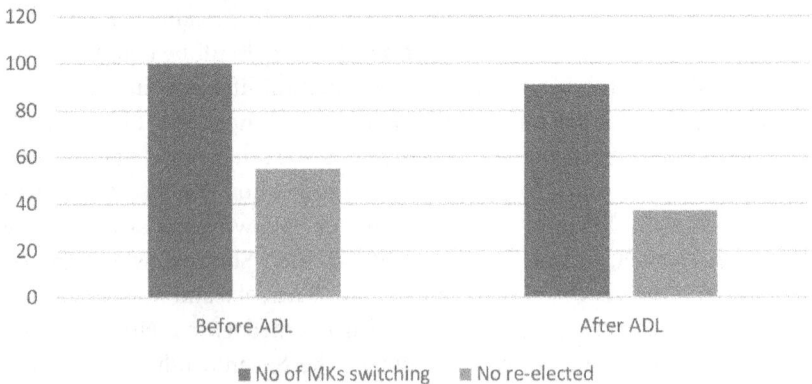

Figure 7.1. Re-election of party switchers in Israel, 1949 to 2019.

who changed their party group ended up returning to the next Knesset, while in a the latter the re-election rate reached a striking 72 percent. The previous chapter showed that the formation of the Kadima Party under the leadership of Ariel Sharon in the Sixteenth Knesset was not only the single largest collective switch but was also responsible for a wave of additional switches in the ranks of other parties. A close look at the re-election rates of the MKs who formed Kadima further shows how powerful the effect of this event was: of the fourteen former Likud MKs who formed the new party, only the Prime Minister and his son, Omri Sharon, were not re-elected, and the former only because of his debilitating illness.

At the other end of the spectrum, we find the Seventeenth and Twentieth Knessets, in which the number of switching MKs was almost the same—three and four, respectively—and the re-election rates were identical with none of the switchers succeeding to return. As we saw in chapter 5, the Seventeenth Knesset witnessed the complete disintegration of the Pensioners' Party, which at first suffered the exit of three of its MKs to be followed by the return of two of them. In the Twentieth Knesset, the four MKs who switched were those who had formed the New Right party, discussed at the start of the chapter, as well as MK Orly Levy-Abukasis, who was actually removed from her party, Yisrael Beitenu, by an adverse decision of the Knesset Committee. Similar to the New Right, Orly Levy-Abukasis also failed to be re-elected to the Twenty-First Knesset, which she contested as the head of her old-new party, Gesher, founded by her father David Levy in the early 1990s. In

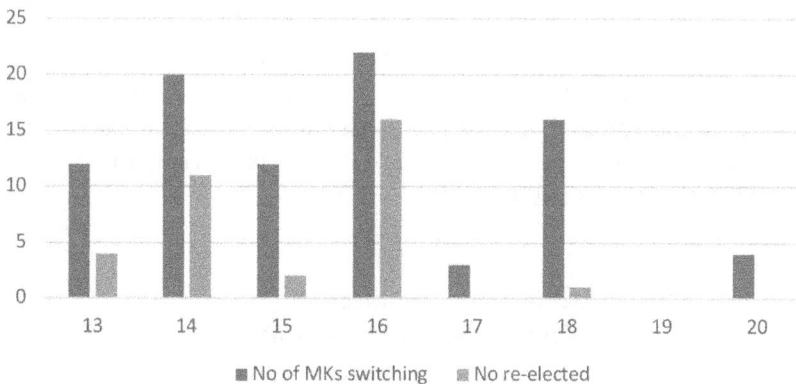

Figure 7.2. The number of switching MKs and their re-election, 1992 to 2019.

the following election, however, she was successfully re-elected as her part of an electoral alliance with the Labor Party.

Although individual politicians may be motivated, at least in part, by their own re-election, the Israeli electoral system is party centered and makes an MK's re-election contingent on which party lists he or she joins and how well, or rather how high, he or she is placed on the party list. In other words, since Israeli elections use a closed-list PR system, voters cannot hold individual politicians directly to account. Therefore, an understanding of the electoral consequences of party switching should also take into account party-level dynamics, specifically, what the electoral fate of new political parties MKs form in the Knesset through party switching.

Since the adoption of the anti-defection law, party switching has resulted in the formation of twenty-four new political parties in the Knesset, on average three new parties per Knesset. Again, as figure 7.3 shows, there has been significant variation in this number across the legislative terms, with the Thirteenth and the Fourteenth Knessets having particularly high numbers, five and eight, respectively. It is important to reiterate that Amendment 31, which was passed with the intention of making the formation of new parties easier in the pre-electoral period, was in effect precisely during these Knessets. As such, the higher than average number of new parties in these parliaments provides evidence in support of the important institutional effect of Amendment 31. Accordingly, once this law was rescinded, the rate of new party formation decreased.

The electoral success of these new parties has also varied considerably, but it is important to emphasize that new parties have been much more successful in terms of their re-election than individual MKs. In contrast to the re-election rate of 40.6 percent among switching MKs, new party groups had a re-election rate of 58 percent (fourteen of the twenty-four new parties were re-elected). In terms of the individual Knesset terms, the Fourteenth, Fifteenth, and Sixteenth Knessets stand out, as they had the highest new party re-election rates, at 88 percent, 100 percent, and 50 percent, respectively.

Understanding the Electoral Success of New Parties and Switching MKs

Under the Israeli electoral system, a political party has two principal avenues to enter the Knesset. The first is to enter the electoral contest on

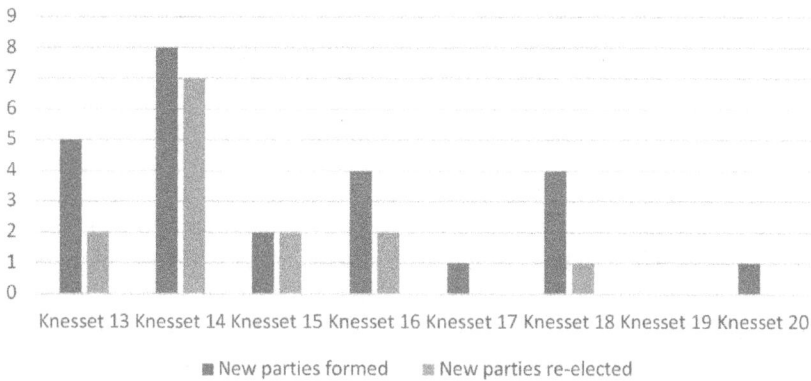

Figure 7.3. The formation and electoral success of new parties, 1992 to 2019.

its own by running a list of its candidates. If the list crosses the electoral threshold, it enters and partakes in the allocation of Knesset seats. The second avenue is for multiple political parties to come together and form a joint electoral list. Therefore, when party switching results in the formation of a new party group in the Knesset, the electoral viability of such a new party depends on (a) whether it will cross the threshold on its own or (b) whether it can enter a broader multiparty electoral alliance that will do so. With regard to the former, two types of new parties enjoy a particular advantage: those that split from a large established party and those that resurrect an older but well-established and well-known party label.

Large parties, by definition, have a larger electoral following that breakaway MKs can tap into when they form a new splinter party. Moreover, large parties, by definition, bring together multiple electoral constituents, some defined by ethnicity, and some by ideological or more narrowly based issue preferences. Breakaway MKs can develop a careful strategy to capture and mobilize these subparty groups and rally them to their support in the next election. Indeed, each and every one of the twenty-four new parties formed between 1992 and 2019 as a result of a breakaway from one of the major parties continued to be electorally successful in the subsequent legislature. Since the previous chapters have already discussed all of these cases in depth, it will be sufficient to simply point them out and ask the reader to refer to the details of each case in the appropriate chapter.

Among the twenty-four new party groups, seven seceded from either the senior government party or the largest opposition at the time. These were the Third Way and Gesher that split from the Labor Party and Likud, respectively, in the Thirteenth Knesset; the Am Ehad that split from the Labor Party, the Center Party that brought together two groups of MKs from Labor and Likud respectively, and Herut that split from Likud in the Fourteenth Knesset; Kadima that split from Likud in the Sixteenth Knesset; and Hatnua that split from Kadima in the Eighteenth Knesset. All of these parties, except for Gesher, which joined an electoral alliance with Likud in the 1996 elections, and Herut, which entered a three-party alliance in the 1999 election, ran in the next election on its own and, most importantly, all were re-elected. In one case, a new Knesset party group was based on the re-establishment of an earlier well-established party label. This was the case of Shinui, a party established in 1980 as a new party group in the Ninth Knesset, which ran successfully for the next twelve years before merging into the new Meretz Party 1992. In the Fourteenth Knesset, MK Avraham Poraz left the Meretz union and re-created Shinui, which another MK, Eliezer Sandberg, also joined. The re-created party contested the 1999 election on its own and won six seats, three times as many as it had won the previous time it competed in a Knesset election in 1988. In short, party origin clearly matters for the electoral success of new Knesset parties.

The remaining seventeen new party groups were formed by MKs who had split from smaller or medium-sized parties. To this group belonged Haatzmaut, formed by group Labor MKs led by Ehud Barak, leader of the Labor Party at the time. By then the Labor Party had slipped from its position of electoral prominence and was only the fourth largest party in the Knesset, with a mere thirteen seats. Of these seventeen new parties, only six proved to be electorally successful, and all of these were re-elected to the Knesset because they formed a viable electoral alliance with other parties. These six party groups were Aliah, Menora, and Emunim in the Fourteenth Knesset, Machar and Taal in the Fifteenth Knesset, and Hitchabrut in the Sixteenth Knesset. The remaining eleven new party groups not re-elected to the Knesset all originated in smaller or medium-sized parties, and either disintegrated before the next election (e.g., Yi'ud in the Thirteenth Knesset or the Justice for the Elderly in the Seventeenth Knesset); ran on their own (e.g., the New Right in 2019); or decided to withdraw from the electoral contest in the absence of viable electoral following (e.g., Haatzmaut in 2012).

Clearly, the electoral fate of new party groups will determine first and foremost the electoral success and re-electability of MKs who switched parties. Put simply, if an MK forms or joins a party group that fails to cross the electoral threshold, then it does not matter what qualifications or assets the MKs might have possessed that otherwise might have made him or her potentially more electable. The literature suggests, however, that the political experience of party switchers, particularly their legislative experience, is an important asset that promotes the chances of their re-election.[2] Indeed, the Israeli data appear to support this. Figure 7.4 breaks down switching MKs into two groups according to their legislative experience: first-time, or rookie, MKs and those with at least some experience of legislative service. It is evident from the bar chart that in both time periods rookie legislators who switched from their original party group were re-elected at a much lower rate than their more experienced colleagues. Prior to the adoption of the anti-defection law, 27.7 percent of rookie switchers were re-elected, and this number has increased only slightly, to 28.2 percent, since 1992. In contrast, 83.8 percent of non-rookie switchers were re-elected before the anti-defection law, but only 50 percent did so since the law took effect. Another way of showing this relative shift is that the ratio of re-elected non-rookie MKs to re-elected rookie MKs has dropped from 5.1 to only 2.4 across the two time periods. In short, this comparison suggests that experience matters: both before and since the adoption of the anti-defection law, rookie switchers were re-elected much less frequently than their more experienced co-legislators.

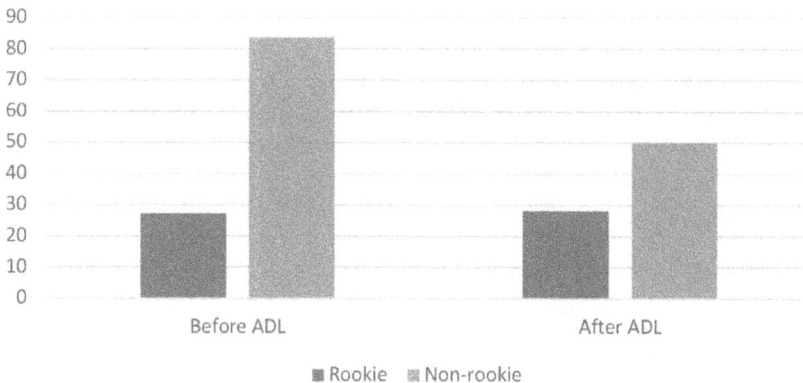

Figure 7.4. Re-election of switching MKs by legislative experience.

The relative decline in the re-election rates of the latter group is consistent with the overall decrease in the re-election rate of party switchers since the anti-defection law took effect. The data show that most of the re-election failures came from among the group of rookie MKs.

Conclusion

This chapter has shown that party switching has carried considerable electoral cost both before and since the adoption of the anti-defection law. While more than half of party switchers were re-elected prior to 1992, this rate has dropped by more than 10 percent in the period since. Rookie legislators who change parties are particularly vulnerable and tend not to be re-elected as often as their more experienced colleagues; however, their participation is almost always pivotal for the formation of new party groups that need to satisfy the criteria for a legal split. Under the anti-defection legislation, the dynamics of party switching has fundamentally changed in favor of collective switches leading to the formation of new party groups in the Knesset. The chapter also pointed to three important factors that are consequential for the electoral viability of the new parties under the structure of the electoral system: the party that they split from, the party label they (re)-create, and their ability to enter into a multiparty electoral alliance.

Chapter 8

Comparative Cases

Anti-Defections Laws and Their Consequences in India, New Zealand, and South Africa

This chapter casts the Israeli case in a broader comparative context by examining the history of anti-defection legislation in three other democracies: India, New Zealand, and South Africa. The circumstances that led to the adoption, and subsequent changes, of these laws in the three countries vary substantially from those that prevailed in Israel. However, they reinforce the profound difficulty that legislators may face elsewhere in designing an anti-defection law that can effectively balance between the competing logics of protecting the political freedom of individual legislators, enhancing the unity of legislative parties, and ensuring the overall integrity of the electoral process so that electoral outcomes are reflected in the composition and the output of the legislature. As we shall see, Israel remains unique in maintaining an anti-defection law that approximates such a balance: while India and South Africa have moved toward privileging political parties over individual legislators by effectively banning party hopping, New Zealand allowed the country's temporary anti-defection law to expire, until its recent re-introduction in 2018, for precisely the opposite reason. At the same time, none of these other anti-defection laws experienced the frequency of change and amendments that characterized the Israeli regulation of defections.

The key institutional variation among the three cases and that of Israel is presented in table 8.1. The columns in the table distinguish anti-defection laws according to their conditionality (conditional vs. cat-

Table 8.1. Typology of Anti-Defection Laws

	Categorical	Conditional
Disqualification (loss of seat)	India after 2003; New Zealand (2001–2005, after 2018); South Africa after 2008	India 1985–2003, South Africa 2002–2008
No disqualification (seat retained)		Israel

Source: Csaba Nikolenyi, "Government Termination and Anti-Defection Laws," 645.

egorical) while the rows sort them according to whether a defector can lose her legislative mandate. Going counter-clockwise from the top left quadrant, the most punitive anti-defection laws are those that are categorical and impose disqualification as the penalty for defection. This type of law essentially revives the delegate model of representation, rooted in the archaic practice of the imperative mandate, that strictly binds the elected representative to follow and faithfully represent the manifest preferences and interests of the elector. By making defections so costly, an anti-defection law of this type seeks to freeze the legislative party system according to the results of the last election: because it is so costly for legislators to defect and change the balance of seats in the inter-election period, the legislative party system is likely to remain stable with government durability unaffected by defections. A variant of such categorical anti-defection laws is in the second, lower-left quadrant that imposes lighter punishments on defectors without causing them to lose their seats in the current legislature.

The third type is a permissive anti-defection law that not only allows defectors to hold onto their seats, while incurring other kinds of penalties, but also allows certain kinds of defection to go unpunished. A permissive anti-defection law retains a key element of the Burkean, or trustee, model of representation in that it treats a defecting legislator's seat as untouchable and cannot be taken away. In other words, while defection can be penalized, it can never lead to disqualification. The Israeli anti-defection law belongs to this category. Such laws permit legislators to strategize and find ways to avoid the penalty of the law and, as a consequence, they are less likely to insulate governments from the harmful effects of defection. Finally, the fourth category is an anti-defection law that combines conditionality with disqualification: while certain defections are tolerated and go unpunished if the stipulated conditions are met, a defector who fails to meet these conditions will pay the heavy price of losing his or her legislative seat. Mapping the main variations in the types of anti-defection measures helps us better understand not only why legislatures vary in their response to government terminating defections but also how effective and successful the different anti-defection measures have become.

The Growing Severity of the
Anti-Defection Law in India, 1985–2003

India adopted its anti-defection law by way of a constitutional amendment in 1985. Similar to Israel, there had been a number of prior calls and suggestions to pass such legislation. However, it required the unique political moment when the Congress Party won its largest-ever landslide parliamentary majority in the 1985 elections for the law to be adopted. The idea of adopting an anti-defection legislation was first floated in the aftermath of the large-scale defections that took place in the spring of 1967. In their immediate aftermath, the Lok Sabha struck a Committee of Defection that involved representatives of political parties as well as constitutional experts.[1] This committee provided a formal definition of what constitutes a defection, which was retained in its essence by the 1985 Amendment. In 1980, a prominent member of opposition, M. Dandavate, moved that the Lok Sabha should draft an anti-defection bill. However, the Congress government of the time showed no interest in pursuing the matter. The two instances when pieces of anti-defection legislation were actually introduced in the national parliament occurred in 1973 and 1978 as parts of the Thirty-Second and Forty-Eighth Constitutional Amendment Bills, respectively. However, neither of these Bills passed. The only successful legislative regulation of defections took place in the state of Jammu and Kashmir through the passage of the Jammu and Kashmir Representation of People' Act of 1979. Interestingly, the anti-defection legislation adopted in Jammu and Kashmir referred issues and cases of disqualification to the judiciary rather than to the office of the Speaker for adjudication. This example was referred to as an important precedent during the parliamentary debates of the 1985 Bill. However, the Congress government insisted on keeping the Speaker in ultimate charge of deciding the status of defecting legislators.

Another similarity with the Israeli case was that the Indian legislation distinguished between "defections," which are penalized, and "splits," which are allowed and recognized. The distinction between the two kinds of switching was the same numerical criterion of one-third of the total number of the party's elected representatives; however, the Indian legislation was much more categorical and did not allow for the kinds of exceptions we saw in Israel. Furthermore, India's anti-defection law was much more stable and did not experience the frequent amendments and re-amendments that characterized Israeli legislation. After nearly two decades, the Indian Parliament did pass an amendment to the anti-defection law in 2003 that eliminated the possibility of a recognized split, and since then all forms of legislative party switching fall under the same set of penalties. The administration of party switching in the two cases has always followed fundamentally different models: instead of allowing a legislative committee to make the relevant decisions, the Indian legislation empowered the Speaker of the respective house, where switching occurs, to adjudicate.

The immediate context for the passage of the anti-defection law of 1985 was provided by the eighth general election to the Lok Sabha.[2] The Congress Party swept the polls riding on a wave of sympathy votes that poured forth after the assassination of Indira Gandhi on October 31, 1984. Within just a few hours of her death, the Congress(I) Parliamentary Board recommended to President Zail Singh to appoint Rajiv Gandhi, son of the slain Prime Minister, as the new head of government. The President complied with the advice and appointed Rajiv Gandhi the same day. On November 2, the Congress(I) Parliamentary Party also elected Rajiv Gandhi as its leader, and on November 12, the Congress(I) Working Committee along with Congress(I) Chief Ministers and state party presidents elected him as co-president of the party alongside with Kamlapathi Tripathi.

The selection of Rajiv Gandhi to the apex of the Congress Party's leadership provided the party with internal stability that was crucial to take full advantage of the sympathy vote. Indeed, the general election that followed the assassination resulted in the best electoral performance of the Congress(I) ever, both in terms of the share of the popular vote it mustered, 48.1 percent, as well as the share of Lok Sabha seats won, 76 percent. The opposition was utterly devastated in the election. The largest opposition party emerging was the Telugu Desam (TD), a state party recognized and running candidates only in the state of Andhra Pradesh, with a mere thirty seats. Of the national parties, the Communist Party of India (Marxist) won the most seats, twenty-two of the sixty-four that it contested.

Yet, despite having no background in political life whatsoever, the novice Prime Minister showed no sign of wanting to be merely an interim leader. The proposed cabinet list that Rajiv Gandhi submitted to President Zail Singh reflected the young Prime Minister's attempt to establish firm control over the government, as more than half of his proposed cabinet consisted of newcomers. While a majority of his ministers with cabinet rank were incumbents, at the rank of ministers of state he nominated sixteen newcomers while retaining only nine incumbents.[3] Thus, the Congress party found itself caught between the Scylla of electoral victory and the Charybdis of an unsettled internal leadership transition. Yet, in stark contrast to earlier instances, the governing party also found itself with a much larger majority of seats under its control in parliament. This presented the new prime minister with an ambiguous situation. On the one hand, he had at his disposal a large legislative majority that allowed him to exercise very effective control over the legislative business and agenda as well as to adopt and pursue government policies that he deemed appropriate. On the other hand, he would also have to cope with the problem of intraparty rebellion and defections. This was certainly not a novel problem and phenomenon in Indian politics; however, it was one that would be of particular concern for a novice political leader yet untrained in the art of securing alliances and intraparty support. The importance of containing defections and ascertaining the new leader's authority over the party was made clear when Rajiv Gandhi felt compelled to speak to this issue in the Lok Sabha in the closing debates of the bill on January 30, 1985:

> What is the hurry in having this Bill? We have been waiting 7 years to have this Bill and a lot of damage has been done. This Bill should have come yesterday, should have come last year, should have come 7 years ago. We are doing it the fastest that we can do. Feel that anybody who does not want this Bill has to have his own integrity examined. Sir, it has been said that this Bill is being brought to keep the Congress Party intact, to strengthen the Congress Party. I would like to point out that the defections are invariably to the Congress Party, and not from the Congress Party. We do not have a problem with people leaving the party: we have a problem with people wanting to join our party. We do not need this to strengthen our party. You can see the strength of our party in front of you.[4]

The Prime Minister re-iterated this point the following day when the debate continued in the upper house of parliament, the Rajya Sabha:

> If you look at the history of defections, the number of peoples that have left the Congress is insignificant. I am not talking of splits, because splits are different. I am talking about defections. . . . So the Bill is not to stop the Congress from breaking up. The Congress has lived and gained strength for a hundred years. We are not going to break up in a few years.[5]

The opposition, however, was quick to point out inconsistencies in these claims. A Communist member of the upper house, Indradeep Sinha pointed out that he

> was surprised at the Prime Minister's remark that there have been more defections towards the Congress than from the Congress. Maybe, it is true. Then it only shows that the ruling party has pursued a systemic policy of instigating defections to its side or of abducting persons elected on the tickets of other parties. . . . According to this [Home Ministry's] report, in 1968, 139 Members [of parliament] had defected from other parties to the Congress and 175 Members had defected from the Congress to other parties.[6]

Sinha further pointed out that the sharp increase in the number of defections over time implied a "two-way traffic" of party switching. The same point has been made by Hardgrave and Kochanek, who note that prior to 1989 there had been "more than 2,700 recorded cases since 1967, most within the state assemblies. Congress had been the principal beneficiary, with as many as 1,900 defections to Congress. . . . Between March 1967 and June 1968, the high days of defection, 16 state governments were brought down by defections. Of the 438 legislators who changed parties during this period, 210 were rewarded with ministerships."[7]

As part of the new government's program, the passage of an anti-defection law was explicitly mentioned in the President's Speech during the inaugural session of the Eighth Lok Sabha in on January 17, 1985. Five days later, and following intense all-party consultations, the new Minister of Law and Justice, A. K. Sen, introduced a Bill to Amend the Constitution. In its initial form, the Bill stipulated that elected or nominated member of the national Parliament or a State Assembly would be disqualified if they *defected* from the party that elected or nominated them; if they *voted* against their party or abstained from voting without permission; or if they were *expelled* from the party. Questions about disqualification on grounds of defections, breaking the party line, or expulsion were proposed to be dealt with by the Speaker, or the presiding officer, of the legislative chamber in question. The constitutional amendment bill was debated in the plenary session of the Lok Sabha on January 30 and passed unanimously that same day. Indicative of the broad support for the anti-defection law, the Rajya Sabha debated and passed the bill the following day with no amendments or modifications. On February 15, the new law came into effect as the fifty-second Amendment to the Constitution of India.

Some of the most serious consequences of defections that deputies noted during the debates included government instability; the undermining of the principles of representative democracy; the "selling" off of ministerial positions; de-stabilizing the party system; and betrayal of Indian political values. With regard to the latter, it was particularly significant, symbolically, that the Bill was debated in the Lok Sabha on the anniversary of Mahatma Gandhi's death. Indeed, several lawmakers pointed out that the Bill aimed at nothing less than the restoration of the Gandhian ideals of clean public life and service. Criticisms of the Bill were few; most of them came from the opposition benches and centered on two points: the power of the Speaker in adjudicating claims of disqualifications, and the power of the caucus vis-à-vis the elected individual MP. The timeline of the passage of the Bill is summarized in table 8.2.

The 1985 Constitutional Amendment Bill was passed in nearly the exact same form as it had been introduced by the Minister of Law and

Table 8.2. The Passage of the Anti-Defection Amendment to the Indian Constitution

Date	Detail	Voting records	Outcome
January 17, 1985	President's speech		
January 23, 1985	Bill is introduced		
January 30, 1985	Lok Sabha debate and vote	418:0	Bill is passed
January 31, 1985	Rayja Sabha debate and vote	192:0	Bill is passed

Source: Csaba Nikolenyi and Shaul Shenhav, "The Constitutionalization of Party Unity."

Justice. The only significant change concerned the expulsion of deputies by a party, which according to the final version no longer constituted an admissible ground for disqualification. The Law states that a member of a legislature, state or national, belonging to any political party shall be disqualified for membership

> if he votes or abstains from voting in such House contrary to any direction issued by the political to which he belongs or by any person or authority authorized by it in his behalf, without obtaining, in either case, the prior permission of such political party, person or authority and such voting or abstention has not been condoned by such political party, person or authority within fifteen days from the date of such voting or abstention; . . . An elected member of a House who has been elected as such otherwise than as a candidate set up by any political party shall be disqualified for being a member of the House if he joins any political party after such election.

Furthermore,

> Where a member of a House makes a claim that he and any other members of his legislature party constitute the group representing a faction which has arisen as a result of a split in his original political party and such a group consists of not less than one-third of the members of such legislature party,
>
> (a) he shall not be disqualified . . .
>
> (b) from the time of such split, such faction shall be deemed to be the political party . . .

Finally,

> a member of a House shall not be disqualified . . . where his original political party merges with another political party and he claims that he and any other members of his original political party;

(a) have become members of such other political party or, as the case may be, of a new political party formed by such merger; or

(b) have not accepted the merger and opted to function as a separate group . . .

. . . the merger of the original political party of a member of a House shall be deemed to have taken place if, and only if, not less than two-thirds of the members of the legislature party concerned have agreed to such merger.

Although often criticized for its inability to clean up political life, India's Anti-Defection Law has been quite successful in terms of reducing the number of defections and splits at both the national and the state levels. From 1985 to 2004, only sixteen requests were submitted to the Speaker to have individual members of the Lok Sabha disqualified. Interestingly, only two of these petitions were allowed by the Speaker, while the remaining fourteen cases were either dismissed or "rendered infractuous" due to the dissolution of the House. The sixteen cases involved thirty-nine individual deputies, but only thirteen of them were actually disqualified on the ground of defection.[8]

Of the five Lok Sabhas in this period, only the one elected in 1999 lasted a full term. It thus may not be surprising that the highest number of disqualification requests (five) were submitted during its term. By comparison, only three such requests were issued during the terms of the Eighth (1984–1989), the Tenth (1991–1996), and the Twelfth (1998–1999), two during the term of the Ninth Lok Sabha (1989–1991), and none during the term of the Eleventh (1996–1997). In the Rajya Sabha, only two disqualification cases occurred during the entire period of nineteen years, but both of them were allowed.

At the state level, there has been great variation in the number of disqualification requests issued and allowed. Between 1985 and 2004, ninety-seven petitions were submitted against 164 members of the different State Assemblies (Vidhan Sabha). Unlike at the national level, the majority of the individual parliamentarians, 113, charged with defection were actually removed from their respective assemblies. The majority of cases (fifty out of ninety-seven) were launched in four states, which shows a remarkable degree of concentration in the problem of defection. These are Uttar Pradesh, the largest state of the India Union, Haryana, and the tiny states of Goa and Manipur. The outcome of the disqualification cases has been highly uneven: while most of the deputies who were charged ended up being disqualified in Goa and Manipur, the majority of them had their cases dismissed in Haryana. In Uttar Pradesh, not a single deputy was disqualified on the grounds of defection.

The Anti-Defection Law was somewhat less effective to keep the number of splits and mergers at bay in the Lok Sabha. In the nineteen years following the adoption of the Law, twenty-two cases of party splits and thirteen cases of party mergers were registered, and all but three of them were allowed. At the state level, however, there were fewer splits and mergers than cases of individual defections.[9] On both counts, the states of Uttar Pradesh and Haryana stood out, accounting for the highest number of cases: the number of splits and mergers was twenty-four and twenty-seven in Uttar Pradesh, and six and eleven in Haryana, respectively. Interestingly, all these cases were allowed.

As the numbers indicate, the anti-defection law was evidently unable to eliminate legislative party switching in India. Building on the formal recommendations submitted by three commissions of inquiry that studied the working of the anti-defection law, among other issues, between 1990 and 2002,[10] the government of the Bharatiya Janata Party ensured unanimous passage of the Ninety-First Amendment to the India constitution in November 2003.[11] The amendment eliminated the category of a recognized split, regulated the size of a Council of Ministers, and explicitly barred parliamentarians who were disqualified on grounds of defection from having an executive appointment until such time that they were re-elected to their seat either in a general election or a by-election. The new law, however, did not alter the role of the Speaker in making the final decision about defections. By closing the loophole of a collective split, the new amendment effectively eliminated legislative party switching, although incidents of floor-crossing and defying the party whip continued, albeit at a much smaller scale. For example, in a well-publicized case, the Congress Party–led United Progressive Alliance coalition government narrowly survived a confidence vote in July 2008, by a margin of nineteen votes, due to cross voting and abstentions. Although several parties expelled their defiant deputies who voted against the party line, including the Speaker of the Lok Sabha, Somnath Chatterjee, most of them were not disqualified.[12]

Electoral Integrity Legislation in New Zealand

Similar to Israel, the history of New Zealand's anti-defection legislation stems from a political crisis associated with the politics of institutional reform in the early 1990s. The original anti-defection legislation expired in accordance with its sunset clause; however, after several attempts over the years, the House of Representatives re-passed it in October 2018. In stark contrast to the Israeli and the pre-2003 Indian cases, the solution that the New Zealand legislation proposed to combat legislative party switching did not allow for the possibility of recognized legal party splits but, instead, treated any form of switching in a uniform fashion. Similar to the Indian legislation, the New Zealand law empowered the Speaker to be the central decision maker and adjudicator of switching and defection cases, unlike the Israeli case where the Knesset Committee plays that role. Moreover, the New Zealand legislation gave explicit powers to parliamentary party leaders to seek the expulsion of renegade members of their party groups, a feature shared by the Indian but not the Israeli law. The original legislation in New Zealand remained in effect for a very short period, from 2001 to 2005. During this period, and thereafter, party switching in the New Zealand legislature has been by and large contained. Yet, the re-adoption of the law in 2018 bears testimony that defection politics in New Zealand remain far from resolved.

The genesis of the anti-defection law in New Zealand can be traced to the result of the 1993 referendum that paved the way to the electoral reform replacing the country's first-past-the-post electoral system with a mixed-member proportional system that was styled after that of Germany.[13] The new electoral system gave every voter two votes, one to be cast for a closed party list of candidates and another to be cast for individual candidates running in the voter's district. As in Germany, the overall allocation of the 120 seats in the House was primarily determined by the outcome of the list-vote results, which reflected the fact that the main concern that electoral reform sought to solve was to introduce proportionality to the country's electoral system. In just a few years after the introduction of the new system, it would be precisely the negative effect that party switching would have on distorting proportionality, the central goal of the new electoral system, that compelled a majority of lawmakers to introduce a special legislation to penalize such perfidy.

The first election under the new electoral system was held in October 1996.[14] As is normally the case under proportional electoral rules, the results of the election did not yield a majority outcome, and after two months of negotiations a coalition government was formed between the Right bloc of parties (led by the National Party and also including ACT New Zealand and the United Party) and New Zealand First, which played a balancing role between the Right and Left blocs. Within the first year of the term of the new House, a member of the opposition Alliance party, Mrs. Alamein Kopu, left her party in a much-publicized incident citing racial discrimination against the Maori people. Although Kopu, like all other Alliance MPs, had signed a blanket statement before the election committing herself to quitting her seat if she would ever leave the party, there was no legal way to enforce this pledge. What made her defection particularly problematic was that she was elected to the House from the party-list tier of the electoral system and, as such, she could not possibly justify her decision on the grounds that she was directly accountable to her constituents: her seat in the House was solely and exclusively the result of her party listing her as a candidate. Moreover, similar to the Israeli party funding law, Kopu was able to claim state funding for the new party she formed and led, Mana Wahine Te Ira Tangata.

Shortly after Kopu's defection, New Zealand suffered a coalition crisis that resembled Israel's "stinking trick." Following the elections, New Zealand First started out on a good working relationship with the National Party, the senior coalition partner, which agreed to offer it several senior positions in government. However, following a palace coup in the National Party that replaced Prime Minister Jim Bolger with Jenny Shipley in December 1997, the relations started to sour. In August 1998, the new Prime Minister sacked Winston Peters, the founding leader of New Zealand First, from his posts of Deputy Prime Minister and Treasurer, which immediately triggered Peters's decision to pull his party from the coalition. However, eight members of his party refused to follow him into the opposition and declared themselves Independent Members of the House supporting the coalition government. Together with Kopu, the New Zealand First defectors were able to keep the government in a bare-majority status, which lasted until the next elections in November 1999.

The defections that occurred in the House between 1996 and 1999 exposed the fragility of the political system that emerged for the new electoral rules. Further, they also showed that if left unchecked, disloyal MPs could easily undermine the principle of proportionality that the new electoral system was supposed to rest on: when MPs switch from the party that they were elected to represent, the proportionality of the vote-seat conversion is compromised. In order to prevent such events from recurring in the future, the Labor and the Alliance parties promised in their campaign during the 1999 election that they would introduce legislation to curb party hopping, which they did once they formed the new coalition minority government. Since Labor and Alliance won only forty-five and ten seats, respectively, their coalition government relied on the external support of the Green Party for the implementation of its legislative program. This meant serious complications for the purposes of passing an anti-party hopping law because the Green Party was adamant against regulating party switching, which it saw, as did the other opposition parties, as a violation of the individual political freedom of MPs. Therefore, even though the coalition partners proposed a very weak Electoral Integrity law, it could not pass the committee stage.

In its initial version, the Electoral (Integrity) Amendment Bill was introduced and passed its first reading in the House of Representatives on December 22, 1999, less than a month after the general election. The proposed bill sought to amend the Electoral Act of 1999 by inserting section Fifty-Five A, which would add a member's voluntary resignation from the party that such member was elected to represent in the last election, as a condition for creating vacancy in the House. The bill stipulated that if the resigning MP held a constituency seat, a by-election would have to be called to fill the vacancy, but if the MP had held a party-list, the candidate next in line from the same list would advance and enter the House. In addition, the bill had a sunset clause, according to which its provision would expire "with the close of the polling day for the second general election" after its passage. The House referred the bill to the Justice and Electoral Committee, which held hearings and received submissions until February 25, 2000.[15] According to its final report, the Committee was split and unable to provide a recommendation, which reflected partisan divisions on the issue of regulating party hopping that would delay the passage of the bill, in a significantly revised version, by another year.

The government parties emphasized that the legislation would not only strengthen public confidence in the integrity of the electoral system following the series of scandalous defections between 1996 and 1999 but also would act to protect the proportionality of the new electoral system. A number of organizations, such as the National Council of Women, Grey Power New Zealand, the Auckland City Council, and Auckland District Council of Social Service, that participated in the consultation process organized by the Justice and Electoral Committee agreed with the stated purposes of the draft legislation. Others, however, were more cautious. For example, the Electoral Commission submitted a brief to the Committee in which it argued that the electoral system was not purely proportional to begin with, and therefore additional legislation to strengthen and lock-in proportionality may not be necessary.[16] Additional points raised during the committee stage of the legislation included that the bill treated list and constituency MPs the same way; that it did not consider the complications that might arise from resignations from a component party of an umbrella party;[17] and that it did not apply to MPs who were elected as Independents.

Several submissions noted that the scope of the bill should be broadened to apply to constructive resignations as well as expulsion of the MP from his or her party. Constructive resignations in this context meant situations wherein an MP openly and publicly opposed his or her party without formally resigning, whereas the inclusion of expulsion suggested both that parties would be empowered to notify the Speaker of a Member's resignation and that an MP who was expelled from his or her party would be requested to notify the Speaker accordingly. These suggestions evidently sought to weaken the independent status of parliamentarians vis-à-vis their parties, raising questions about the limits of MPs' political freedoms, and the Committee noted that such limitations would violate the New Zealand Bill of Rights.[18] Three opposition parties, the Nationals, ACT, and the Green Party, remained united in their opposition to the bill, which they saw as a bad law that only served the purpose of weakening the independence of MPs and enhancing "party power."[19]

Given the divisions and the inability of the Justice and Electoral Committee to support the bill, the government parties had to change strategy; they thus reached out to the opposition New Zealand First party, which was so badly damaged by defections in the previous House, and sought to pass a much stricter anti-defection law. In exchange for its support, New Zealand First demanded a beefed-up version of the bill, which passed its second and third reading in the House on December 21, 2001, with a narrow majority of sixty-four in favor to fifty-six against. The sixty-four votes in support of the legislation were cast by MPs of the Labor Party (forty-nine), the Alliance (ten), and New Zealand First (five).

The central objective of the new Electoral (Integrity) Amendment Law, 2001, was to impose the penalty of disqualification on defecting MPs. While it preserved the voluntary aspect of the draft legislation, it also included another provision by which a MP could be disqualified. This second route empowered the leader of a parliamentary party group to initiate the process against any member of the party caucus by informing him or her that according to the leader's reasonable belief, the MP had "acted in a way that has distorted, and is likely to continue to distort, the proportionality of political party representation in Parliament as determined in the last general election."[20] Upon receiving such notice, the accused MP had twenty-one days to provide a written response, after which the leader needed to provide his or her evidence to all members of the party group in the House. If the leader secured the consent of two-thirds of the party group's membership, a written notice would be served to the Speaker to the effect that the member left the party and, consequently, his or her seat would be declared vacant. An important part of the new legislation was the incorporation of a sunset clause according to which it was going to expire after the second general election held following its passage. In practice, this meant that the Electoral (Integrity) Amendment Law automatically expired as of September 17, 2005.

The 2005 elections returned the Labor Party (fifty seats) to government, albeit at the head of a minority coalition with the Progressive Party (one seat) that rested on the external support of New Zealand First (seven seats) and the United Future Party (three seats). Labor and New Zealand First reaffirmed their commitment to fighting party hopping and signed a confidence and supply agreement in which they pledged to support the resurrection of the Electoral (Integrity) Amendment Law.[21] The new Bill, which departed from the earlier expired version in that it no longer included a sunset clause and sought to make the penalties against party hopping a permanent feature of the Electoral Act, passed its first reading in the House on December 6. 2005, with a wafer-thin majority of sixty-one votes in favor and was subsequently referred to the Justice and Electoral Committee. During the next three months, the Committee read fifteen written and heard seven oral submissions.[22] Having concluded its deliberations on February 28, 2006, the Committee issued a majority recommendation that the Bill should not proceed any further. Consequently, the Labor government did not proceed.

Although the New Zealand legislation succeeded to eliminate legislative party switching, the two cases that tested the new law also showed the price to be paid to preserve legislative party unity in the House. The first price was what Geddis[23] has called the representational lock-in. In a curious twist of fate, the Alliance party, one of the chief proponents of the law, suffered a major internal schism toward the end of the 1999–2002 parliamentary cycle over the issue, and the method of the party's continued cooperation with Labor in the coalition government. The "moderate" group that emphasized coalition collegiality was led by the leader of the party's legislative group, Jim Anderton, and included six of the party's ten MPs, while the more radical "activist" group, which sought a stronger differentiation of the Alliance from the coalition's policies, was led by party president Matt McCarten and included four MPs. The division eventually led to Anderton's removal from the party organization; however, the extra-parliamentary party could not effectively remove him from his post as legislative party leader since a majority of the caucus supported him. For his part, Anderton was not in a position to initiate the disqualification process against the "activists," since he did not command the two-third majority required under the new law. Therefore, thanks to the mechanical effect of the legislation, the two factions had no choice but to serve out the remainder of the term of the House as a legislative party group united only in name.

The second case reaffirmed the principle that a party could effectively expel an MP even if the preservation of proportionality did not appear to be clearly at stake. This case pitted Mrs. Awatere Huata, who was elected to the House in the 2002 election from the list-tier as a representative of the ACT Party.[24] Mrs. Huata gained notoriety for allegations of misusing public funds that earned her suspension form the caucus. When she failed to renew her party membership following her suspension, the party's legislative leader, Richard Prebble, notified the Speaker that Mrs. Huata was no longer a member of the party. To satisfy the requirements of the anti-defection law, the caucus leader also initiated the disqualification process, and having secured the unanimous support of the caucus membership, the Speaker was served another notice to that effect. Mrs. Huata took the party to court, arguing that she was not leaving the party but rather the party was effectively expelling her. While the lower court was split over the case, the Supreme Court sided with ACT and in so doing allowed the extra-parliamentary party organization to have direct control over the status of its MP's legislative membership status.

The re-introduction of the Electoral Integrity Bill did not return to the political agenda until recently. Following the 2017 general elections, the Labor Party once again formed a minority coalition government with the New Zealand First party, propped up from the outside by a supply-and-provision agreement with the Green Party. The coalition agreement between Labor and New Zealand First contained a specific clause that obliged the parties to re-pass the Electoral Integrity Bill with no provisions for a sunset clause. Although the two parties did not have a majority to implement this commitment, they were able to persuade the Green Party to give up its traditional opposition to the bill and support it. The Electoral Integrity Act was successfully re-passed in September 2018 by a narrow margin of sixty-three to fifty-seven, which showed a clear division of votes between the governing coalition (in favor) and the opposition (against).

Anti-Defection Law in a New Democracy: South Africa

Unlike the other three countries under discussion (Israel, India, and New Zealand), South Africa is a new Third Wave democracy where the politics of legislating against party switching has been intimately connected with the politics of building and consolidating a new competitive party system. As a result of this difference, the issue in South Africa was not whether to restrict or ban party hopping, or floor-crossing, but rather whether to allow it at all. Both the Interim Constitution of 1994 and the Final Constitution adopted in 1996 contained specific clauses (Articles 43b and 133/1/b) that categorically required members of the national, provincial, and the municipal assemblies to resign their seats if they left the political party that got them elected. The key justification, similar to New Zealand, was to protect the integrity of the country's electoral system, which, similar to Israel, is a nationwide closed party-list rule. Although this effective ban on party hopping was suspended for a period of six years, between 2002 and 2008, the *status quo ante* was re-established in 2008 with the passage of the Fourteenth and Fifteenth Amendments to the Constitution. In short, for all but six years in the political life of post-apartheid South Africa, party switching at all three levels of the political system was categorically forbidden.

The first post-apartheid elections in 1994 resulted in a landslide victory by the African National Congress (ANC), which grabbed 252 of the 400 seats (62.5%) in the National Assembly, the first chamber of the bicameral national legislature, and sixty of the ninety seats in the Senate.[25] Given its overwhelming majority, close to the two-thirds margin required for passing constitutional changes, and the complete fragmentation of the opposition, the ANC was in complete control over the writing of the country's new constitution, which came into effect in February 1997.[26]

Similar to India, where the super-majority won by the Indian National Congress in the 1984 election prompted the party leadership to pass the anti-defection amendment to the constitution so as to protect the party's large legislative group from breaking up, the ANC used its constitution-alizing majority to impose a ban on party switching. Accordingly, the 1997 South African constitution provided that any member of a legislative assembly, at any level, who left that party that he or she was elected to represent in the election would have to vacate the seat. While the central arguments in favor of the anti-defection clauses in the new constitution stressed the protection of the proportionality of the electoral system, the ban on party hopping served the dual purposes of keeping the large ANC parliamentary party group together and the already fragmented opposition divided.

The movement to relax the anti-defection provision of the Constitution stemmed from the results of the second post-apartheid election in the province of Western Cape, which was one of the two provinces of the country where the ANC did not immediately become a dominant party after the transition to democracy.[27] In the 1994 elections, the Western Cape elections were won by the National Party (NNP), which had been the ruling party of the former apartheid regime. Five years later, in the 1999 elections, however, the renamed New National Party not only lost its majority in the province but the ANC actually became the largest party there, having won eighteen seats in the province's forty-two seat legislature. Yet, in spite of the improvement of the ANC's position in the former heartland of the National Party, the latter was able to stay in government by forming a bare-majority minimum winning coalition with the Democratic Party. In the 1999 national elections, which were held together with the provincial polls, the ANC further improved on its previous electoral results by winning 266 (66.6%) seats in the National Assembly and, given the party's overall success in the provincial polls, increased its mandates in the National Council of Provinces to sixty-three.

In the context of the gradual consolidation of the ANC's dominance in the party system, the fragmented opposition started to develop institutional mechanisms for electoral and legislative coordination. Building on their experience of running the Western Cape coalition government, the New National and the Democratic Parties decided to create a new united umbrella party, the Democratic Alliance (DA), which also included a third much smaller opposition party, the Federal Alliance. The formalization of establishing the DA had to be rushed through in preparation for the country-wide municipal elections in 2000 because once the elections were over, councilors and legislators were locked in and could not change their party affiliations under the anti-defection clause of the Constitution. Although the DA was formally established and contested the local polls as a united party, its creation was an anomaly: the DA existed and functioned as a unitary actor at the municipal level; however, its three component parties were forced to retain their respective independent statuses in the provincial and national legislatures by the anti-defection provisions of the Constitution.[28]

In order to resolve this procedural abnormality, the DA proposed amending the anti-defection law, but the ANC government showed no interest in supporting the initiative. The ANC's attitude, however, became favorable when the cracks in the ranks of the DA started to show and resulted in the eventual withdrawal by the NNP in late 2001.[29] As part of its divorce from the DA, the NNP also terminated its coalition with the DP in the province of Western Cape and entered into an agreement of "cooperative governance" with the ANC. Since the component parties of the DA had existed as separate parties at the provincial and national levels, no complications arose from the dissolution of the DA at these levels of government. In the municipalities, however, the NNP councilors were locked in their local DA units, making it impossible for them to leave without incurring the high switching costs imposed by the anti-defection clause of the Constitution. To use Geddis's word, this was representational lock-in at its "best."

Evidently, the ANC now stood to gain from allowing the relaxation of the defection ban. The government thus passed four pieces of legislation in 2002, two constitutional amendments and two ordinary acts, which introduced the possibility of party switching at all three levels of government. The First Amendment of the Constitution provided that floor-crossing would be allowed twice during the term of a municipal council, in the second and fourth years following its election, and as long as a minimum of 10 percent of a party group's members participated in the switch. In addition, the Act provided for an exceptional one-time, fifteen-day window for floor-crossing that would be scheduled immediately after its passage. A compendium amendment to the Local Government Act removed all references to the prohibition of floor-crossing at the local level and made all other necessary legal arrangements in the light of the First Amendment.[30] The third piece of legislation was the Loss or Retention of Membership in National and Provincial Legislatures

Act, which extended the same new provisions about floor-crossing to these respective levels of government, whereas the fourth new law, the Second Amendment of the Constitution, allowed for changes to be made to the composition of the National Council of Provinces in the light of the floor-crossings that would take place.

This package of laws was passed with an overwhelming majority of 86 percent in the National Assembly.[31] Yet, the idea of allowing floor-crossing, albeit in a highly controlled and circumscribed form, did not enjoy unquestionable support. For example, the Institute for Democracy in South Africa, as well as the Election Commission, produced a submission arguing in favor of the continuation of the floor-crossing ban.[32] Among the political parties, the Inkatha Freedom Party and the United Democratic Movement took their opposition to the new law to the courts.[33] Their case eventually went up to the Constitutional Court, which ruled that allowing for floor-crossing was neither in conflict with the South African Constitutions nor with the general notion of democracy.[34] However, the Court agreed with the petitioners that the amendment to the Loss or Retention of Membership in National and Provincial Legislatures Act was passed by parliament as an ordinary piece of legislation, whereas it should be passed as a constitutional amendment act. Acting on the directive to the Court, the government re-introduced the bill as the Fourth Amendment Act of the Constitution, later renumbered as the Tenth Amendment of the South African Constitution, which was passed with a majority of 87 percent in the National Assembly on February 25, 2003.[35] One month later, on March 18, the National Council Of Provinces also passed the Act unanimously. Since the constitutional challenge only affected the Bill to change the rules about floor-crossing in the provincial and national legislatures, defection could already be carried out in the municipalities as of 2002.

The actual periods for floor-crossing established by the Tenth Amendment fell from the first to the fifteenth of the second and the fourth September after each general election. Since the Tenth Amendment took effect in March 2003, by which time the second and fourth Septembers following the 1999 elections had already passed, it made a special authorization that allowed floor-crossings to take place in the current legislatures between March 21 and April 4, 2003. Following the 2004 elections, however, there were two duly scheduled floor-crossing periods, in September 2005 and 2007, respectively, when legislators and councilors were allowed to switch their parties without penalty. Table 8.3 shows the number of members at the three levels of government who switched their parties during five of the six years (2002–2007) when floor-crossing was allowed. According to the data, floor-crossing was clearly a much more prevalent feature of local than either provincial or national politics.

Similar to both India and Israel, the South African legislation also had a numerical clause, although the threshold for legal defection was set at 10 percent instead of one-third of the number of members of a given party's legislative group. The provision clearly favored the continued unity of larger parties, where the 10 percent rule was much more difficult to satisfy. Indeed, the net losers under the floor-crossing laws were the smaller parties, such as the UDM, which was reduced from fourteen to four seats in 2003, while the net beneficiaries were the larger parties, specifically the ANC, which not only gained new members without losing any in each of the periods but also achieved a two-thirds legislative majority in the National Assembly as a result of floor-crossings.[36] In spite of its gains from defections, the ANC witnessed internal discontent about the practice of floor-crossing both on normative grounds as well as on the practical level that defectors were often more handsomely rewarded for joining the dominant party than loyal ANC members. Eventually, the ANC's Fifty Second National Conference, held on December 20, 2007, in Polokwane, resolved that "floor crossing should be abolished and that public representatives of of other political parties should be encouraged to join the ANC regardless of whether or not they retain their seats."[37] According to the resolution, the ANC government proceeded to submit and pass the Fourteenth and Fifteenth Amendments to the Constitutions,

Table 8.3. Party Switching in South Africa, 2002–2007

	National Assembly	Provincial assemblies	Municipal councils
2002	na	na	417
2003	23	21	na
2004	na	na	493
2005	26	26	na
2007	7	—	250

Source: Sueanne Issac, "Summary and Analysis of Floor-Crossing Legislation," *Research Unit of the Parliament of South Africa*, July 24, 2008. (Data for 2006 were not included in the original source.)

which restored the *status quo ante* at all levels of government by subjecting a member who crossed the floor to the loss of his or her seat.[38]

Conclusion

The three case studies in this chapter clearly establish the singular nature of the Israeli anti-defection law. Compared to the three comparator cases, Israel is the only one where the anti-defection law is neither categorical—that is, certain types of party switches are legally allowed—nor does it carry the severe penalty of disqualification. In contrast, both India and South Africa have come to entrench in their constitutions clauses that *de facto* rule out any change in the composition of legislative parties. As such, in the latter two cases individual legislators have lost a significant amount of their political freedoms to their parties. Similarly, following a thirteen-year hiatus, the Parliament of New Zealand also re-introduced its earlier severe and categorical anti-defection law. In short, Israel continues to occupy an intermediate position between the extremes of banning defections and allowing the free movement of legislators, which points to the possibility of an interesting mixed model of legislative representation that can be a lesson to other countries.

The comparative discussion in this chapter also raises the important counterfactual question about the likely consequences of a more stringent form of anti-defection law in Israel. In other words, if the Knesset had adopted, or were to adopt in the future, a more stringent categorical anti-defection law that would present disloyal MKs with the threat of disqualification, would it be plausible to expect the numbers and types of party switching to change in the Israeli legislature? The evidence from the three other countries quite convincingly suggests that such a categorical anti-defection law works well to contain the scope of party switching even if they do not offer a perfect panacea. Since Israeli legislators are elected from close party lists, disqualification could be fairly easily administered by allowing parties to replace their defecting MKs with another candidate form the party's candidate list in the last election. The adoption of this most severe form of penalty would be particularly effective to discourage early-term party switches in the Knesset, which the Edelstein amendment addressed. A more stringent anti-defection law would also imply that the leadership of the legislative party group will become more powerful vis-a-vis their MKs whose exit threat would seriously weaken in the face of increased exit costs. In turn, however, this would also make Israeli government less likely to be able to manipulate the cohesion in the ranks of their parliamentary opposition. In short, the dynamics of party switching could indeed be changed very significantly if the anti-defection law were more stringent.

It is worth noting that the recent adoption of the so-called Norwegian Law by the Knesset may partly achieve the objective of containing party exits, albeit in a limited and indirect way. Subject to limitations according to the size of party groups, this Law allows a party's minister in government to resign his or her Knesset seat and transfer it to another candidate from the electoral list of the minister's party until such time that the minister leaves government and wants to take up his or her legislative seat once again.[39] Clearly, the so-called "Norwegian," that is, replacement legislators, will have a strong incentive to remain loyal to their party leadership, and to the minister in particular, to whom they owe their opportunity to serve in the Knesset. Party switching by such legislators would also make little sense because they could be very easily removed from the Knesset by the minister who remains the technical owner of the seat. Evidently, the effect of the Norwegian Law to contain party switching is limited in that it applies only to parties in the governing coalition and its enforcement is fundamentally subject to the voluntary decision of the government minister in question.

Another counterfactual scenario to consider is what the record of party switching might have been in Israel over the past thirty years if the Knesset had not adopted an anti-defection law in the first place. The previous chapters documented that the formal regulation of party switching resulted in an increase in the number of switches, even at the cost of declining re-election rates among the switchers. Plausibly, several MKs who only ended up exiting from their party group in order to help their fellow switchers meet the one-third condition for a legal split would have stayed put and by so doing would have helped to contain the overall number of switches. Similarly, in the absence of the anti-defection law, pre-electoral switching would have been more likely to be motivated by prospective electoral considerations and less by strategic considerations to avoid the penalty in case the one-third condition was not met. With all of this said, it is important to recall that the Israel party system has become significantly more fragmented, volatile, and much more personalized since the 1990s than what it had been in the decades prior to the "stinking trick." As such, the post-1990s party system has presented a more favorable environment for changes in politician's party affiliations and the formation of new parties and party groups. In this context of increasingly less cohesive and more personalized political parties, it is understandable that Israeli legislators held onto a weak, and progressively weakening, regulation of party switching that ultimately maintained their freedom to change their party label. Although a more stringent and categorical kind of anti-defection law might have kept Israeli parties together better precisely at the time when parties were becoming weaker, the adoption of such legislation was hardly in the legislators' interest.

Conclusion

In response to the "stinking trick" that brought down Prime Minister Yitzhak Shamir's government in the spring of 1990, the Knesset adopted a package of laws to restrict and regulate party switching in the future. Although defections were not a novel phenomenon in Israeli legislative politics, it took a major political crisis at the apex of the country's political establishment, and a large-scale public outcry, before the national legislature would take action. In the decades that followed, political parties and their MKs have continuously presented the Knesset with new strategies and realities that have required modifications to the ways in which the defections were defined and penalized under the original legislation. In addressing these challenges, the Knesset has struggled to maintain a balance between protecting the mandates that political parties received from the electorate with the political freedom of individual legislators as it continued to amend the various laws that made up the original anti-defection package.

The chapters in the book have provided evidence for the ambivalent effects of the anti-defection law. On the one hand, the sheer number of MKs who have switched parties has actually increased compared to the period before the adoption of the law. At the same time, party switching has assumed a much more regular, and regulated, pattern both in terms of the number of MKs switching, the types of switches, and the timing of the switches. The anti-defection law has all but eliminated solo switches and it also ended the practice of MKs directly hopping directly form one party group to another. The overwhelming majority of party switching has been collective and led to the formation of new party groups in the Knesset, which in turn led to growing instability in party system while also inflating the number of MKs who leaving their original party groups.

It is important to stress that the Israeli anti-defection law has clearly succeeded on one very important dimension: party switching and defections have never again undermined the stability of an incumbent government the way they did in the Twelfth Knesset. In short, the anti-defection law has successfully eliminated *kalanterism* in the narrow technical sense of the term. The fact that it did so without imposing the kind of categorical ban on party hopping that was the case in India and South Africa, or without formally empowering political parties to expel their MKs, as the law in New Zealand does, shows the paramount concern and respect that the Israeli law-makers have given to maintaining the freedom of individual legislators while trying to preserve party unity.

Yet, *kalanterism*, in the broader sense of power- and office-oriented defection and party switching may not be entirely a matter of the past as evinced by the complex developments that took place in the Israeli party system between April 2019 and July 2021. In fact, the processes that led up to the formation and subsequent termination of the Thirty-Fifth Israeli government, followed by the investiture of the Thirty-Sixth government in July 2021 showcased most of the main themes that were discussed in this book: the ongoing significance of pre-electoral party switches, the powerful effect of the one-third rule; and the continued interest of Israeli governments to change the legislative regulation of party switching in order to make it easier to drive wedges and divisions in the opposition.

Party Switching, Anti-Defection Laws, and the Political Instability of 2019–2021

Following the early termination of Israel's Thirty-Fourth government, Israeli voters had to go to the polling stations three times in a quick succession (April 2019, September 2091 and again in March 2020) before a new government, the Thirty-Fifth, was eventually formed. Even so, the investiture of the new government was predicated upon several MKs changing their party affiliations and extracting additional changes in the legislative regulation of party switching. In the end, the Thirty-Fifth government proved to be one of the shortest-lived of all Israeli governments and collapsed in December 2020 due to the failure of the coalition partners to agree on passing a new budget. The ensuing Knesset election, held in March 2021, did produce a national unity coalition government four months later, however, its composition was extremely unusual: the new coalition government not only brought together political parties from the

Left, Right, Center and, for the first time, also an Arab political party, but thanks to a rotation agreement it also allowed Naftali Bennett, the leader of one of the smallest Knesset parties, Yamina, to serve as Prime Minister for the first half of the duration of the government.

Although the prolonged instability that started with the April 2019 elections was in large measure caused by the emergence of a new political cleavage that cut across the traditional divisions in the party system, inter-party relations also became increasingly more volatile under the pressure with the onset of the global Covid-19 pandemic that presented the Israeli political leadership with extremely difficult challenges. The new cleavage that assumed a focal role in the party system was the personal political record and leadership credentials of Prime Minister Benjamin Netanyahu whose pending indictment by Attorney General Amichai Mandeblit for charges of fraud, breach of trust and attempted bribery in three separate cases provided the impetus for broadly based popular mobilization demanding his replacement as well as the formation of new political parties and alliances that sought to capitalize on the Prime Minister's growing vulnerability.

The political formation that led the electoral challenge against the Prime Minister and his Likud party in the successive elections of April and September 2019 and in March 2020 was the Blue and White alliance jointly led by Benny Gantz, former Chief of Staff of the Israeli Defense Force, and Yair Lapid, leader and founder of the Yesh Atid party. Technically, Blue and White was a formal partnership among three political parties, two of which, Gantz's own Resilient Israel and Telem led by Moshe Yaalon, a former Likud MK and Minister of Defense until his forced resignation in 2016, were formed right before the April 2019 election. The third member of the Blue and White alliance was Yesh Atid led by Yair Lapid.[1] According to their agreement, the three partners formed a united electoral list that was headed by their three respective leaders and included candidates from each party in proportion to their current base of electoral and financial support. As such, the thirty-five Blue and White candidates who were elected to the Knesset in the April 2019 election comprised fifteen MKs each from Resilience Israel and Yesh Atid and five MKs from Telem. In the September 2019 and March 2020 polls the Blue and White Alliance managed to win only thirty-three seats with Yesh Atid losing two candidates each time.

The April 2019 elections resulted in a neck-to-neck tie between Blue and White and Likud each of them winning thirty-five Knesset seats. Following his mandatory consultation with the representatives of the newly elected Knesset party groups, President Reuven Rivlin gave Prime Minister Netanyahu the mandate to try and form the next government because the combined total strength of the party groups that recommended him was significantly larger, sixty-five seats, than that of the party delegations recommending Gantz, forty-five seats.[2] Notwithstanding his initial advantage, Netanyahu was unable to secure a majority coalition because of the deep and seemingly irreconcilable division between the ultra-orthodox parties and the secular right-wing Yisrael Beitenu over the issue of drafting ultra-orthodox youth in the army. In order to prevent the possibility of the formation of an alternative government by Gantz, the Prime Minister managed to secure passage of a bill to dissolve the Knesset and hold fresh elections in September.[3]

The Twenty-Second Knesset election was held in September 2019 and resulted in a slight edge for Blue and White which won thirty-three seats against Likud's thirty-two. This so-called "second election" did not result in a new government either. Although Netanyahu was once again recommended by a larger coalition of parties to form a government than Gantz was, the incumbent Prime Minister's ten-seat advantage after the April election had been eroded to a wafer-thin margin of only one seat: the number of MKs whose party delegations supported Netanyahu was fifty-five as opposed to Gantz's fifty-four. There were two key changes that resulted in this dramatically different scenario: first, Yisrael Beitenu toughened its position vis-à-vis the Prime Minister and its former ultra-orthodox coalition partners by refusing the endorse either Netanyahu or Gantz as candidates for Prime Minister; and second, three of the four Arab parties that re-united under the Joint List umbrella in the September elections had broken with their earlier position of neutrality between the two leaders by formally recommending Gantz.[4] President Rivlin once again followed the formal playbook of the Israeli government formation process and extended an invitation to Netanyahu to try and form a government. However, this time he insisted that in case of a failed attempt by Netanyahu the mandate would be passed to Gantz rather than allow the Prime Minister force another early election.[5] These important changes notwithstanding, neither Netanyahu nor Gantz were able to overcome the deadlock and neither of them showed any genuine interest in forming a unity grand coalition government even though President Rivlin had strongly encouraged them to do so. After Gantz's mandate also expired, the Knesset assumed the responsibility of trying to find a politician who could muster sufficient support to break the impasse, however, this was also to no avail.

The third snap election was held on March 23, 2021 and this time it resulted in the formation of a new government. However, the political gridlock could be overcome only because several MKs broke ranks with their party groups and, as a result, the formation of the new government appeared to bring back *kalanterism* in its true form. The elections results suggested that Likud led by Netanyahu was emerging with renewed strength from the past eleven months of prolonged political instability as the party registered its best electoral performance yet with thirty-six seats won. In contrast, Blue and White appeared to be stagnating as the alliance failed to improve on its previous share of Knesset seats. Yet, further changes in the partisan line-up of support for the two leaders actually suggested that Gantz's chances to form a government were much improved. Prior to the elections, Yisrael Beitenu indicated that it was going to recommend Gantz to form the new government, the previously divided Joint List of Arab parties also closed ranks in Gantz's favor in a united fashion, while the only change in Netanyahu's favor was a split in the three-party alliance of Labor, Meretz and Gesher with the latter refusing to endorse either leader for Prime Minister. For the first time since April 2019, Gantz was not only recommended by a larger coalition of parties to form a government than Netanyahu but his supporting coalition also reached the critical threshold of a sixty-one seat Knesset majority.[6]

Although President Rivlin asked Gantz to try and form the next government, the negotiations very quickly came to a halt because three MKs, Zvi Hauser and Yoaz Hendel (both Blue and White) and Orly Levy-Abukasis (Gesher) were resolutely opposed to supporting a government that would either include or would depend on the support of the Arab parties.[7] Instead, the three politicians suggested that Gantz and Netanyahu should form a national unity grand coalition government with the Prime Ministership to rotate between them similar to the arrangement between Likud and the Alignment after the deadlocked 1984 elections. Although no fan of the prospect of sharing power with Netanyahu, whose displacement was at the very core of his repeated electoral campaigns, Gantz had to realize that a unity coalition needed to be considered very seriously because without the support of Hauser, Hendel and Levy-Abukassis, his supporting coalition was reduced to fifty-eights seats, exactly the same number that Netanyahu commanded.

In order to enhance the credibility of their positions, all three MKs decided to leave their respective party groups. In Levy-Abukassis' case, this was a straightforward move since her own Gesher party was linked to Labor and Meretz only through an electoral alliance. In the case of Hendel and Hauser, however, the situation was complicated by the fact of the timing of their departure. The two legislators formally belonged to Telem, the smallest of the three constituent parties in the Blue and White alliance. Since Telem had five candidates among the thirty-three elected from the Blue and White list, Hendel and Hauser could exit without facing the penalty of not being able to run on any existing party's ticket in the next election since they met the criterion of the one-third rule. However, according to the reintroduction of the Edelstein amendment to the Party Funding legislation in 2014, which denied allocation of funds for current expenses to MKs who change their party groups in the first two years after the general election, the two Telem MKs would have been deprived of a key source of party funding. Therefore, while the formal exit from Telem and their formation of a new two-member party group called Derek Eretz (Common Sense) was approved by the Knesset Arrangements Committee on March 29, 2020, it was evident that they would demand some sort of compensation for the funds that they were going to lose.[8]

The formation of Derek Eretz was not the only loss that the Blue and White alliance suffered during the coalition formation talks. In fact, the two senior leaders, Gantz and Lapid, fundamentally disagreed about the feasibility of a national unity coalition with Likud under Netanyahu's leadership; whereas Gantz was becoming increasingly more open to this solution to the deadlock, Lapid flatly rejected it. Therefore, when Gantz signaled his readiness to enter into formal talks to set up a grand coalition, the Blue and White alliance effectively ended. According to the agreement between the two partners, Gantz's Resilient Israel group inherited the Blue and White label and would continue to function in the Knesset as such, while Lapid and his followers would regroup as Yesh Atid. The only additional change was a friendly swap of two MKs between the two parties: Penina Tamanu, the first ever female Ethiopian politician elected to the Knesset, who was a Yesh Atid MK ever since the party entered the Knesset in 2013—was allowed to switch her affiliation from Yesh Atid to Blue and White, and Gadeer Kamal-Mreeh—elected as a candidate from the Israel Resilience Party and the first-ever female Druze Member in the Knesset—was allowed by the Committee to switch and join Yesh Atid.

When all the changes in the composition of the various party groups and alliances were finalized, Gantz found his position vis-a-vis Netanyahu significantly weakened. The parties that were still willing to support him in and join a grand national unity coalition with Likud, and its allies, included the rump Blue and White, Derek Eretz, Labor and Gesher, however, Yesh Atid, Meretz, and Yisrael Bietenu resolved to move into opposition. Compared with the immediate post-election line-up of parties' positions, when Gantz enjoyed the support of sixty-one MKs, this represented a staggering loss of forty-three MKs. Although Gantz's negotiating team was able to extract significant concession from Likud during the formation of the grand coalition, including the commitment to rotation of the Prime Ministership and a "paritetic," i.e., parity-based, allocation of portfolios between the two blocs of parties, the national unity coalition rested and fundamentally suffered from a deep asymmetry as the combined strength of the party groups that were still supporting Netanyahu in a grand coalition numbered fifty-three MKs.[9]

The formation of Israel's Thirty-Fifth government also led to changes in the ranks of Yamina, an alliance of three political parties that ran on a joint list in the election to represent the Religious Zionist electoral constituency. Notwithstanding the apparently solid and consistent commitment of the Religious Zionist parties to helping Netanyahu form a new government, the Prime Minister designate could not accommodate their expectations in terms of the number and types of portfolios in the unity coalition government. As a result, Yamina resolved to stay in the opposition and, consequently, on May 17, 2020, five of its six MK voted against the investiture of the new government. The sixth and dissenting MK was Rabbi Rafi Peretz, former Chief Rabbi of the Israel Defense Force, who also headed and was the sole representative of his Jewish Home party in the Yamina alliance. Similar to the disintegration of Blue and White, Rafi Peretz's departure from Yamina was a straightforward matter since it merely constituted the parting of way by the electoral allies. Had the Jewish Home been represented by more MKs, the situation might have been more complicated.[10]

In sum, the formation of the Thirty-Fifth Government was evidently predicated upon politicians changing the party affiliations that they had presented to the voters in the last election. Three of the eight party lists that entered the Twenty-Third Knesset split up (Blue and White, Labor-Gesher-Meretz, and Yamina), two MKs had formed a brand new political party (Derek Eretz) and two further MKs (Tamanu and Kamal-Mreeh) switched parties during the break-up of Blue and White. Moreover, since Derek Eretz would have been deprived of state funding under the existing legislation, the coalition partners agreed to pass an amendment to the Party Funding Law that specifically authorized a new party that was formed in the Twenty-Third Knesset before the formation of the new government to receive state funds in order to cover its current expenses.[11] Once again, the legal framework of the existing anti-defection legislation fell victim to the office-seeking compulsion of politicians.

In addition to these changes all of which received the approval and authorization from the Knesset Arrangements Committee, there was one other change in the Twenty-Third Knesset that did not result in a formal party switch. The three MKs who remained to represent the Labor Party after the Labor-Meretz-Gesher alliance splintered did not have consensus on whether or not to support the government. Two Labor MKs, party chairman Amir Peretz and Itzhik Shmuli, were in favor of supporting the coalition and accordingly voted in its favor and received portfolios in the new government.[12] The third Labor MK, Meerav Michaeli, remained in steadfast opposition to a Netanyahu-led government and joined with Meretz in voting against its investiture. Although such action might very well have triggered an anti-defection charge against Michaeli, the issue was neither picked up formally by the other Labor MKs nor did Michaeli proceed to exit. Instead, she chose to remain an opposition voice within the coalition in order to strike the difficult balance between loyalty to her party and to the voters.[13] Her decision paid-off in the long-run as she successfully wrested the leadership from Peretz after the fall of the government in late 2020 and she led Labor successfully not only back to the Twenty-Fourth Knesset but also into fold of the anti-Netanyahu coalition government that was formed in the summer of 2021.

The Thirty-Fifth government collapsed on December 23, 2020 following its failure to pass the state budget. In terms of party switching, the most significant development in the pre-electoral period was the formation of the New Hope party led by Likud stalwart Gideon Sa'ar who had unsuccessfully challenged Netanyahu for party leadership two years earlier. Along with three other Likud MKs (Michal Shir, Sharen Haskel, and Zeev Elkin) Sa'ar formally resigned his Knesset seat in order to avoid any complications that might emerge with respect to the interpretation of the anti-defection law by Likud lawmakers and their allies in the Knesset Committee. A fifth Likud MK, Yifat Shasha Biton, whom Sa'ar later appointed to the second spot on the New Hope list, came very close to becoming precisely such victim to a Likud leadership that was bent to rein in any form of dissent and indiscipline.[14] On the same day when Shasha Biton announced her decision to join Sa'ar's New Hope, the Likud Knesset faction immediately notified the Knesset Committee that they sought to formally brand her as a defector with all the appropriate sanctions to apply. As we saw earlier in book, party groups rarely resorted to initiating such a hostile move against renegade MKs; the most recent such events were those of Orly Levy-Abukassis in 2017 and Michael Nudelman in 2006. Following a heated debate in the Knesset Committee, the Likud request was eventually dropped and Shasha Biton was allowed to finish her term as an MK.[15] In addition to Shasha Biton, the two MKs of the Derek Erezt party group also announced their decision to join Sa'ar's new party and contest the next Knesset election as electoral allies on the same list. Since Derek Eretz operated as a fully funded Knesset party group, its alliance with the New Hope provided Gideon Sa'ar's newly formed party with much need funds to run the electoral campaign.

The results of the Twenty-Fourth election seemed to revert back to the same inconclusive mandates that had characterized the previous three polls. Once again, Netanyahu secured the most votes recommending him to form a government, and once again he failed. In stark contrast to the earlier processes, however, the second attempt at forming a post-election government bore result. Yair Lapid, who received the mandate from President Rivlin following Netanyahu's failure, managed to cobble together an eight-party wafer-thin majority coalition which passed the investiture vote with a margin of sixty votes in favor and fifty-nine against. According to the coalition agreement, the Prime Ministership was to rotate between Naftali Bennett and Yair Lapid. The formation of this second national unity government immediately prompted Amichai Chikli, a rookie MK in the new Prime Minister's Yamina party, to rebel and vote against not only its investiture but also its subsequent policies. It is instructive to note that while the one-third rule of the anti-defection law formally locked Chikli in as a member of his party group, Yamina could not afford to brand him a defector either at this time given the extremely tight and delicate balance of powers in the Knesset between the governing coalition and the opposition.

The Bennett government's extremely narrow parliamentary majority meant that both the coalition and the opposition were motivated to woo defectors over to their respective side. In an evident attempt to encourage and enable other Likud lawmakers to follow Gideon Sa'ar's example and join the coalition, the new government immediately passed an amendment to the anti-defection rules by lowering the minimum number of MKs who can collectively leave their party group without sanctions and penalties to four.[16] The amendment, which was much more radical in its scope than the Mofaz Law had been, sought to make it extremely easy for as few as four disgruntled Likud MKs to jump ship. Yet, at the time of writing when the Bennett government has just completed its seventh month in office, even this relaxed anti-defection law did not succeed in providing the necessary stimulus and the opposition parties remained solidly united in their ranks.

Although the period between 2019 and 2021 was highly unusual in terms of the level of political instability produced by the party system, the anti-defection law continued to operate in much the same way as it had before. The repeated elections showed that the political deadlock could not be overcome at the ballot box which in turn forced elected politicians to make difficult choices with regards to forming and supporting governments that they normally would not have. In this context, it is perhaps not surprising to find that some of these hard choices by necessity involved party switching and the formation of new political parties in the Knesset. The existing anti-defection legislation could only restrict but not entirely prevent these maneuvers from happening. Indeed, if and when MKs decided to change their party groups, they did so according to the stipulations of the anti-defection legislation and sought to avoid its negative sanctions. While some of these party switches were clearly motivated by the office-seeking incentive of entering government and securing a portfolio, e.g., Derek Eretz and Pnina Tamanu, none of them were pivotal to the formation of the new government that they supported by their switch. Therefore, they could not be properly considered as examples of perfidious *kalanterism*; the government would have been formed with or without their switch. Since preventing *kalanterism* was the key objective of the original anti-defection law, one can conclude that the legislation met its original intent on this score as well.

The 2019–2021 period reinforced yet another characteristic of the anti-defection legislation, namely its tremendous vulnerability to manipulation by a governing majority that seeks to create more favorable conditions to encourage party switching. Within a short span of thirteen months, the anti-defection legislation was changed twice: in May 2020 to ensure that the newly formed Derek Eretz party group would not be denied state funding, and again in July 2021 to lower the number of MKs required for a permissible party split. In stark contrast to India, where the anti-defection legislation has constitutional status making it extremely difficult to change, the Israeli legislation remains subject to the interests of the shifting legislative majorities whose political control remains unchecked in the absence of an entrenched written constitution.

In Closing . . .

Justifying his defection from the Conservative to the Liberal Party in the British House of Commons in 1904, Sir Winston Churchill famously claimed that "[s]ome men change their party for the sake of their principles, others their principles for the sake of their party.[17] Churchill's words provide justification for the kind of principle-driven party switching that was compatible with Sir Edmund Burke's vision of the parliamentary representative's free mandate. However, these words are much more difficult to accept in the context of a contemporary political system, such as Israel's, where both the electoral system and the organization of the legislature reinforce the centrality of political parties making an unfettered right by the individual deputies to leave their party groups difficult to defend. Given these complexities, the efforts by the Israeli legislature to balance between the rights and political freedoms of MKs on the one hand and the interests of political parties on the other show that there is no easy solution to the problem of regulating party switching in a modern party-centered democracy. As such, the very fact that *kalanterism* has been largely eliminated and that Israeli governments are no longer at the mercy of unstable parties and fickle MKs are in and of themselves important legislative, and political, achievements to celebrate and for other democracies to learn from.

Appendix

The List of Party Switches in the Knesset, 1949–2019

Source: "Mergers and Splits Among Parliamentary Groups," Official website of the Knesset, www.knesset.gov.il/faction/eng/FactionHistoryAll_eng.asp

(Note: Only those cases are listed here that meet the definition of party switching as explained in the Introduction. The dates indicated below use the following convention: day.month.year.)

First Knesset

8.6.49   Eliezer Preminger left the Israel Communist Party and established the Hebrew Communists.

15.8.49   The Hebrew Communists joined the United Workers' Party.

20.2.51   Ari Jabotinsky left the Herut Movement.

20.2.51   Hillel Kook left the Herut Movement.

Second Knesset

10.9.51   The Sephardim and Oriental Communities and Yemenite Association of Israel merged with General Zionists.

20.2.52   Rostam Bastia, Avraham Berman, and Moshe Sneh split from the United Workers' Party and established the Left Faction.

20.1.53   Hannah Lamdan and David Livschitz left the United Workers'
           Party and established the Faction Independent from Ahdut
           Ha'avoda.

13.1.54   The Faction Independent from Ahdut Ha'avoda joined Work-
           er's Party of Eretz Yisrael (Mapai).

23.8.54   Moshe Aram, Israel Bar-Yehuda, Yitzhak Ben-Aharon, and
           Aharon Zisling left the United Workers' Party and established
           Ahdut Ha'avoda—Poalei Zion.

1.11.54   The Left Faction ceased to exist: Avraham Berman and Moshe
           Sneh moved to Israel Communist Party, Rostam Bastuni
           returned to the United Workers' Party.

29.6.55   Shimon Garidi (Yemenite Association of Israel) announced
           that he split from the General Zionists.

Fifth Knesset

22.12.64   Yona Kesse's resignation from Mapai and his status as a single
           MK was approved, although the House Committee did not
           approve his becoming a single member parliamentary group
           by the name of "Min Hayesod."

16.3.65   Members of the Liberal Party of Israel who were in the Progres-
           sive Party in the past—Rachel Cohen-Kagan, Benno Cohen,
           Itzhak Golan, Yizhar Harari, Moshe Kol, Pinhas Rosen, and
           Yehuda Shaari—left and formed the Independent Liberals.

14.7.65   Joseph Aharon Almogi, David Ben-Gurion, Gideon Ben-Israel,
           Moshe Dayan, Amos Degani, Hannah Lamdan, Shimon Peres,
           and Yizhar Smilansky left Mapai and established Rafi.

1.9.65   Emil Habibi and Tawfik Toubi left the Israel Communist Party
           and established the New Communist List.

Sixth Knesset

29.3.67   The Free Center—Eliezer Shostak, Shmuel Tamir (Katznelson),
           and Avraham Tiar—split from the Herut-Liberal Bloc.

11.4.67   The Druze Party (Jabr Moade) split from Shituf Ve-achva.

23.1.68   Rafi (all members except David Ben Gurion) and Alignment merged and formed the Israel Labor Party.

27.5.68   Yizhar Harari left the Independent Liberals and joined the Israel Labor Party.

22.10.68   The Jewish-Arab Brotherhood (Elias Nahale) split from Kidma vPituach.

11.2.69   Shlomo Cohen-Tsiddon left the Herut-Liberal Bloc and joined the Free Center. (He had requested to establish a single-member parliamentary group by the name of the "Popular Faction.")

Seventh Knesset

4.1.72   Shalom Cohen split from Ha-olam Hazeh—Koah Hadash and became a Single MK.

25.4.72   Meir Avizohar left the National List and became a Single MK.

22.5.73   Avner-Hai Shaki left the National Religious Party and became a Single MK.

17.7.73   Single MK Meir Avizohar joined the Alignment.

Eighth Knesset

26.2.74   Kidma Vepituah and the Arab List for Bedouin and Villagers joined the Alignment.

18.3.75   Benjamin Halevi left the Likud to become a Single MK.

29.4.75   Arie Lova Eliav left the Alignment to become a Single MK.

27.1.76   Arie Lova Eliav and Marcia Freedman left Ya'ad—Movement for Civil Rights and established a parliamentary group called the Social-Democratic Faction. Shulamit Aloni and Boaz Moav returned to the name Civil Rights Movement (Ratz).

8.6.76   Seif-El-Din El-Zubi and Jabr Moade left the Alignment and returned to the name Kidma Vepituah.

26.10.76   Shmuel Tamir and Akiva Nof split from the Likud and established the Free Center.

4.1.77   Hamad Abu-Rabiah left the Alignment and reestablished the Arab List for Bedouin and Villagers.

15.2.77   Hillel Seidel left the Independent Liberals and joined the Likud.

15.3.77   Mordechai Ben-Porat left the Alignment and became a Single MK.

Ninth Knesset

5.7.77   Shlomtzion (Itzhak Itzhaky and Ariel Sharon) joined the Likud.

5.7.77   Moshe Dayan left the Alignment and became a Single MK.

15.5.79   Moshe Shamir left the Likud and became a Single MK.

17.7.79   Geula Cohen left the Likud and together with Moshe Shamir established Bnai.

31.12.79   Josef Tamir left the Likud and joined the Movement for Change and Initiative.

5.2.80   Mordechai Elgrably left the Democratic Movement and became a Single MK.

13.5.80   Meir Amit and David Golomb left the Movement for Change and Initiative and joined the Alignment.

8.7.80   Shafik Asaad and Shlomo Eliahu left the Democratic Movement and established Achva.

17.9.80   Akiva Nof left the Democratic Movement and joined Achva.

14.10.80   Itzhak Itzhaky left the Likud and became a Single MK.

11.11.80   Saadia Marciano split off from the Left Camp of Israel and established a Single-Member Parliamentary Group.

26.1.81   Igael Hurvitz, Yitzhak Peretz, and Zalman Shoval split from the Likud and established Rafi.

28.1.81   Akiva Nof left Achva and joined the Likud.

17.3.81   Shmuel Tamir became a Single MK; (Yigal Yadin did not request any special Knesset status—he remained a minister in the government, but by default became a Single MK).

11.5.81   Josef Tamir split from Shinui—Center Party and became a Single MK.

19.5.81   Mordechai Elgrably joined Equality in Israel-Panthers which then changed its name to the Unity Party.

19.5.81   Moshe Dayan joined the Movement for National Renewal—Telem.

27.5.81   Yitzhak Peretz returned to the Likud.

15.6.81   Shafik Asaad left Achva and joined Telem—Movement for National Renewal.

Tenth Knesset

16.11.81   The Civil Rights Movement (Ratz) (Shulamit Aloni) joined the Alignment.

26.10.82   Amnon Linn and Yitzhak Peretz left the Likud and joined the Alignment.

10.10.83   Haim Meir Druckman left the National Religious Party and became a Single MK (he had requested to set up a parliamentary group called the National Religious Camp, but his request was denied).

14.5.84   The Civil Rights Movement (Ratz) split from the Alignment.

29.5.84   Gesher—Zionist Religious Center (Yehuda Ben-Meir and Zevulon Hammer) split off from the National Religious Party.

12.6.84   Gesher—Zionist Religious Center returned to the National Religious Party.

Eleventh Knesset

22.10.84   Yahad joined the Alignment.

22.10.84   Yossi Sarid left the Alignment and joined the Civil Rights Movement (Ratz).

29.7.86   Haim Meir Druckman split off and joined the National Religious Party.

5.8.87   Mordechai Virshubski left Shinui and joined the Civil Rights Movement.

16.11.87   Rafael Eitan split from Tehiya.

15.2.88   Abdulwahab Darawshe split off from the Alignment and formed a single-member parliamentary group.

15.3.88   Yitzhak Artzi left the Alignment and joined Shinui—the Center Movement.

12.7.88   Muhammed Wattad left the National Workers' Party and joined Hadash.

29.8.88   The Movement for the Heritage of Israel (Tami) (Aharon Abuhatssira) merged with the Likud.

27.9.88   Rafi-Ometz (Igael Hurvitz) merged with the Likud.

27.9.88   Shimon Ben-Shlomo left Shas and became a Single MK.

Twelfth Knesset

15.3.90   Yosef Goldberg, Pinhas Goldstein, Pesach Grupper, Yitzhak Moday, and Avraham Sharir split off from the Likud and established the Party for the Advancement of the Zionist Idea.

18.6.90   Avraham Sharir left the Party for the Advancement of the Zionist Idea and returned to the Likud.

4.12.90   Yosef Goldberg left the Party for the Advancement of the Zionist Idea and returned to the Likud.

25.12.90   Yitzhak Haim Peretz left Shas and founded Moriah.

25.12.90   Charlie Bitton left Hadash, and the name for his new parliamentary group was not yet approved.

25.12.90   Efraim Gur left the Alignment and established Unity for Peace and Immigration.

25.12.90   Eliezer Mizrachi split off from Agudat Yisrael and established Geulat Yisrael.

17.5.92   Unity for Peace and Immigration joined the Likud.

Thirteenth Knesset

7.2.94   Alex Goldfarb, Esther Salmovitz, and Gonen Segev split off from Tzomet and established Yi'ud.

24.7.95   Shaul Gutman left Moledet and established Right Israel.

27.11.95   Alex Goldfarb and Esther Salmovitz split off from Yi'ud and established Atid.

28.2.96   Joseph Azran left Shas and became a Single MK.

7.3.96   Nava Arad left the Alignment and became a Single MK.

7.3.96   Efraim Gur left the Likud and became a Single MK.

7.3.96   Avigdor Kahalani and Emanuel Zisman split off from the Labor Party and founded The Third Way.

11.3.96   David Levy and David Magen split off from the Likud and established Gesher.

12.3.96   Joseph Bagad left Moledet and became a Single MK.

Fourteenth Knesset

17.1.99   Avraham Poraz left Meretz and established Shinui—Center Party.

23.2.99   Michael Nudelman and Yuri Shtern split off from Yisrael Be'aliyah and formed Aliah—For a Renewed Israel.

23.2.99   Ze'ev Binyamin Begin, Michael Kleiner, and David Re'em split off from Likud Gesher Tzomet and formed Herut—National Movement.

23.2.99   Hagai Meirom and Nissim Zvili left the Labor Party and established Israel in the Center (a).

23.2.99   David Magen, Dan Meridor, Itzchak Mordechay, and Eliezer Sandberg left Likud Gesher Tzomet and formed Israel in the Center (b).

4.3.99   Moshe Peled left Tzomet and established Mehora which immediately merged with Moledet.

4.3.99   Zvi Hendel and Hanan Porat left the National Religious Party and established Emunim.

17.3.99   David Zucker left Meretz and became a Single MK.

22.3.99   Eliezer Sandberg left Israel in the Center and formed Hatzeirim.

25.3.99   Amir Peretz, Rafik Haj Yahia, and Addisu Messele split off from the Labor Party and established Am Ehad.

29.3.99   Shinui—Center Party (Avraham Poraz) and Hatzeirim (Eliezer Sandberg) merged and kept the name Shinui.

29.3.99   Emanuel Zisman split off from the Third Way and became a Single MK.

Fifteenth Knesset

20.7.99   Roman Bronfman and Alexander Tsinker split off from Yisrael Be'aliyah, but the name for their new parliamentary group was not yet approved.

21.12.99   The Arab Movement for Renewal (Ta-al) (Ahmad Tibi) split off from the National Democratic Assembly (Balad).

1.2.00   Ichud Leumi split into Ichud Leumi—Moledet—Tekuma and Herut—National Movement (Michael Kleiner).

19.2.01   Muhamad Kanan and Tawfik Khatib split off from the United Arab List and established the National Arab Party.

6.3.01   The New Way (Amnon Lipkin-Shahak, Dalia Rabin-Pelossof, and Uri Savir) split off from Center Party.

7.5.01   The New Way merged into One Israel.

6.11.02   Roni Milo and Yechiel Lasry left the Center Party and established Lev, which then merged with the Likud.

10.12.02   Hashem Mahameed split off from the United Arab List (towards elections) and established National Unity—National Progressive Alliance.

Sixteenth Knesset

10.3.03   Yisrael Be'aliyah (Yuli-Yoel Edelstein and Marina Solodkin) merged into the Likud.

21.3.05   Hitchabrut (Effie Eitam and Yitzhak Levy) split off from the National Religious Party.

18.5.05   Joseph Paritzky split off from Shinui—the Secular Movement and established Zionism Liberalism Equality.

23.5.05   David Tal split off from Am Ehad and established Noy.

23.11.05   14 MKs from the Likud split off and formed Achrayut Leumit.

23.11.05   Noy (David Tal) merged with Achrayut Leumit.

1.2.06   Michael Nudelman left Ichud Leumi and remained a Single MK.

1.2.06   Igal Yasinov split off from Shinui, and formed Ha-olim, which then merged with Ichud Leumi-Yisrael Beitenu-Moledet-Tekuma.

5.2.06   Chemi Doron and Eliezer Sandberg left the Secular Faction and established Habayit Haleumi.

Seventeenth Knesset

2.6.08   Three MKs from the Gil Pensioners Party (Elhanan Glazer, Sara Marom Shalev, and Moshe Sharoni) split and formed the Justice for the Elderly parliamentary group.

27.10.08   Two MKs from Justice for the Elderly (Sara Marom Shalev, and Moshe Sharoni) remerged with Gil Pensioners Party. The third MK, Elhanan Glazer, split and formed a single member parliamentary group called the Right Way.

Eighteenth Knesset

17.1.11   The Labor Under Ehud Barak parliamentary group divided into two new groups: Haatzma'ut (Ehud Barak, Orit Noked, Shalom Simhon, Matan Vilnai, and Einat Wilf), and the Israel Labor Party (Binyamin (Fouad) Ben-Eliezer, Daniel Ben Simon, Avishay Braverman, Eitan Cabel, Isaac Herzog, Raleb Majadele, Amir Peretz, and Shelly Yachimovich).

19.11.12   Two Knesset members (Michael Ben Ari and Arieh Eldad) split off from Ichud Leumi and established a new parliamentary group called Otzma Leyisrael.

3.12.12   Seven Knesset members split off from Kadima and established a new parliamentary group called Hatenua Chaired by Tzipi Livni.

3.12.12   MK Talab El-Sana split off from Ra'am-Ta'al and re-established the Arab Democratic Party ("Mada") parliamentary group.

3.12.12   MK Chaim Amsellem left Shas and began serving as a Single MK parliamentary group.

Twentieth Knesset

15.3.17   Orly Levi-Abekasis split off from the Yisrael Beitenu faction and became a Single MK.

31.12.18   Naftali Bennett, Ayelet Shaked and Shuli Moalem-Refaeli quit the Habayit *Hayehudi* (Jewish Home) parliamentary group and formed *The New Right* parliamentary group.

Notes

Introduction

1. See Gideon Rahat, *The Politics of Regime Structure Reform in Democracies: Israel in Comparative and Theoretical Perspective* (Albany, NY: SUNY Press, 2008).

2. Reuven Hazan, "Presidential Parliamentarism: Direct Popular Election of the Prime Minister; Israel's New Electoral and Political System," *Electoral Studies* 15, no. 1 (1996): 21–37.

3. Reuven Hazan and Gideon Rahat, "Israel: The Politics of Extreme Proportionality," in Michael Gallagher and Paul Mitchell, eds. *The Politics of Electoral Reform* (Oxford: Oxford University Press, 2005), 333–335; Gideon Rahat and Ofer Kenig, *From Party Politics to Personalized Politics? Party Change and Political Personalization in Democracies* (Oxford: Oxford University Press, 2018).

4. For the concept of party system institutionalization, see Scott Mainwarring and Timothy R. Scully, *Building Democratic Institutions: Party Systems in Latin America* (Stanford, CA: Stanford University Press, 1995).

5. For an excellent overview of these cases, see G. C. Malhotra, *Anti-Defection Law in India and the Commonwealth* (New Delhi: Metropolitan Book Co., 2005).

6. Zdzislaw Kedzia and Agata Hauser, *The Impact of Political Party Control over the Exercise of the Parliamentary Mandate* (Geneva: Inter-Parliamentary Union, 2012).

7. In his famous Speech to the Electors of Bristol, Sir Edmund Burke argued that parliament was a deliberative body of free agents and not a congress of ambassadors of various interests. As he put it: "You choose a member indeed; but when you have chosen him, he is not a member of Bristol, but he is a member of Parliament." See Edmund Burke, "Speech to the Electors and Bristol, 3 November, 1774," in Philip B. Kurland and Ralph Lerner, *The Founders' Constitution.* http://press-pubs.uchicago.edu/founders/documents/v1ch13s7.html

8. For a discussion and a list of states that place an outright ban on restricting the political freedom of individual parliamentarians, see European Commission for Democracy through Law (Venice Commission), *Report on Democracy, Limitation of Mandates and Incompatibility of Political Functions*, Strasbourg, France, 2013. www.venice.coe.int/webforms/documents/default.aspx?pdffile=CDL-AD(2012)027rev-e

9. See, for example, Conference on Security and Cooperation in Europe, *Document of the Copenhagen Meeting, 1990* at www.osce.org/odihr/elections/14304?download=true p. 7; European Commission for Democracy through Law (Venice Commission), *Report on the Imperative Mandate and Similar Practices*, Strasbourg, France, 2009; Kedzia and Hauser, *The Impact of Political Party Control.*

10. For the formula and discussion of the effective number of parties, see Markku Laakso and Rein Taagepeara, "'Effective' Number of Parties: A Measure with Application West Europe," *Comparative Political* Studies 12, no. 1 (1979): 3–27.

11. Hazan and Rahat, "Israel: The Politics of Extreme Proportionality."

Chapter 1

1. Giovanni Sartori, *Comparative Constitutinal Engineering: An Inquiry into Structures, Incentives and Outcomes* (New York: New York University Press, 1997), 94.

2. Ergun Özbudun, *Party Cohesion in Western Democracies: A Causal Analysis* (London: Sage, 1970), 305.

3. Reuven Hazan, "Does Cohesion Equal Discipline? Toward a Conceptual Delineation," *Journal of Legislative Studies* 9, no. 4 (2003): 4.

4. John Owens, "Explaining Party Cohesion and Discipline in Democratic Legislatures: Purposiveness and Contexts," *Journal of Legislative Studies* 9, no. 4 (2003): 12–40; Shaun Bowler, David M. Farrell, and Richard S. Katz, eds., *Party Discipline and Parliamentary Government* (Columbus: Ohio State University Press, 1999).

5. Hazan, "Does Cohesion Equal Discipline?"

6. Bowler, Farrel, and Katz, eds., *Party Discipline and Parliamentary Government*, 5.

7. Jim F. Couch, "An Empirical Examination of the Impetus for Political Party Defection," *International Journal of Business and Social Science*, 4, no. 3 (2013): 109–113; Scott Desposato, "Parties for Rent? Ambition, Ideology, and Party Switching in Brazil's Chamber of Deputies," *American Journal of Political Science* 50, no. 1 (2006): 62–80; Christian Grose and Antoine Yoshinaka, "The Electoral Consequences of Party Switching by Incumbent Members of Congress, 1947–2000," *Legislative Studies Quarterly* 28, no. 1 (2003): 55–75; William Heller and Carol Mershon, "Party Switching in the Italian Chamber of Deputies, 1996–2001," *Journal of Politics* 67, no. 2 (2005): 536–559; William Heller and

Carol Mershon, "Dealing in Discipline: Party Switching and Legislative Voting in the Italian Chamber of Deputies," *American Journal of Political Science* 52, no. 4 (2008): 910–925; William Heller and Carol Mershon, eds., *Political Parties and Legislative Party Switching* (New York: Palgrave Macmillan, 2009); William Heller and Carol Mershon, "Integrating Theoretical and Empirical Models of Party Switching," Heller and Mershon, eds., *Political Parties and Legislative Party Switching*; William Heller and Carol Mershon, "Introduction: Legislative Party Switching, Parties, and Party Systems," in Heller and Mershon, eds., *Political Parties and Legislative Party Switching*; William Heller and Carol Mershon, "Legislator Preferences, Party Desires: Party Switching and the Foundations of Policy Making in Legislatures," Heller and Mershon, eds., *Political Parties and Legislative Party Switching*; William Heller and Carol Mershon,"Party Switching in the Italian Chamber of Deputies, 1996–2001," *Journal of Politics*, 67, no. 2 (2005): 536–559; Seth C. McKee and Antoine Yoshinaka, "Late to the Parade: Party Switchers in Contemporary US Southern Legislatures," *Party Politics* 21, no. 6 (2013): 957–969; Carol Mershon and Olga Shvetsova, *Party System Change in Legislatures Worldwide* (Cambridge: Cambridge University Press, 2015); Diana Z. O'Brien and Yael Shomer, "A Cross-National Analysis of Party Switching," *Legislative Studies Quarterly* 38, no. 1 (2013): 111–141; Owens, "Explaining Party Cohesion and Discipline"; Antoine Yoshinaka, "House Party Switchers and Committee Assignments: Who Gets "What, When, How?," *Legislative Studies Quarterly* 30, no. 3 (2005): 391–406.

8. Heller and Mershon, "Introduction: Legislative Party Switching, Parties, and Party Systems," 8.

9. Jon Fraenkel, "Party Hopping Laws in the Southern Hemisphere," *Political Science* 64, no. 2 (2011): 106–120; Andrew Geddis, "Gang Aft A-Gley: New Zealand's Attempt to Combat 'Party Hopping' By Elected Representatives," *Election Law Journal* 1, no. 4 (2002): 557–571; Andrew Geddis, "Proportional Representation 'Party Hopping' and the Limits of Electoral Regulation: A Cautionary Tale from New Zealand," *Common Law World Review* 35, no. 1 (2006): 24–50; Martin Goeke and Christof Hartmann, "The Regulation of Party Switching in Africa," *Journal of Contemporary African Studies* 29, no. 3 (2009): 263–280; Kenneth Janda, "Laws against Party Switching, Defecting, or Floor-Crossing in National Parliaments," paper delivered at the 2009 World Congress of the International Political Science Association in Santiago, Chile; Z. Kedzia and A. Hauser, *The Impact of Political Party Control Over the Exercise of the Parliamentary Mandate* (Geneva: Inter-Parliamentary Union, 2012); G. C. Malhotra, *Anti-Defection Law in India and the Commonwealth* (New Delhi: Metropolitan Book Co., 2005); Eric McLaughlin, "Electoral Regimes and Party-Switching: Floor-Crossing in South Africa's Local Legislatures," *Party Politics* 18, no. 4 (2011): 563–579; Eric McLaughlin, "Did Floor-Crossing Alienate South African Voters? Evidence from Municipal Legislatures," *Politikon: South African Journal of Political Studies* 41, no. 2 (2014): 289–310; Sarah Miskin,. "Politicians Overboard: Jumping the Party Ship,"

Research Paper No. 4. Department of the Parliamentary Library, Australia, 2003; Csaba Nikolenyi and Shaul Shenhav, "The Constitutionalisation of Party Unity: The Origins of Anti-Defection Laws in India and Israel," *Journal of Legislative Studies* 21, no. 4 (2015); R. Subramanian, *Developing and Testing a Theory of Legislative Party Fragmentation* (University of Wisconsin-Madison. Unpublished PhD dissertation, 2008); Venice Commission, *Report on the Imperative Mandate and Similar Practices* (Strasbourg: Council of Europe, 2009); Vineeta Yadav, "Legislative Institutions and Corruption in Developing Country Democracies," *Comparative Political Studies* 45, no. 8 (2012): 1027–1058.

10. Michael Laver and Kenneth Benoit, "The Evolution of Party Systems Between Elections," *American Journal of Political Science* 47, no. 2 (2003): 215–233; Michael Laver and Junko Kato, "Dynamic Approaches to Government Formation and the Generic Instability of Decisive Structures in Japan," *Electoral Studies* 20, no. 4 (2001): 509–527; Michael Laver and John Underhill, "The Bargaining Advantages of Combining with Others," *British Journal of Political Science* 12, no. 1 (1982): 27–42; Carol Mershon, "Legislative Party Switching and Executive Coalitions," *Japanese Journal of Political Science* 9, no. 3 (2008): 391–414. Mershon and Shvetsova, *Party System Change in Legislatures Worldwide.*

11. Shane Martin, "Why Electoral Seats Don't Always Matter: The Impact of Mega-Seats on Legislative Behaviour in Ireland," *Party Politics* 20, no. 3 (2014): 467–479.

12. Carol Mershon and Olga Shvetsova, "Timing Matters: Incentives for Party Switching and Stages of Parliamentary Cycles," in Heller and Mershon, eds., *Political Parties and Legislative Party Switching.*

13. See, for example, Grose and Yoshinaka 2003; Heller and Mershon 2009; Miskin, 2003.

14. Elad Klein, "Explaining Legislative Party Switching in Advanced and New Democracies," *Party Politics* 27, no. 2 (2021): 329–340.

15. Dafydd Fell, "Do Party Switchers Pay an Electoral Price? The Case of Taiwan," *Parliamentary Affairs,* 70, no. 2 (2017): 377–399; Sergiu Gherghina, "Rewarding the "Traitors"? Legislative Defection and Re-Election in Romania," *Party Politics,* 22, no. 4 (2016): 490–500; Jordan Hamzawi, "Policy Preferences and Party Switching: Evidence from the 2012 Japanese Election," *Party Politics* 27, no. 6 (2021): 1268–1278.

16. Antoine Yoshinaka, *Crossing the Aisle: Party Switching by U.S. Legislators in the Postwar Era* (Cambridge: Cambridge University Press, 2016).

17. Heller and Mershon, "Dealing in Discipline: Party Switching and Legislative Voting in the Italian Chamber of Deputies"; Elisa Volpi, "Ideology and Party Switching: A Comparison of 12 West European Countries," *Parliamentary Affairs* 72, no. 1 (2019): 1–20.

18. O'Brien and Shomer, "A Cross-National Analysis of Party Switching."

19. Maurice Duverger, *Political Parties, Their Organization and Activity in the Modern State* (London: Methuen, 1969).

20. Mershon and Shvetsova, *Party System Change in Legislatures Worldwide*.

21. Marie Kaldahl Nielsen, Ann Mogeltolt Andersen, and Helena Helboe Pedersen, "Balancing Costs of Legislative Party Switching in the Danish Parliament, 1953–2015," *Parliamentary Affairs* 72, no. 1: (2019): 42–58.

22. Elad Klein, "The Personal Vote and Legislative Party Switching," *Party Politics* 24, no. 5 (2018): 501–510.

23. Daniela Giannetti and Michael Laver, "Party System Dynamics and the Making and Breaking of Italian Governments," *Electoral Studies* 20, no. 4 (2001): 529–553.

24. Jordan Hamzawi, "Policy Preferences and Party Switching: Evidence from the 2012 Japanese Election"; Ethan Scheiner, "Pipelines of Pork: Japanese Politics and a Model of Local Opposition Party Failure," *Comparative Political Studies* 38, no. 7 (2005): 799–823.

25. Bowler, Farrell and Katz, eds, *Party Discipline and Parliamentary Government*; Hazan, "Does Cohesion Equal Discipline?"

26. Dan Avnon, "Parties Laws in Democratic Systems of Government," *Journal of Legislative Studies* 1, no. 2 (1995): 283–300; Ingrid van Biezen, "Party Regulation and Constitutionalization: A Comparative Overview," in Benjamin Reilly and Per Nodlund, eds., *Political Parties in Conflict-Prone Societies* (New York: United Nations University Press., 2008), 25–47; Ingrid van Biezen and Petr Kopecky, "The State and the Parties: Public Funding, Public Regulation and Rent-Seeking in Contemporary Democracies," *Party Politics* 13, no. 2 (2007): 235–254. Richard S. Katz and Peter Mair, "Changing Models of Party Organization and Party Democracy: The Emergence of the Cartel Party," *Party Politics* 1, no. 1 (1995): 5–28; Lauri Karvonen, "Legislation on Political Parties: A Global Comparison," *Party Politics* 13, no. 4 (2007): 437–455; Wolfgang Muller, "The Relevance of the State for Party System Change," *Journal of Theoretical Politics* 5, no. 4 (1993): 419–454. Wolfgang Muller and Ulrich Sieberer, "Party Law," in Richard S. Katz and William J. Crotty, eds., *Handbook of Party Politics* (London: Sage, 2006), 435–445.

27. Kenneth Janda, "Adopting Party Law," in *Political Parties and Democracy in Theoretical and Practical Perspectives* (Washington, DC: National Democratic Institute for International Affairs, 2005); Malhotra, *Anti-Defection Law in India and the Commonwealth*; Miskin, "Politicians Overboard: Jumping the Party Ship."

28. Susan Booysen, "The Will of the Parties versus the Will of the People? Defections, Elections and Alliances in South Africa," *Party Politics* 12, no. 6 (2006): 727–746.

29. Csaba Nikolenyi and Shaul Shenhav, "The Constitutionalization of Party Unity: The Origins of the Anti-Defection Laws in India and Israel," *Journal of Legislative Studies* 21, no. 3 (2015): 390–407.

30. Benjamin Reilly, "Political Engineering and Party Politics in Papua New Guinea," *Party Politics* 8, no. 6 (2002): 701–718.

31. Malhotra, *Anti-Defection Law in India and the Commonwealth*.

32. Janda, "Laws against Party Switching."

33. Muller and Sieberer, "Party Law," 435.

34. Janda, "Adopting Party Law."

35. Biezen and Kopecky, "The State and the Parties"; Katz and Mair, "Changing Models of Party Organization and Party Democracy"; Petr Kopecky and Peter Mair, "Political Parties and Government," in Mohamed A. Salih, ed., *Political Parties in Africa* (London: Pluto, 2003), 275–292; Petr Kopecky, "Political Parties and the State in Post-Communist Europe," *Journal of Communist Studies and Transition Politics* 22, no. 3 (2006): 251–273.

36. Muller and Sieberer, "Party Law," 435.

37. See Karvonen, "Legislation on Political Parties: A Global Comparison"; Muller and Sieberer, "Party Law"; Biezen, "Party Regulation and Constitutionalization."

38. Thomas Carothers, *Confronting the Weakest Link: Aiding Political Parties in New Democracies* (Washington, DC: Carnegie Endowment for International Peace, 2006).

39. Avnon, "Parties Laws in Democratic Systems of Government."

40. Karvonen, "Legislation on Political Parties: A Global Comparison"; Katz and Mair, "Changing Models of Party Organization"; Ben Clift and Justin Fisher, "Comparative Party Finance Reform: The Cases of France and Britain," *Party Politics* 10, no. 6 (2004): 677–699; 2004; Jonathan Hopkin, "The Problem with Party Finance: Theoretical Perspectives on the Funding of Party Politics," *Party Politics* 10, no. 6 (2004): 627–651; Susan E. Scarrow, "Explaining Political Finance Reforms: Competition and Context," *Party Politics* 10, no. 6 (2004): 653–675.

41. Janda, "Adopting Party Law."

42. Janda, "Laws against Party Switching."

43. Miskin, "Politicians Overboard: Jumping the Party Ship," 23.

44. Booysen, "The Will of the Parties Versus the Will of the People? Defections, Elections and Alliances in South Africa."

45. Miskin, "Politicians Overboard: Jumping the Party Ship."

46. Manuel Sanchez de Dios, "Parliamentary Party Discipline in Spain," in Bowler, Farrell, and Katz, eds., *Party Discipline and Parliamentary Government*, 141–166.

47. Malhotra, *Anti-Defection Law in India and the Commonwealth*.

48. Biezen and Kopecky, "The State and the Parties: Public Funding, Public Regulation and Rent-Seeking in Contemporary Democracies," 246–247.

49. Biezen, "Party Regulation and Constitutionalization"; Vernon Bogdanor, "The Constitution and the Party System in the Twentieth Century," *Parliamentary Affairs* 57, no. 4 (2004): 717–733.

50. Biezen, "Party Regulation and Constitutionalization"; Biezen and Kopecky, "The State and the Parties"; Muller and Sieberer, "Party Law."

51. Biezen and Kopecky, "The State and the Parties."

52. Janda, "Laws against Party Switching."

53. Although Israel has no formal written constitution, key elements of the country's anti-defection legislation are included in the Basic Law: the Knesset and the Basic Law: the Government. The Basic Law have functions as a de facto constitution. See Amnon Rubeinstein and Barak Medina, *The Constitutional Law of the State of Israel* (Jerusalem: Shoken Books, 2005). (In Hebrew.)

54. This number includes Zimbabwe, although the state was expelled from the Commonwealth in 2003.

55. Michael Fitzsimmons, *The Remaking of France: The National Assembly and the Constitution of 1791* (Cambridge: Cambridge University Press, 1994), 33–69; Alice M. Holden, "The Imperative Mandate in the Spanish Cortes of the Middle Ages," *American Political Science Review* 24, no. 4 (1930): 886–912; Leif Lewin, *Ideology and Strategy: A Century of Swedih Politics*. Cambridge: Cambridge University Press, 1988), 51–53; Pasquale Pasquino, "One and Three: Separation of Powers and the Independence of the Judiciary in the Italian Constitution," in John Ferejohn, Jack N. Rakove, and Jonathan Riley, eds., *Constitutional Culture and Democratic Rule* (Cambridge: Cambridge University Press, 2001), 205–222.

56. Conference on Security and Cooperation in Europe, *Document of the Copenhagen Meeting, 1990*, www.osce.org/odihr/elections/14304?download=true 2018, p. 7. Emphasis added.

57. European Commission for Democracy through Law (Venice Commission), *Report on the Imperative Mandate and Similar Practices* (Strasbourg: Council of Europe, 2009), 8.

58. Relevant examples include the *Pact against Floor Crossing* in Spain (see Venice Commission 2009: 6) and the requirement by Slovakia's HZDS in 1992 that the party's deputies would be pre-committed to paying an exceedingly large sum of money to the party in case of defection (see Tim Haughton, *Constraints and Opportunities of Leadership in Post-Communist Europe* [Aldershot & Burlington, VT: Ashgate, 2005]), 31.

59. This sanction has also been raised yet rejected in the Israeli parliament, the Knesset. See Rhanan Har Zahav, "Constitutional Amendments—A Review from the Knesset," *Hamishpat* 1 (1993): 112. (In Hebrew.)

60. Nikolenyi and Shenhav, "The Constitutionalization of Party Unity."

61. For example, the constitution of Fiji requires that any such expulsion must take place in accordance with the "rules of the party relating to party discipline," and the constitution of Panama states the "reasons for the termination of the mandate and the applicable procedure must have been established in the party by-laws." The Thai constitution even specifies that expulsion can result in a deputy's loss of mandate only if a resolution to that effect is passed by a qualified three-quarters majority of the party's Executive Committee and its current legislative representatives.

62. The prohibition of any imperative mandate is actually enshrined in the constitutions of several states such as Malawi and Niger even though party switch-

ing is penalized. There are only six states (Guyana, India, Pakistan, Bangladesh, Zimbabwe, and Sierra Leone) where the constitution penalizes both defection and voting against the party line.

63. Cited in Marc van der Hulst, *The Parliamentary Mandate: A Global Comparative Study* (Geneva: Inter-Parliamentary Union, 2000), 7.

64. Suzie Navot, *The Constitution of Israel: A Contextual Analysis* (Oxford & Portland: Hart Publishing, 2014), 108–109.

65. Csaba Nikolenyi, "Government Termination and Anti-Defection Laws in Parliamentary Democracies," *West European Politics* 45, no. 6 (2022): 638–662.

Chapter 2

1. George Tsebelis, *Nested Games: Rational Choice in Comparative Politics* (Berkeley: University of California Press, 1990), 104–110.

2. "Levatel et Tziruto shel Preminger beAsafat Ha-Mekonenet Tovea Merkaz Maki," [The Maki Central Committee demands to Cancel Preminger's Mandate in the Constituent Assembly] *Kol Haam*, February 14, 1949, 2.

3. "Communist Party Purge" *Palestine Post*, February 14, 1949, 3,

4. "Constituent Assembly in Session," *Palestine Post*, February 16, 1949, 2.

5. These factions were the Fighters List, WIZO, and the Yemenite Association.

6. Divrei Haknesset [Knesset Proceedings], April, 12, 1951, 1680–1683.

7. "Communists Dissolve Party, Urge Members to Join Mapam," *Chicago Sentinel*, August 18, 1949, 3.

8. *Knesset Committee Protocols*, November 22, 1949. https://fs.knesset.gov.il/1/Committees/1_ptv_399113.PDF

9. "New Jerusalem Coalition Minus Orthodox Parties," *Jerusalem Post*, August 27, 1956. 1.

10. A similar private member bill submitted by Aguda MK Menahem Porush in July 1969 was also defeated by the coalition. This bill sought to stabilize the mayor's position by requiring that a motion of no-confidence be submitted three weeks prior to its vote and that the removal of the mayor should require an absolute majority of two-thirds of the local councilors. Although these attempts at a formal legislative regulation against defections failed, the two largest political blocs of the day, Gahal and Alignment, actually signed a political agreement in 1963 committing themselves not to participate in and condone any *kalanteristic* deals in the future. Eventually, the Knesset did resolve the issue of the rampant instability of local governments by introducing direct elections to the mayoral offices throughout the country.

11. "I.L.P. Leader Wants Party to Join Labour Group," *Jerusalem Post*, December 26, 1967, 3.

12. "ILP Votes Against Tie-Up with Labour; Only 8 in Favour," *Jerusalem Post*, May 24, 1968, 8.

13. "Harari of ILP Crosses Floor to Join Labour Party Ranks," *Jerusalem Post* May 28, 1968, 1.

14. Knesset Committee Protocols, No. 120, Sixth Knesset, June 11, 1968. https://fs.knesset.gov.il/6/Committees/6_ptv_425610.PDF

15. Asher Wallfish, "Knesset Marranos' Danger of Anti-Floor-Crossing Law," *Jerusalem Post*, November 21, 1968, 8.

16. Knesset Committee Protocols, No. 130, Sixth Knesset, July 30, 1968. https://fs.knesset.gov.il/6/Committees/6_ptv_425630.PDF

17. Between 1959 and 1964, Dayan had also served as Minister of Agriculture.

18. "Dayan Seeks Independent Knesset Status," *Jerusalem Post,* June 15, 1977, 1.

19. Knesset Committee Protocols, No. 3. July 12, 1977. http://fs.knesset.gov.il//9/Committees/9_ptv_441707.PDF

20. Knesset Plenary Protocols, June 20, 1977, 69. http://fs.knesset.gov.il//9/Plenum/9_ptm_254065.pdf

21. Knesset Committee Protocols, No. 2. July 5, 1977. http://fs.knesset.gov.il//9/Committees/9_ptv_441705.PDF

22. Ibid, 4.

23. Knesset Committee Protocols, No. 3. July 12, 1977. http://fs.knesset.gov.il//9/Committees/9_ptv_441707.PDF

24. Moshe Kohn, "Dayan to Sit as Independent MK," *Jerusalem Post,* July 13, 1977, 2.

25. Knesset Committee Protocols, No. 3. July 12, 1977, 15. http://fs.knesset.gov.il//9/Committees/9_ptv_441707.PDF

26. Divrei Ha-Knesset [Knesset Proceedings], The Eleventh Session of the Ninth Knesset, July 12, 1977, 258–259.

27. In March 1982, the government actually tied on a no-confidence vote with the opposition and coalition parties polling fifty-eight votes each in the Knesset. Although Prime Minister Begin informally offered his resignation, the cabinet did not accept it.

28. Sarah Honig, "Was it Kalanterism," *Jerusalem Post*, May 19, 1982, 1.

29. "Nissim Considers Law Against Kalanterism," *Jerusalem Post*, May 23, 1982, 2.

30. Asher Wallfish, "Proposal Would Stop MKs from Bolting Their Factions," *Jerusalem Post,* September 7, 1982, 2.

31. Shevach Weiss, 1987, Explanation to a Bill Proposal, the 11th Knesset, 03/0882/A/024. https://main.knesset.gov.il/Activity/Legislation/Laws/Pages/LawBill.aspx?t=lawsuggestionssearch&lawitemid=151847

32. For an excellent and comprehensive discussion, see Dani Koren, *A Time in Grey* (Tel Aviv: Zemorah, 1994). (In Hebrew.)

33. Knesset Committee Protocols, 12th Knesset, Session no. 100 on February 26, 1990, Session no. 103 on March 6, 1990; Session no. 104 on March 14, 1990, and Sessions No. 107 and 108 on March 15, 1990.

34. Avraham Sharir, who served as Minister of Tourism and a Minister of Justice in the Eleventh Knesset, harbored particularly strong resentment against Prime Minister Shamir, who unceremoniously left him out of his National Unity government after the 1988 elections. See Dan Petreanu, "Likud in Uproar over Unity Deal," *Jerusalem Post*, December 21, 1988, 1.

35. Sarah Honig and Michal Yudelman, "Despite Peretz-Deri Blowup, Shas Leans to Likud—without Shamir," *Jerusalem Post*, March 19, 1990, 1; Michal Yudelman, "Peretz Stands Firm—Shas Rift Deepens," *Jerusalem Post*, March 21, 1990, 1.

36. The votes in favor of the government came from Likud, PAZI, Moledet, Tzosmet, Tehiya, the NRP, Degel Hatorah, and Y. Peretz, while those supporting the no-confidence motion included all members of the Left and Arab bloc parties and one party, Aguda, in the religious bloc.

37. It is worth noting that the two MKs received spiritual and political guidance from the Lubavitcher Rebbe Menachem Mandel Schneerson, who clearly was in favor of a Likud-led coalition at this time. See Chaim Herzog, *Living History* (New York: Pantheon Books, 1996), 365.

38. Eventually Verdiger changed his mind and continued in the Knesset as an Aguda MK.

39. Similar to Sharir, Goldberg also left PAZI and returned to Likud in December 1990.

40. These included Uriel Lynn, Tzahi Hanegbi, Uzi Landau, David Levy, and Benny Begin. See Asher Wallfish, "Shamir Asks Party to Back Moda'i Deal," *Jerusalem Post*, April 20, 1990, 1.

41. These demand safe spots for all five defectors on the Likud candidate list in the next election, the allocation of three portfolios and one deputy ministership to the party in case Likud were to form the next government, the overall restoration of the 1965 Gahal agreement regarding the nomination of Knesset candidates, and, to make things credible, PAZI further demanded that Likud should deposit $10 million in its account as a safety deposit. As the Likud leadership was scrambling to try to meet these demands, the two senior members of PAZI, Moda'i and Sharir, started to negotiate with Labor as well in a game of playing the two large parties off against each other. See Sarah Honig, "Five Liberal Defectors Ready to Talk Coalition with Labor," *Jerusalem Post*, March 29, 1990, 1.

42. Asher Wallfish, "Bill Targets Perfidious, Corrupt MKs," *Jerusalem Post*, June 22, 1990, 9.

43. Ibid.

44. Csaba Nikolenyi and Shaul Shenhav, "The Constitutionalization of Party Unity: The Origins of the Anti-Defection Laws in India and Israel," *Journal of Legislative Studies* 21, no. 3 (2015): 390–407.

45. Amendment No. 12 to the Basic Law: The Knesset. https://fs.knesset.gov.il/12/law/12_lsr_210826.PDF

46. Amendment No. 31 to the Law on the Election of the Knesset and the Prime Minister. https://fs.knesset.gov.il/13/law/13_lsr_211239.PDF

47. Constitution, Law and Justice Committee Protocols, No. 464, Thirteenth Knesset, February 21, 1996. https://fs.knesset.gov.il/13/Committees/13_ptv_476322. PDF

48. David Zev Harris, "MKs Back Plan to Limit Party Splits," *Jerusalem Post*, January 20, 2000, 4.

49. Uriel Lynn, "In Defense of Electoral Reform," *Jerusalem Post*, December 12, 2000, 8.

50. In fact, Am Ehad had indicated its conditional openness to entering Sharon's government in the first place.

51. Gil Hoffman, "Opposition Growing to Labor-Am Ehad Merger," *Jerusalem Post*, July 10, 2003, 3.

52. Ibid.

53. *Reshumot* (Official Government Records), Amendment to the Knesset Election Law, February 11, 2004, 40.

54. Gil Hoffman, "Knesset Passes David Tal Law," *Jerusalem Post*, March 2, 2004, 2.

55. Divrei ha-Knesset [Knesset Proceedings], One Hundred and Thirteenth Session of the Sixteenth Knesset, March 1.

56. Gil Hoffman, ""Livni Ambushes Mofaz in Kadima Faction Meeting," *Jerusalem Post*, March 3, 2009, 4.

57. The Likud-Yisrael Beitenu coalition agreement contained a provision in its Article 36 that had direct relevance for the legislation on party unity. According to this Article, the two parties agreed to advance legislation that would allow one-third of a legislative party group or seven MKs, whichever is less, to split with impunity. The Article clearly sought to make it easier for splinter factions to exit from larger parties with more than twenty-one MKs. In the Eighteenth Knesset, this specifically applied to Likud and Kadima. http://main.knesset.gov.il/mk/government/documents/coal2009YisraelBeitenu.pdf

58. Mazal Mualem, "Knesset Passes Land Reform and 'Mofaz Law,'" *Haaretz*, August 3, 2009. www.haaretz.com/1.5085713

59. "Knesset Passes Governance Laws, Electoral Threshold Raised," *Knesset News*, March 11, 2014. https://m.knesset.gov.il/en/news/pressreleases/pages/pr11193_pg.aspx

60. Amendment No. 62 to the Law on the Election of the Knesset. https://fs.knesset.gov.il/19/law/19_lsr_301595.pdf

Chapter 3

1. Diana O'Brien and Yael Shomer, "A Cross-National Analysis of Party Switching," *Legislative Studies Quarterly* 38, no. 1 (2013): 111–141.

2. Giovanni Sartori, *Political Parties and Party Systems: A Framework for Analysis* (Cambridge: Cambridge University Press, 1976).

3. Mershon and Shvetsova, *Party System Change in Legislatures Worldwide*.

4. Reuven Hazan and Gideon Rahat, "Representation, Electoral Reform, and Democracy: Theoretical and Empirical Lessons from the 1996 Elections in Israel," *Comparative Political Studies* 33, no. 10 (2000): 1310–1336; Reuven Y. Hazan and Abraham Diskin, "The 1999 Knesset and Prime Ministerial Elections in Israel," *Electoral Studies* 19, no. 4 (2000): 628–637; Reuven Hazan, "The Unintended Consequences of Extemporaneous Electoral Reform: The 1999 Elections in Israel," *Representation* 37, no. 1 (2000): 39–47; Reuven Hazan, "The Israeli Mixed Electoral System: Unexpected Reciprocal and Cumulative Consequences," in Matthew Soberg Shugart and Martin Wattenberg, eds., *Mixed-Member Electoral Systems: The Best of Both Worlds?* (Oxford: Oxford University Press, 2003).

5. Reuven Hazan, "Constituency Interests without Constituency: The Geographical Impact of Candidate Selection on Party Organization and Legislative Behavior in the 14th Israeli Knesset, 1996–99," *Political Geography* 18, no. 7 (1999): 791–811; Reuven Hazan, "The 1996 Intra-Party Elections in Israel: Adopting Party Primaries," *Electoral Studies* 16, no. 1 (1997): 95–103; Gideon Rahat, "Determinants of Party Cohesion: Evidence from the Israeli Parliament," *Parliamentary Affairs* 60, no. 2 (2007): 279–296.

6. Hazan, "Constituency Interests without Constituency."

7. Ofer Kenig, 2012, "The Primary System in Israel: A Balance Sheet." https://en.idi.org.il/articles/6883

8. Claude Habermann, "Israel's Likud Passes Torch, Naming Netanyahu Leader," *New York Times*, March 25, 1993. www.nytimes.com/1993/03/26/world/israel-s-likud-passes-torch-naming-netanyahu-leader.html

9. For example, Levy was denied a coveted appointment to the Knesset Foreign Affairs and Defense Committees.

10. Michal Yudelman, "Levy: Fix Primary System of I'll Quit Likud," *Jerusalem Post*, May 30, 1995, 1; Michal Yudelman, "Countdown to Likud's Self-Destruction Begins," *Jerusalem Post*, June 2, 1995, 8; Sarah Honig, "Netanyahu Sweeps Likud Party Vote," *Jerusalem Post*, 1996, June 6, 1.

11. Sarah Honig, "Likud No Longer My Home," *Jerusalem Post*, December 12, 1995, 12; Michal Yudelman, "David Levy Launches his Gesher Party," *Jerusalem Post*, February 21, 1996, 1; Sarah Honig and Liat Collins, "Levy Prepares for 'New Way,'" *Jerusalem Post*, June 7, 1995, 2; Sarah Honig, "Magen to Announce He Is Joining Levy Today," *Jerusalem Post*, December 11, 1995, 12; Michal Yudelman, "David Levy to Announce New Party in December," *Jerusalem Post*, August 13, 1995, 1.

12. Knesset Committee Protocols No. 377, Thirteenth Knesset. March 11, 1996. https://fs.knesset.gov.il/13/Committees/13_ptv_477584.PDF. The vote was unanimous 2 in favor and 0 against Levy and Magen.

13. Liat Collins, "Knesset OKs Hebron Pact," *Jerusalem Post*, January 17, 1997, 1

14. Herb Keinon, "Force 17 Tests Netanyahu," *Jerusalem Post*, February 21, 1997, 7.

15. Evelyn Gordon, "High Court Throws Out Kleiner's Hebron Petition," *Jerusalem Post*, November 21, 1996, 2.

16. Jonathan Tepperman, "Levy-Netanyahu: The Latest Round," *Jerusalem Post*, June 30, 1997, 3.

17. Sarah Honig, "Magen Resigns as Deputy Finance Minister," *Jerusalem Post*, May 21, 1997, 1; Sarah Honig, "Magen to Quit Government," *Jerusalem Post*, May 22, 1997, 1.

18. Sarah Honig, "Rubicon Crossed," *Jerusalem Post*, June 19, 1997, 3.

19. Begin's father was former Prime Minister Menachem Begin, while Meridor's father, Eliahu, was also a former Irgun fighter who was exiled to Africa by the British during the Mandate. Eliahu Meridor served in the Fourth through the Sixth Knessets until his death in 1966.

20. Sarah Honig, "Milo, We'll Split the Party," *Jerusalem Post*, November 18, 1997, 1.

21. Reportedly, Communications Minister Limor Livnat, a strong rightwing critic of the government's Hebron policy and a protege of Ariel Sharon's, also appeared to be on the verge of quitting the cabinet and join Milo's plan. Sarah Honig, "Livnat Quells Anti-Netanyahu Mutiny by Staying On," *Jerusalem Post*, November 26, 1997, 1.

22. Liat Collins, "17 Likudniks Needed for Part Split," *Jerusalem Post*, November 20, 1997, 2.

23. Jeff Barak and Danna Harman, "Cabinet Ratifies Wye Deal, Arafat: PNC will Annul Anti-Israel Clauses," *Jerusalem Post*, November 12, 1998, 1. The ministers who voted against the agreement were Rafael Eitan (Tzomet), Yitzhak Levy (NRP), Shaul Yahalom (Likud), and Yuli Edeslstein (Yisrael Be'aliyah). Those who abstained were Limor Livnat, Moshe Katsav, Silvan Shalom, Yehoshua Matsa, and Tzahi Hanegbi (all of them Likud).

24. Nina Gilbert, "It All Started with the Wye Agreement: How the Coalition Fell Apart," *Jerusalem Post*, December 22, 1998, 4.

25. Nina Gilbert, "Knesset Approves Early Elections," *Jerusalem Post*, January 5, 1999, 1.

26. Knesset Committee Protocols No. 225, Fourteenth Knesset, February 23, 1999. https://fs.knesset.gov.il/14/Committees/14_ptv_486649.PDF

27. Knesset Committee Protocols, No. 226, Fourteenth Knesset, February 23, 1999. https://fs.knesset.gov.il/14/Committees/14_ptv_486652.PDF

28. On the brief history of the Center Party, see Efraim Torgovnik, "The Centre Party," *Israel Affairs* 7, nos. 2–3 (2000): 135–152.

Chapter 4

1. The story is reported by the *Jerusalem Post* on July 18, 1994. See "Government Gets Five Days to Explain why Yi'ud Members are Getting Government Posts," *Jerusalem Post*, July 18, 1994, 12.

2. In the 1984 elections, Tzomet ran in alliance with Tehiya. Although the electoral alliance won five seats, Raful, the single Tzomet member elected from the joint list, split and would contest the 1988 election independently.

3. Dan Izenberg, "A Doctor Turned Farmer-Politician," *Jerusalem Post*, June 9, 1992, 2.

4. Alisa Odenheimer, "MK Segev Asks Court to Cancel Rabinovitch Posting," *Jerusalem Post*, January 12, 1992, 3.

5. Dan Izenberg, "Tzomet MK Asks High Court to Block Treaty," *Jerusalem Post*, September 10, 1993, 3.

6. Sarah Honig and Dan Izenberg, "Tzomet Dissidents Charge Financial Irregularities in Party," *Jerusalem Post*, January 25, 1995, 12.

7. Sarah Honig, "Tzomet Showdown Expected on Sunday," *Jerusalem Post*, January 27, 1994, 14.

8. Michal Yudelman, "Tsomet Splits, 3 MKs Form New Party," *Jerusalem Post*, February 3, 1994, 1.

9. Ibid. Also see "Pilug Be-Siyah Tzomet," *Yediot Ahronot* February 3, 1994, 1.

10. Knesset Committee Protocol No. 105, Thirteenth Knesset. February 7, 1994. The formation of Yi'ud was recognized with a vote of ten in favor, three against, and one abstention.

11. Dan Izenberg, "Coalition Would Welcome Tsomet Breakaways," *Jerusalem Post*, February 3, 1994, 2; Michal Yudelman, "Labor, Yi'ud to Form Joint Histadrut List," *Jerusalem Post*, April 5, 1994, 12; Dan Izenberg, "Rafael Eitan's 'Wild Animals,'" *Jerusalem Post*, July 13, 1994, 12.

12. Dan Izenberg, "Yi'ud Seen Split Over Joining Coalition," *Jerusalem Post*, June 22, 1994, 1; Dan Izenberg, "Yi'ud's Salmovitz May Refuse to Follow Faction into Coalition Talks," *Jerusalem Post*, July 6, 1994, 12; Dan Izenberg, "Salmovitz Creates Interesting Anomaly," *Jerusalem Post*, July 13, 1994, 12.

13. Sarah Honig, "MK Salmovitz Wants Out of 'Marriage from Hell'" with Yi'ud," *Jerusalem Post*, December 19, 1994, 2.

14. Evelyn Gordon, "Court Forbids Appointment of Yi'ud MKs to Gv't Post," *Jerusalem Post*, July 15, 1994, A14.

15. Evelyn Gordon, "High Court to Rule Today Whether Yi'ud MKs Can Serve in Gv't," *Jerusalem Post*, July 25, 1994, 12; Michal Yudelman, "Yi'ud Still Part of Coalition Despite Court Ruling," *Jerusalem Post*, July 26, 1994, 1–2.

16. Evelyn Gordon, "Court Ruling on Yi'ud Draws Fire from MKs," *Jerusalem Post*, July 26, 1994, 12.

17. Dan Izenberg, "Yi'ud Cleared to Join Government," *Jerusalem Post*, December 20, 1994, 12.

18. Sarah Honig, "Yi'ud Party, Knesset Faction Disintegrating *Jerusalem Post*, February 21, 1995, 1.

19. Sarah Honig, "Segev Ousted and Yi'ud Chief," *Jerusalem Post*, May 18, 1995, 2; Sarah Honig, "Salmovitz Accuses Segev of Fraud, Forgery," *Jerusalem Post*, June 21, 1995, 2.

20. Sarah Honig, "Yi'ud Shrinks to Last MK," *Jerusalem Post*, October 26, 1995, 12; Liat Collins, "Goldfarb, Salmovitz Quit Yi'ud," *Jerusalem Post*, November 28, 1995, 2.

21. Evelyn Gordon, "Golan Bill Defeated in Cliffhanger Tie," *Jerusalem Post*, July 27, 1995, 1; Michal Yudelman, "Goldfarb: Nonentity Who Saved the Government," *Jerusalem Post*, July 27, 1995, 1, 2. The Golan bill was a private member bill submitted by three Labor Party MKs, Avigdor Kahalani, Emanuel Zisman, and Yaacov Sheffi. It sought to tie any territorial concessions on the Golan Heights either to support by a qualified majority of seventy MKs or 50 percent of all eligible voters in a referendum. Goldfarb had left the Knesset plenum and missed the first round of the roll call but then returned to cast the last vote, which broke the tie in favor of the government.

22. Michal Yudelman, "Goldfarb Leaves Margins to Rescue Government," *Jerusalem Post*, October 6, 1995, 15.

23. Ibid.

24. www.haaretz.com/print-edition/features/just-a-farmer-in-cuba-1.192046

25. Uri Dan, "What Makes Rafi Run," *Jerusalem Post*, March 2, 2006, 14.

26. Ibid.

27. Ibid.

28. See http://main.knesset.gov.il/mk/government/documents/Coal2006gil.pdf.

29. Yariv Katz and Yuval Karni, "Bikoret Be-Miflagat Ha-Gamlaim: Rafi Eitan Buba Shel Olmert," [Criticism in the Pensioners' Party: Rafi Eitan is Olmert's Puppet], *Yediot Ahronot*, November 17, 2006, 6 (in Hebrew).The dissenting Gil MKs who voted against Lieberman's appointment to the government were Moshe Sharoni and Itshak Galantee. For the detailed results of the vote, see Seventeenth Knesset, Minutes of the Fifty-First Session of the Plenary, October 30, 2006 (in Hebrew), http://main.knesset.gov.il/Activity/plenum/Pages/SessionItem.aspx?itemID=178107. Also see Sheera Claire Frenkel and Gil Hoffman, "Newly Sworn-In Lieberman Already Set to Visit US," *Jerusalem Post*, October 31, 2006, 19.

30. Gil Hoffman, "Party Registrar Makes Gaydamak, Eldad Parties Official," *Jerusalem Post*, December 10, 2007, 3.

31. Gil Hoffman, "Pensioner Party Rebel Row Foils Gaydamak's Ministerial Hopes," *Jerusalem Post*, April 9, 2008, 5.

32. Knesset Committee Protocols, Seventeenth Knesset, No. 233. https://main.knesset.gov.il/Activity/committees/Pages/AllCommitteeProtocols.aspx

33. Shely Paz, "Labor MKs Pressure Barak to Rule Out Serving Alongside Lieberman," *Jerusalem Post*, February 6, 2009, 4.

34. Gil Hoffman, "Peretz to Try to Oust Barak as Labor Head," *Jerusalem Post*, February 15, 2009, 1.

35. Divrei HaKnesset, Thirteenth Sitting of the Eighteenth Knesset, March 31, 2008, http://main.knesset.gov.il/Activity/plenum/Pages/SessionItem.aspx-?itemID=322083. In addition to the five Labor MKs, Ahmed Tibi, also abstained.

36. The Labor minsters in the new government were Ehud Barak, Shalom Simhon, Avishay Braverman, Benyamin Ben-Eliezer, and Isaac Herzog. The two deputy ministers were Matan Vilnai and Orit Noked.

37. See https://main.knesset.gov.il/mk/government/documents/coal2009Avoda.pdf.

38. Gil Hoffman, Joshua Newman, and Carrie Sheffield, "Last Minute Deal to prevent Labor Split," *Jerusalem Post*, August 6, 2009, 1.

39. Gil Hoffman, "Pines-Paz's Exit Deals Death Blow to Labor Rebellion," *Jerusalem Post*, January 8, 2010, 1; Gil Hoffman, "Einat Wilf Opposes Major Changes," *Jerusalem Post*, January 11, 2010, 5.

40. Gil Hoffman, "New Labor MK Ghaleb Majadleh: Party Must Leave," *Jerusalem Post*, April 13, 2010, 9.

41. Gil Hoffman, "Labor to Get New Secretary-General Today," *Jerusalem Post*, October 14, 2010, 4.

42. Gil Hoffman, "Labor Activists to Push Ben-Eliezer to Lead Party," *Jerusalem Post*, October 31, 2010, 2; Rebecca Anna Stoil, "Ben-Eliezer Calls for Candidates Outside Labor to Contend for the Party Leadership," *Jerusalem Post*, November 4, 2010, 10.

43. Gil Hoffman, "Ben-Simon Blames Barak for Losing Knesset Committee. Labor MK Calls his Fellow Party Members 'dishrags,'" *Jerusalem Post*, November 2, 2010, 2.

44. Gil Hoffman, "Ben-Simon to be Punished for Budget Vote," *Jerusalem Post*, January 2, 2011.

45. Yuval Karni, "Ha-Targil," *Yediot Ahronot*, January 18, 2011, 11. (In Hebrew.)

46. Gil Hoffman, "Ben-Simon Barred from Leaving Labor Party," *Jerusalem Post*, January 18, 2011.

47. 18th Knesset, Knesset Committee Protocols, No. 144, January 17, 2011.

48. See Knesset website. www.knesset.gov.il/vote/heb/Vote_Res_Map.asp?vote_id_t=15213

49. Yuval Karni, "Kitzur Haderek shel Barak" [Barak's Shortcut] in Hebrew, *Yediot Ahronot*, May 9, 2011, 11.

50. Yuval Karni, "Haatzmaut Im Salmon" [Independence with Salmon], in Hebrew, *Yediot Ahronot*, May 13, 2011, 6.

51. Jodi Rudoren, "Israeli Defense Minister Says He is Leaving Politics," *New York Times*, November 26, 2012. www.nytimes.com/2012/11/27/world/middleeast/ehud-barak-israeli-defense-minister-to-quit-politics.html

Chapter 5

1. Carol Mershon and Olga Shvetsova, *Party System Change in Legislatures Worldwide*, chapters 3 and 5.

2. Knesset Committee Protocol no. 412, 20th Knesset, December 30, 2018. https://main.knesset.gov.il/Activity/committees/Pages/AllCommitteeProtocols.aspx

3. Herb Keinon, "Shas Council to Meet before Knesset Vote," *Jerusalem Post*, July 13, 1992, 1; Herb Keinon, "Two Shas Men May Abstain in Vote Tomorrow," *Jerusalem Post*, July 12, 1992, 1.

4. Dan Izenberg, "*Jerusalem Post* POST," January 13, 1993, 2; Dan Izenberg, "Knesset Debates PLO Contacts Bill," *Jerusalem Post*, January 19, 1993, 1; Dan Izenberg, "Knesset Repeals Ban on Meetings with Terror Groups," *Jerusalem Post*, January 20, 1993, 1; Dan Izenberg, "Labor Hawks Put Coalition on Notice," *Jerusalem Post*, January 22, 1993, 9.

5. Dan Izenberg, "Human Rights Bill Compromise Collapses," *Jerusalem Post*, February 16, 1993, 4; Dan Izenberg, "Coalition Leaders Reach Compromise on Human Rights Bill," *Jerusalem Post*, January 26, 1993, 12; Dan Izenberg, "Basic Law Presented Despite Opposition," *Jerusalem Post*, March 24, 1993, 4.

6. Sarah Honig, "Shas' Azran Says He Won't Rejoin Coalition," *Jerusalem Post*, May 20, 1994; Sarah Honig, "Labor May Woo Shas with Religious Legislation," *Jerusalem Post*, June 20, 1994, 3; Michal Yudelmand and Dan Izenberg, "Yi'ud, Labor Initial Coalition Agreement: Shas Expected to Follow After Tisha Be'av," *Jerusalem Post*, July 13, 1994, 1; Michal Yudelman, "Meretz Split Over Whether to Veto Labor Agreement with Shas," *Jerusalem Post*, July 24, 1994.

7. Dan Izenberg, "Azran Will Surrender Post, to Escape Shas," *Jerusalem Post*, November 8, 1994, 12; Dan Izenberg," Shas Continues Battle to Remove Azran from Knesset," *Jerusalem Post*, November 9, 1994, 12; Dan Izenberg, "Law Would Remove Azran from Post," *Jerusalem Post*, November 16, 1994, 4.

8. Knesset Committee Protocols No. 373, Thirteenth Knesset. The vote was 4 in favor and 1 against Azran's request to recognize his defection. https://fs.knesset.gov.il/13/Committees/13_ptv_477527.PDF

9. See http://fs.knesset.gov.il//13/law/13_ls1_292588.PDF. The amendment was passed on the second and third reading on the same day it was introduced.

10. Evelyn Gordon, "Party Financing Law Challenged in High Court," *Jerusalem Post*, May 15, 1996, 3.

11. Dan Izenberg, "New 'Centrist' Labor group Launched," *Jerusalem Post*, May 25, 1994, 1.

12. Tzur was not an MK in the Thirteenth Knesset but was appointed to head the Agriculture portfolio. See also Sarah Honig, "Tzur Quits Third Way," *Jerusalem Post*, June 20, 1994, 2.

13. Sarah Honig and Liat Collins," Kahalani, Zissman, Seffi Call on Government to Resign," *Jerusalem Post,* June 12, 1995, 1; Sarah Honig," Third Way Rejects Oslo 2," *Jerusalem Post,* September 29, 1995, 2.

14. Liat Collins, "Kahalani, Zissman Warn Rabin to Keep Them in Committee Post," *Jerusalem Post,* October 8, 1995, 1.

15. Sarah Honig, "Zissman, Kahalani Will Leave Labor for Third Way," *Jerusalem Post,* September 22, 1995, 5

16. Sarah Honig, "Labor Fails to Dissuade Third Way from Running," *Jerusalem Post,* November 9, 1995, 2; Sarah Honig, "Third Way Officially Declares Itself a Party," *Jerusalem Post,* February 14, 1996, 2; Liat Collins, "Maverick Zissman Ready for a Divorce from Labour," *Jerusalem Post,* October 6, 1995, 8;

17. Knesset Committee Minutes, Session no. 232, Fourteenth Knesset, March 29, 1999, 4–11. https://fs.knesset.gov.il/14/Committees/14_ptv_486670.PDF

18. Knesset Committee Minutes, Session no. 232, Fourteenth Knesset, March 25, 1999, 10. https://fs.knesset.gov.il/14/Committees/14_ptv_486667.PDF

19. Danna Harman, "Third Way's Zissman Joins One Israel," *Jerusalem Post,* March 30, 1999, 3.

20. Liat Collins, "Likud-Tsomet Deal Falls Through," *Jerusalem Post,* March 25, 1999, 3; Danna Harman, "Center Party Announces List of Candidates," *Jerusalem Post,* March 17,1999, 1.

21. Knesset Committee Minutes, Session No. 230, Fourteenth Knesset, March 22, 1999, 1–4. The split was approved by a unanimous 2-0 vote. https://fs.knesset.gov.il/14/Committees/14_ptv_486664.PDF

22. For the Shinui candidate list in the 1999 Knesset elections, see https://www.gov.il/apps/elections/Elections-knesset-15/heb/index.html.

23. Avraham Diskin and Efraim Podoksik, "Israel," *European Journal of Political Research Political Data Yearbook* 52, no. 1 (2013): 112.

24. Jeremy Saltan, "Kadima MK Breakdown: Who Supports Livni vs Mofaz?" http://www.jewishpress.com/indepth/analysis/kadimamkbreakdownwhosupportsl vsmofaz/2012/01/29. Livni's supporters were the following MKs: Ronnie BarOn, Marina Solodkin, Majallie Whbee, Gideon Ezra, Yoel Hasson, Shlomo Molla, Nino Abesadze, Rachel Adatto, Doron Avital, Nachman Shai, Robert Tiviaev, and Orit Zuaretz. Gideon Ezra passed away in lung cancer a few months later and was replaced by Druze MK Akram Hasson, a supporter of Mofaz. Avi Dichter had entered the primaries but dropped out of the race before polling started and threw his support behind Mofaz. Itzhik remained neutral throughout the period.

25. Elad Benari, "Mofaz Wins Kadima Leadership, Calls on Livni to Stay," *Israel National News,* March 28, 2012. https://www.israelnationalnews.com/news/154231

26. The Tal Law, named after Supreme Court Justice Tzvi Tal who headed the non-parliamentary committee recommending the legislation, was passed by the Knesset in 2002. Its objective was to provide a legislative framework for the

exemption of the ultra-orthodox youth from military service. The Supreme Court rendered the Tal Law unconstitutional in 2012 and instructed the Knesset to amend it. For a critical review, see Etta Bick, "The Tal Law: A Missed Opportunity for "Bridging Social Capital" in Israel," *Journal of Church and State* 52, no. 2 (2010): 298–322.

27. "Agreement to Establish a National Unity Government." https://main.knesset.gov.il/mk/government/documents/coalition2012.pdf

28. See https://main.knesset.gov.il/Activity/Legislation/Laws/Pages/LawBill.aspx?t=lawsuggestionssearch&lawitemid=435177.

29. Attila Somfalvi, "Netanyahu Dissolves Plesner Committee," *Y-Net News,* July 2, 2012. www.ynetnews.com/articles/0,7340,L-4250215,00.html

30. Attila Somfalvi, "Kadima Faction Votes to Quit Coalition," *Y-Net News* July 17, 2012. www.ynetnews.com/articles/0,7340,L-4256736,00.html

31. Attila Somfalvi, "PM Offers Portfolios to Kadima MKs," *Y-Net News* July 23, 2012. www.ynetnews.com/articles/0,7340,L-4259030,00.html

32. Knesset Committee Protocols, Session 301, Eighteenth Knesset, July 24, 2012. https://main.knesset.gov.il/Activity/committees/Pages/AllCommittee-Protocols.aspx

33. Moram Azoulay, "Livni Returns to Politics, Unveils New Party," *Y-Net News*, November 27, 2012. www.ynetnews.com/articles/0,7340,L-4312312,00.html

34. Moram Azoulay, "Livni Returns to Politics, Unveils New Party," *Y-Net News*, November 27, 2012. www.ynetnews.com/articles/0,7340,L-4312312,00.html

35. Mati Tuchfeld, "This Could Be The End of a Beautiful Friendship," *Israel Hayom*, October 5, 2012. www.israelhayom.com/2012/10/05/this-could-be-the-end-of-a-beautiful-friendship

36. Livni made the official announcement about forming her new party three days before the deadline to register the list of Knesset candidates, which clearly left her no time to have the party legally registered as well.

37. Mati Tuchfeld, "Netanyahu's Advantage," *Israel Hayom*, December 21, 2012. www.israelhayom.com/2012/12/21/netanyahuas-advantage

38. Kadima continued to contest the legality of the Livni-Poraz deal and formally requested the State Attorney to investigate the matter. Mati Tuchfeld, "Lachkor Bedhifut Et Dil Livni-Poraz" [Livni-Poraz Deal to be Urgently Investigated], *Israel Hayom*, December 21, 2012, 9. (In Hebrew.) www.israelhayom.co.il/article/61519

Chapter 6

1. In a surprise move, Prime Minister Sharon requested a roll-call vote on the induction of ministers in his new coalition government. For the detailed result of the roll-call vote, see www.knesset.gov.il/vote/heb/vote_gov100105.htm.

2. Knesset Committee Protocols, No. 6306, Sixteenth Knesset, March 10, 2003.

3. Likud MK Michel Eitan noted that he had proposed a private member bill in the Fifteenth Knesset that proposed that when a faction splits, the two successors should also divide between them proportionally the additional party funding unit that the new faction is entitled to.

4. See Ariel Sharon's speech at the Fourth Herzliya Conference in December 2003. http://mfa.gov.il/MFA/PressRoom/2003/Pages/Address%20by%20PM%20 Ariel%20Sharon%20at%20the%20Fourth%20Herzliya.aspx

5. Joshua Brillant, "Sharon Sacks Hawkish Ministers," *United Press International*, June 4, 2004. www.upi.com/Defense-News/2004/06/04/Sharon-sacks-hawkish-ministers/96181086372015

6. Nina Gilbert and Gil Hoffman, "PM Survive No-Confidence Votes," *Jerusalem Post*, June 29, 2004, 2.

7. Tovah Lazaroff, "NRP Split Over Leaving Government," *Jerusalem Post*, June 7, 2004, 1.

8. Tovah Lazaroff, "PM Loses Majority as Eitam, Levy Quit," *Jerusalem Post*, June 9, 2004, 1.

9. Herb Keinon and Gil Hoffman, "Sharon Appoints Substitute Ministers," *Jerusalem Post*, July 5, 2004, 3.

10. "The Paritzky Affair," *Jerusalem Post*, July 11, 2004, 13.

11. Nina Gilbert, "Shinui Flip-flops on Paritzky's Fate," *Jerusalem Post*, December 14, 2005, 4; "Likud Working to Free Paritzky from Shinui," *Jerusalem Post*, January 19, 2005, 5.

12. Gil Hoffman, "Shinui to Paritzky: Take NIS 1 Mil and Leave," *Jerusalem Post*, October 12, 2004, 3.

13. "How They Voted," *Jerusalem Post*, October 27, 2004, 1.

14. Abigail Radoszkowicz, "Rabbis: NRP Can Stay in Gov't," *Jerusalem Post*, October 28, 2004, 3.

15. The budget bill failed to pass as forty-two MKs voted in favor but seventy-one against. The former included thirty-seven MKs Likud and five from UTJ. David Tal from Am Ehad broke ranks with his party and abstained. The only other case of indiscipline was Limor Livnat, Minister of Education, Sport and Culture, who championed the Dovrat Commission on unified education, which the budget bill de facto killed by making the generous allocation to the haredi sector. https://main.knesset.gov.il/Activity/plenum/Votes/Pages/vote.aspx?voteId=3430

16. Nina Gilbert, "Likud Working to Free Paritzky from Shinui," *Jerusalem Post*, January 19, 2005, 5.

17. Knesset Committee Protocols, no. 284, Sixteenth Knesset, May 18, 2005. https://main.knesset.gov.il/Activity/committees/Pages/AllCommitteesAgenda. aspx?Tab=3&ItemID=100211

18. In a tight race, Peretz defeated two other Labor Party heavyweights: interim chairman Shimon Peres and former chairman Benyamin (Fuad) Ben-Eliezer.

19. Tovah Lazaroff, "Eitam, Levy Weight Leaving NRP," *Jerusalem Post*, January 21, 2005, 4; Nina Gilbert, "Eitam Moves to Break from NRP," *Jerusalem Post*, January 24, 2005, 2; "Eitam, Orlev on Collision Course," *Jerusalem Post*, January 25, 2005, 3.

20. Gil Hoffman, "NRP Boots Out Eitam from Chairman Post," *Jerusalem Post*, February 15, 2005, 4.

21. Gil Hoffman, "Eitam, Levy Form New Religious Zionist Party," *Jerusalem Post*, February 24, 2005, 1.

22. For an analysis of the formation of Kadima and its effect on the party system, see Reuven Hazan, "Kadima and the Centre: Convergence in the Israeli Party System," *Israel Affairs* 13, no. 2 (2007): 266–288.

23. Michael Nudelman and David Tal defied their parties on this vote as well: the former voted with the government; the latter abstained. See Nina Gilber, "Disengagement Passes 59-40: Knesset Vote Also Rejects Referendum," *Jerusalem Post*, February 17, 2005, 1.

24. Herb Keinon and Gil Hoffman, "Netanyahu Quits Over PM's 'Blind' Insistence on Pullout," *Jerusalem Post*, August 8, 2005, 1.

25. Gil Hoffman, "Sharon Prevails in Likud Showdown: Staves off Netanyahu's Bid for Early Leadership Contest by 104," *Jerusalem Post*, September 27, 2005, 1.

26. Gil Hoffman and Claire Sheera Frenkel, "PM Vows Consequences against Rebels: MKs Vote Down Bar-On, Boim Bids; Approve Olmert," *Jerusalem Post*, November 8, 2005, 1.

27. Formally, the Labor Party Central Committee voted to quit the coalition on November 20. See Gil Hoffman, "Labor Party Votes to Quit Coalition," *Jerusalem Post*, November 21, 2005, 1.

28. Gil Hoffman, "Knesset Resignations Set Off Chain Reaction," *Jerusalem Post*, January 16, 2006, 3; Herb Keinon and Gil Hoffman, "Peres Quits Knesset by Fax after 47 Years: Enables Him to Return as Kadima MK," *Jerusalem Post*, January 16, 2006, 3.

29. Knesset Committee Protocol # 284, 2006 February 1, Sixteenth Knesset. https://main.knesset.gov.il/Activity/committees/Pages/AllCommitteeProtocols.aspx

30. Gil Hoffman, "Nudelman, Landver Quit Knesset," *Jerusalem Post*, February 7, 2006, 4.

31. Reuven Hazan, "Analysis: Israel's New Constructive Vote of No-Confidence." https://m.knesset.gov.il/en/News/PressReleases/Pages/Pr11200_pg.aspx

32. See, for example, Tal Lento and Reuven Y. Hazan, "The Vote of No-Confidence: Towards a Framework for Analysis," *West European Politics* 45, no. 3 (2022): 502–527; Ayelet Rubabshi-Shitrit and Sharon Hasson, "The Effect of the

Constructive Vote of No-Confidence on Government Termination and Government Durability," *West European Politics* 45, no. 3 (2022): 576–590.

Chapter 7

1. Protocol no. 412 of the Knesset Committee, The Twentieth Knesset, December 30, 2018.

2. Sergiu Gherghina, "Rewarding the 'Traitors'? Legislative Defection and Reelection in Romania," *Party Politics* 22, no. 4 (2016): 490–500.

Chapter 8

1. Lok Sabha debates, January 30, 1985, 70.

2. This section is based on Nikolenyi and Shenhav, "The Constitutional-ization of Party Unity."

3. *Keesing's Contemporary Archives* 1985: 33466.

4. Lok Sabha debates, January 30, 1985, 183.

5. Rajya Sabha debates, January 31, 1985, 95.

6. Rajya Sabha debates, January 31, 1985, 99–102.

7. Robert Hardgrave and Stanley Kochanek, *India: Government and Politics in a Developing Nation* (Fort Worth, TX: Harcourt Brace Jovanovich, 2000), 273.

8. Malhotra, "Anti-Defection Law in India and the Commonwealth," 753.

9. The number of splits and mergers at the state level were sixty-eight and eighty-one, respectively.

10. These were the Committee on Electoral Reforms in 1990; the 170th Report of the Law Commission of India in 1999; and the National Commission for the Review of the Working of the Constitution in 2002.

11. "Lok Sabha Passes Anti-Defection Bill," *Times of India, Delhi Edition*, December 13, 2003, 13.

12. Manoj Mitta, "Disqualifying Expelled MPs, Speaker to Decide," *Times of India, Delhi Edition*, July 24, 2008, 11.

13. There is a large literature on the electoral reform in New Zealand. For examples, see Jack Vowles, "The Politics of Electoral Reform in New Zealand," *International Political Science Review* 16, no. 1 (1995): 95–115; Jack Vowles, "Systemic Failure, Coordination, and Contingencies: Understanding Electoral System Change in New Zealand," in Andre Blais, ed., *To Keep or Change First Past the Post: The Politics of Electoral Reform* (Oxford: Oxford University Press, 2008), 163–183; Fiona Barker and Stephen Levine, "The Individual Parliamentary Member and Institutional Change: The Changing Role of the New Zealand Member of Parliament," *Journal of Legislative Studies* 5, nos. 3–4 (1999): 105–130.

14. The following paragraphs are based on Andrew Geddis, "Gang Aft A-Gley: New Zealand's Attempt to Combat 'Party Hopping' By Elected Representatives" and Andrew Geddis, "Proportional Representation, 'Party Hopping' and the Limits of Electoral Regulation: A Cautionary Tale from New Zealand."

15. The Committee received nineteen written and nine oral submissions. See appendix A of the House of Representatives Justice and Electoral Committee *Report on the Electoral (Integrity) Amendment Bill*. www. parliament.nz/en/pb/bills-and-laws/bills-proposed-laws/document/BILL_75706/ electoral-integrity-amendment-bill

16. House of Representatives Justice and Electoral Committee *Report on the Electoral (Integrity) Amendment Bill, 2001*, 2–3.

17. Similar to Israel, an umbrella party is one that brings together several component parties for the purposes of contesting the election.

18. House of Representatives Justice and Electoral Committee *Report on the Electoral (Integrity) Amendment Bill, 2001*, 11–12. www.parliament.nz/en/ pb/bills-and-laws/bills-proposed-laws/document/BILL_75706/electoral-integrity-amendment-bill

19. House of Representatives Justice and Electoral Committee *Report on the Electoral (Integrity) Amendment Bill, 2001*, 23. www.parliament.nz/en/pb/ bills-and-laws/bills-proposed-laws/document/BILL_75706/electoral-integrity-amendment-bill

20. Geddis, "Proportional Representation," 39.

21. Electoral (Integrity) Amendment Bill, 2005. Bills Digest 1312, 1.

22. Electoral (Integrity) Amendment Bill, 2005. Bills Digest 1312, 6.

23. See Geddis, "Gang Aft A-Gley" and "Proportional Representation."

24. New Zealand Parliamentary Library, *Electoral (Integrity) Amendment Bill 2005*, Bills Digest No. 1312. www.parliament.nz/en/pb/bills-and-laws/ bills-proposed-laws/document/BILL_75706/electoral-integrity-amendment-bill

25. Members of the Senate, renamed as the National Council of Provinces in 1997, were chosen by the provincial legislatures. In all but two provinces, the African National Congress won either legislative majorities or pluralities.

26. The largest opposition party, the National Party, won only eighty-two seats in the Assembly and seventeen seats in the Senate.

27. The other province was KwaZulu Natal, where the Inkatha Freedom Party was the strongest party.

28. Joseph Smiles, "Floor Crossing in South Africa: A Controversial Democratic Process," *Insight on Africa* 3, no. 2 (2011): 162–163.

29. Susan Boyseen, "Will of the Parties versus the Will of the People? Defections, Elections and Alliances in South Africa," 736–738.

30. G. E. Devenish, "Political Musical Chairs—The Saga of Floor-Crossing and the Constitution," *Stellenbosch Law Review*, 15, no. 52 (2004): 54.

31. See Proceedings of the National Assembly, February 25, 2003, 57.

32. Boyseen, "Will of the Parties versus the Will of the People?," 738.

33. G. E. Devenish, "Political Musical Chairs—The Saga of Floor-Crossing and the Constitution," *Stellenbosch Law Review,* 15, no. 52 (2004): 52–65.

34. Boyseen, Will of the Parties versus the Will of the People?," 738–739.

35. Proceedings of the National Assembly of South Africa, February 25, 2003.

36. Sueanne Issac, "Summary and Analysis of Floor-Crossing Legislation," *Research Unit of the Parliament of South Africa.* July 24, 2008.

37. Resolutions by ANC, 20 December 2007, 52nd National Conference, Polokwane. www.sahistory.org.za/archive/resolutions-anc-20-december-2007-52nd-national-conference-polokwane

38. Proceedings of the National Assembly, August 20, 2008.

39. Fifty-First Amendment to the Basic Law: The Knesset. https://fs.knesset. gov.il/24/law/24_lsr_603565.pdf

Conclusion

1. It appeared for a while that the Orly Levy-Abukasis Gesher Party might be also part of this alliance; however, the negotiations between the two sides did not effect a concrete result. Gesher thus ran on its own because under the terms of the anti-defection legislation, the party's leader could not be a candidate on the list of any party represented in the outgoing Knesset.

2. Yaal Friedman, "Netanyahu Achieves 65 Recommendations to Form Government," *Y-net News,* April 16, 2019. www.ynet.co.il/articles/0,7340,L-5495244,00.html. [In Hebrew] The two Arab party lists, Raam-Balad and Hadash-Taal, refused to endorse either candidate.

3. The three political parties that supported Gantz's candidacy for prime minister (Blue and White, Labor, and Meretz) voted against the dissolution, while all other parties that supported Netanyahu, including Yisrael Beitenu, as well as the Arab parties, voted in favor. With one MK absent, Roy Folkman (Kulanu), the roll-call vote resulted in a decisive majority of seventy-four in favor and forty-five against, and the Knesset was dissolved. Knesset Plenary Protocols, Twelfth Session of the Twenty-First Knesset, May 29, 2020. https://main.knesset.gov.il/Activity/plenum/Pages/SessionItem.aspx?itemID=2080595

4. The only party in the Joint List that remained noncommittal after the September elections was Balad.

5. Raoul Wootliff, "With 'Paritetic' Proposal, Rivlin Looks to the Past for Power-Sharing Model," *Times of Israel,* September 26, 2019. www.timesofisrael. com/with-paritetic-proposal-rivlin-looks-to-the-past-for-power-sharing-model

6. "Rivlin to Give Gantz Mandate to Form Government on Monday," *Times of Israel,* March 15, 2020. www.timesofisrael.com/liveblog_entry/rivlin-to-give-gantz-mandate-to-form-government-on-monday

7. Moran Azoulay, Yuval Karmi, and Tova Tzimuki, "Top Blue & White MKs Oppose Arab-Backed Government," *Y-Net News*, March 9, 2020. www.ynetnews.com/article/BJT711umBL

8. Knesset Arrangements Committee Protocols, Twenty-Third Knesset, March 29, 2020. https://main.knesset.gov.il/Activity/committees/Pages/AllCommittees Agenda.aspx?Tab=3&ItemID=2086941

9. "Coalition Agreement to Establish an Emergency National Unity Government." https://main.knesset.gov.il/mk/government/Documents/CA35-Likud-BW-200420.pdf

10. The Knesset Committee made the formal decision to approve of the dissolution of Yamina only after the government had been formed. See Knesset Committee, Protocol No. 30, Twenty-Third Knesset, July 14, 2020. https://main.knesset.gov.il/Activity/committees/Pages/AllCommitteesAgenda.aspx?Tab=3&ItemID=2142496

11. *Reshumot*, May 7, 2020. https://fs.knesset.gov.il/23/law/23_lsr_570150.pdf

12. Amir Peretz was sworn in as Minister of the Economy and Industry; Itzik Shmuli received the portfolio of Labor and Social Affairs and Social Services.

13. Havi Rettig Gur, "Labor's 1-Woman Opposition: No to a Religious, Occupying, Non-Democratic State," *Times of Israel*, June 18, 2020. www.timesofisrael.com/labors-1-woman-opposition-no-to-a-religious-occupying-non-democratic-state

14. As chair of the Knesset's Special Committee on the Corona Virus Pandemic, Bitton had already raised the ire of her party's whip by charting an independent course in her role instead of allowing her party's policy to dictate the committees' decisions. In fact, as a result of evident breach of party discipline, Bitton was removed from her post as Committee chair.

15. Knesset Committee, Protocol No. 102, Twenty-Third Knesset, December 28, 2020. https://main.knesset.gov.il/Activity/committees/Pages/AllCommittees Agenda.aspx?Tab=3&ItemID=2151769

16. "Knesset Plenum approves bill enabling four MKs to break away from their faction, even if they do not constitute one third of it." *Knesset News*, July 7, 2021. https://m.knesset.gov.il/EN/News/PressReleases/Pages/press070721b.aspx

17. Devenish, "Political Musical Chairs," 52.

Works Cited

Alon, Gideon. "Just a Farmer in Cuba." *Haaretz*. July 3, 2006. www.haaretz.com/1.4848695

Avnon, Dan. "Parties Laws in Democratic Systems of Government." *Journal of Legislative Studies* 1, no. 2 (1995): 283–300.

Azoulay, Moran. "Livni Returns to Politics, Unveils New Party." *Y-Net News*. November 27, 2012. www.ynetnews.com/articles/0,7340,L-4312312,00.html

Azoulay, Moran, Yuval Karmi, and Tova Tzimuki. "Top Blue & White MKs Oppose Arab-Backed Government." *Y-Net News*, March 9, 2020. www.ynetnews.com/article/BJT711umBL

Barak, Jeff, and Danna Harman. "Cabinet Ratifies Wye Deal, Arafat: PNC Will Annul Anti-Israel Clauses." *Jerusalem Post*. November 12, 1998, 1.

Barker, Fiona, and Stephen Levine. "The Individual Parliamentary Member and Institutional Change: The Changing Role of the New Zealand Member of Parliament." *Journal of Legislative Studies* 5, nos. 3–4 (1999): 105–130.

Benari, Elad. "Mofaz Wins Kadima Leadership, Calls on Livni to Stay." *Israel National News*. March 28, 2012. www.israelnationalnews.com/news/154231

Bick, Etta. "The Tal Law: A Missed Opportunity for 'Bridging Social Capital' in Israel." *Journal of Church and State* 52, no. 2 (2010): 298–322.

Biezen, Ingrid van. "Party Regulation and Constitutionalization: A Comparative Overview," in Benjamin Reilly and Per Nodlund, eds., *Political Parties in Conflict-Prone Societies*. New York: United Nations University Press, 2008, 25–47.

Biezen, Ingrid van, and Petr Kopecky. "The State and the Parties: Public Funding, Public Regulation and Rent-Seeking in Contemporary Democracies." *Party Politics* 13, no. 2 (2007): 235–254.

Bogdanor, Vernon. "The Constitution and the Party System in the Twentieth Century." *Parliamentary Affairs* 57, no. 4 (2004): 717–733.

Booysen, Susan. "The Will of the Parties versus the Will of the People? Defections, Elections and Alliances in South Africa." *Party Politics* 12, no. 6 (2006): 727–746.

Bowler, Shawn, David M. Farrell, and Richard S. Katz, eds., *Party Discipline and Parliamentary Government*. Columbus: The Ohio State University Press, 1999.

Brillant, Joshua. "Sharon Sacks Hawkish Ministers." *United Press International*. June 4, 2004. www.upi.com/Defense-News/2004/06/04/Sharon-sacks-hawkish-ministers/96181086372015

Burke, Edmund Sir, "Speech to the Electors and Bristol, 3 November, 1774," in Philip B. Kurland and Ralph Lerner, *The Founders' Constitution*. http://press-pubs.uchicago.edu/founders/documents/v1ch13s7.html

Carothers, Thomas. *Confronting the Weakest Link: Aiding Political Parties in New Democracies*. Washington DC: Carnegie Endowment for International Peace, 2006.

Clift, Ben, and Justin Fisher. "Comparative Party Finance Reform" The Cases of France and Britain." *Party Politics* 10, no. 6 (2004): 677–699.

Collins, Liat. "Maverick Zissman Ready for a Divorce from Labour." *Jerusalem Post*. October 6, 1995, 8.

Collins, Liat. "Kahalani, Zissman Warn Rabin to Keep Them in Committee Post." *Jerusalem Post*. October 8, 1995, 1.

Collins, Liat. "Goldfarb, Salmovitz Quit Yi'ud." *Jerusalem Post*. November 28, 1995, 2.

Collins, Liat. "Knesset Oks Hebron Pact." *Jerusalem Post*. January 17, 1997, 1.

Collins, Liat. "17 Likudniks Needed for Part Split." *Jerusalem Post*. November 20, 1997, 2.

Collins, Liat. "Likud-Tsomet Deal Falls Through." *Jerusalem Post*. March 25, 1999, 3.

"Communist Party Purge." *Palestine Post*. February 14, 1949, 3.

"Communists Dissolve Party, Urge Members to Join Mapam." *Chicago Sentinel*. August 18, 1949, 3.

Conference on Security and Cooperation in Europe, *Document of the Copenhagen Meeting, 1990*. www.osce.org/odihr/elections/14304?download=true

"Constituent Assembly in Session." *Palestine Post*. February 16, 1949, 2.

Couch, Jim F. "An Empirical Examination of the Impetus for Political Party Defection," *International Journal of Business and Social Science*, 4, no. 3 (2013): 109–113.

"Dayan Seeks Independent Knesset Status." *Jerusalem Post*. June 15, 1977, 1.

Desposato, Scott. "Parties for Rent? Ambition, Ideology, and Party Switching in Brazil's Chamber of Deputies." *American Journal of Political Science* 50, no. 1 (2006): 62–80.

Devenish, G. E. "Political Musical Chairs—The Saga of Floor-Crossing and the Constitution." *Stellenbosch Law Review* 15, no. 52 (2004): 54.

Dios, Manuel Sanchez de. "Parliamentary Party Discipline in Spain," in S. Bowler, D. Farrell, and R. Katz, eds., *Party Discipline and Parliamentary Government*. Columbus: The Ohio State University Press, 1999, 141–166.

Diskin, Avraham, and Efraim Podoksik. "Israel." *European Journal of Political Research Political Data Yearbook*. 52, no. 1 (2013): 112.

Duverger, Maurice. *Political Parties, Their Organization and Activity in the Modern State*. London: Methuen, 1969.

European Commission for Democracy through Law (Venice Commission), *Report on Democracy, Limitation of Mandates and Incompatibility of Political Functions*, Strasbourg, 2013. www.venice.coe.int/webforms/documents/default. aspx?pdffile=CDL-AD(2012)027rev-e

Fell, Dafydd. "Do Party Switchers Pay an Electoral Price? The Case of Taiwan." *Parliamentary Affairs*, 70, no. 2 (2017): 377–399.

Fitzsimmons, Michael. *The Remaking of France: The National Assembly and the Constitution of 1791*. Cambridge: Cambridge University Press, 1994.

Fraenkel, Jon. "Party Hopping Laws in the Southern Hemisphere." *Political Science* 64, no. 2 (2011): 106–120.

Frenkel, Sheera Claire, and Gil Hoffman. "Newly Sworn-In Lieberman Already Set to Visit US." *Jerusalem Post*. October 31, 2006, 19.

Friedman, Yaal. "Netanyahu Achieves 65 Recommendations to Form Government." *Y-net News*. April 16, 2019. www.ynet.co.il/articles/0,7340,L-5495244,00. html. [in Hebrew]

Geddis, Andrew. "Gang Aft A-Gley: New Zealand's Attempt To Combat 'Party Hopping' By Elected Representatives." *Election Law Journal* 1, no. 4 (2002): 557–571.

Geddis, Andrew. "Proportional Representation 'Party Hopping' and the Limits of Electoral Regulation: A Cautionary Tale from New Zealand." *Common Law World Review* 35, no. 1 (2006): 24–50.

Gherghina, Sergiu. "Rewarding the "Traitors"? Legislative Defection and Re-Election in Romania." *Party Politics* 22, no. 4 (2016): 490–500.

Giannetti, Daniela, and Michael Laver. "Party System Dynamics and the Making and Breaking of Italian Governments." *Electoral Studies* 20, no. 4 (2001): 529–553.

Gilbert, Nina. "It All Started with the Wye Agreement: How the Coalition Fell Apart." *Jerusalem Post*. December 22, 1998, 4.

Gilbert, Nina. "Knesset Approves Early Elections." *Jerusalem Post*. January 5, 1999, 1.

Gilbert, Nina. "Likud Working to Free Paritzky from Shinui." *Jerusalem Post*. January 19, 2005, 5.

Gilbert, Nina. "Eitam Moves to Break from NRP." *Jerusalem Post*. January 24, 2005, 2.

Gilbert, Nina."Eitam, Orlev on Collision Course." *Jerusalem Post*. January 25, 2005, 3.

Gilbert, Nina. "Disengagement Passes 59-40: Knesset Vote Also Rejects Referendum." *Jerusalem Post*. February 17, 2005, 1.

Gilbert, Nina. "Shinui Flip-flops on Paritzky's Fate." *Jerusalem Post*. December 14, 2005, 4.

Gilbert, Nina, and Gil Hoffman. "PM Survive No-Confidence Votes." *Jerusalem Post*. June 29, 2004, 2.

Goeke, Martin, and Christof Hartmann, "The Regulation of Party Switching in Africa." *Journal of Contemporary African Studies* 29, no. 3 (2009): 263–280.

Gordon, Evelyn. "Court Forbids Appointment of Yi'ud MKs to Gv't Post." *Jerusalem Post.* July 15, 1994, A14.

Gordon, Evelyn. "High Court to Rule Today Whether Yi'ud MKs Can Serve in Gv't." *Jerusalem Post.* July 25, 1994, 12

Gordon, Evelyn. "Court Ruling on Yi'ud Drawsfire from MKs." *Jerusalem Post.* July 26, 1994, 12.

Gordon, Evelyn. "Golan Bill Defeated in Cliffhanger Tie." *Jerusalem Post.* July 27, 1995, 1.

Gordon, Evelyn. "Party Financing Law Challenged in High Court." *Jerusalem Post.* May 15, 1996, 3.

Gordon, Evelyn. "High Court Throws Out Kleiner's Hebron Petition." *Jerusalem Post.* November 21, 1996, 2.

"Government Gets Five Days to Explain Why Yi'ud Members Are Getting Government Posts." *Jerusalem Post.* July 18, 1994, 12.

Grose, Christian, and Antoine Yoshinaka. "The Electoral Consequences of Party Switching by Incumbent Members of Congress, 1947–2000," *Legislative Studies Quarterly* 28, no. 1 (2003): 55–75.

Gur, Havi Rettig. "Labor's 1-Woman Opposition: No to a Religious, Occupying, Non-Democratic State." *Times of Israel,* June 18, 2020. www.timesofisrael.com/labors-1-woman-opposition-no-to-a-religious-occupying-non-democratic-state

Habermann, Claude. "Israel's Likud Passes Torch, Naming Netanyahu Leader." *New York Times* March 25, 1993. www.nytimes.com/1993/03/26/world/israel-s-likud-passes-torch-naming-netanyahu-leader.html

Hamzawi, Jordan. "Policy Preferences and Party Switching: Evidence From the 2012 Japanese Election," *Party Politics* 27, no. 6 (2021): 1268–1278.

Hardgrave, Robert, and Stanley Kochanek. *India: Government and Politics in a Developing Nation.* Fort Worth, TX: Harcourt Brace Jovanovich, 2000.

Harman, Danna. "Center Party Announces List of Candidates." *Jerusalem Post.* March 17, 1999, 1.

Harman, Danna. "Third Way's Zissman Joins One Israel." *Jerusalem Post.* March 30, 1999, 3.

"Harari of ILP Crosses Floor to Join Labour Party Ranks." *Jerusalem Post.* May 28, 1968, 1.

Harris, David Zev. "MKs Back Plan to Limit Party Splits." *Jerusalem Post.* January 20, 2000, 4.

Har-Zahav, Rhanan. "Constitutional Amendments—A Review From the Knesset." *Hamishpat* 1 (1993): 112. [in Hebrew]

Haughton, Tim. *Constraints and Opportunities of Leadership in Post-Communist Europe.* Aldershot & Burlington, VT: Ashgate, 2005.

Hazan, Reuven. "Presidential Parliamentarism: Direct Popular Election of the Prime Minister; Israel's New Electoral and Political System." *Electoral Studies* 15, no. 1 (1996): 21–37.

Hazan, Reuven. "The 1996 Intra-Party Elections in Israel: Adopting Party Primaries." *Electoral Studies* 16, no. 1 (1997): 95–103.

Hazan, Reuven. "Constituency Interests without Constituency: The Geographical Impact of Candidate Selection on Party Organization and Legislative Behavior in the 14th Israeli Knesset, 1996–99." *Political Geography* 18, no. 7 (1999): 791–811.

Hazan, Reuven. "The Unintended Consequences of Extemporaneous Electoral Reform: The 1999 Elections in Israel." *Representation* 37, no. 1 (2000): 39–47.

Hazan, Reuven. "Does Cohesion Equal Discipline? Toward a Conceptual Delineation." *Journal of Legislative Studies* 9, no. 4 (2003): 4.

Hazan, Reuven. "The Israeli Mixed Electoral System: Unexpected Reciprocal and Cumulative Consequences," in Matthew Soberg Shugart and Martin Wattenberg, eds. *Mixed-Member Electoral Systems: The Best of Both Worlds?* Oxford: Oxford University Press, 2003.

Hazan, Reuven. "Kadima and the Centre: Convergence in the Israeli Party System." *Israel Affairs* 13, no. 2 (2007): 266–288.

Hazan, Reuven Y., and Abraham Diskin. 2000. "The 1999 Knesset and Prime Ministerial Elections in Israel." *Electoral Studies* 19, no. 4 (2000): 628–637.

Hazan, Reuven. "Analysis: Israel's New Constructive Vote of No-Confidence." *Knesset News.* March 18, 2014. https://m.knesset.gov.il/en/News/PressReleases/Pages/Pr11200_pg.aspx

Hazan, Reuven, and Gideon Rahat. "Representation, Electoral Reform, and Democracy: Theoretical and Empirical Lessons from the 1996 Elections in Israel." *Comparative Political Studies* 33, no. 10 (2000): 1310–1336.

Hazan, Reuven, and Gideon Rahat, "Israel: The Politics of Extreme Proportionality," in Michael Gallagher and Paul Mitchell, eds. *The Politics of Electoral Reform.* Oxford: Oxford University Press, 2005, 333–335.

Heller, William, and Carol Mershon. " 'Party Switching in the Italian Chamber of Deputies, 1996–2001," *Journal of Politics* 67, no. 2 (2005): 536–559.

Heller, William, and Carol Mershon. "Dealing in Discipline: Party Switching and Legislative Voting in the Italian Chamber of Deputies." *American Journal of Political Science* 52, no. 4 (2008): 910–925.

Heller, William, and Carol Mershon, eds. *Political Parties and Legislative Party Switching.* New York: Palgrave Macmillan, 2009.

Heller, William, and Carol Mershon. "Integrating Theoretical and Empirical Models of Party Switching," in W. Heller and C. Mershon, eds., *Political Parties and Legislative Party Switching.* New York: Palgrave Macmillan, 2009, 29–51.

Heller, William, and Carol Mershon, "Introduction: Legislative Party Switching, Parties, and Party Systems," in W. Heller and C. Mershon, eds., *Political*

Parties and Legislative Party Switching. New York: Palgrave Macmillan, 2009, 3–28.

Heller, William, and Carol Mershon, "Legislator Preferences, Party Desires: Party Switching and the Foundations of Policy Making in Legislatures," in W. Heller and C. Mershon, eds., *Political Parties and Legislative Party Switching.* New York: Palgrave Macmillan, 2009, 173–200.

Herzog, Chaim. *Living History.* Pantheon Books, New York, 1996.

Hoffman, Gil. "Opposition Growing to Labor-Am Ehad Merger." *Jerusalem Post.* July 10, 2003, 3.

Hoffman, Gil. "Knesset Passes David Tal Law." *Jerusalem Post.* March 2, 2004, 2.

Hoffman, Gil. "Shinui to Paritzky: Take NIS 1 Mil and Leave." *Jerusalem Post.* October 12, 2004, 3.

Hoffman, Gil. "NRP Boots Out Eitam from Chairman Post." *Jerusalem Post.* February 15, 2005, 4.

Hoffman, Gil. "Eitam, Levy Form New Religious Zionist Party." *Jerusalem Post.* February 24, 2005, 1.

Hoffman, Gil. "Sharon Prevails in Likud Showdown: Staves off Netanyahu's Bid for Early Leadership Contest by 104." *Jerusalem Post.* September 27, 2005, 1.

Hoffman, Gil. "Labor Party Votes to Quit Coalition." *Jerusalem Post.* November 21, 2005, 1.

Hoffman, Gil. "Knesset Resignations Set Off Chain Reaction." *Jerusalem Post.* January 16, 2006, 3.

Hoffman, Gil. "Nudelman, Landver Quit Knesset." *Jerusalem Post.* February 7, 2006, 4.

Hoffman, Gil. "Party Registrar Makes Gaydamak, Eldad Parties Official." *Jerusalem Post.* December 10, 2007, 3.

Hoffman, Gil. "Pensioner Party Rebel Row Foils Gaydamak's Ministerial Hopes." *Jerusalem Post.* April 9, 2008, 5.

Hoffman, Gil. "Peretz to Try to Oust Barak as Labor Head." *Jerusalem Post.* February 15, 2009, 1.

Hoffman, Gil. "Livni Ambushes Mofaz in Kadima Faction Meeting." *Jerusalem Post.* March 3, 2009, 4.

Hoffman, Gil, Joshua Newman, and Carrie Sheffield. "Last Minute Deal to Prevent Labor Split." *Jerusalem Post.* August 6, 2009, 1.

Hoffman, Gil. "Pines-Paz's Exit Deals Death Blow to Labor Rebellion." *Jerusalem Post.* January 8, 2010, 1.

Hoffman, Gil. "Einat Wilf Opposes Major Changes." *Jerusalem Post.* January 11, 2010, 5.

Hoffman, Gil. "New Labor MK Ghaleb Majadleh: Party Must Leave." *Jerusalem Post.* April 13, 2010, 9.

Hoffman, Gil. "Labor to Get New Secretary-General Today." *Jerusalem Post.* October 14, 2010, 4.

Hoffman, Gil. "Labor Activists to Push Ben-Eliezer to Lead Party." *Jerusalem Post*. October 31, 2010, 2

Hoffman, Gil. "Ben-Simon Blames Barak for Losing Knesset Committee. Labor MK Calls his Fellow Party Members 'Dishrags." *Jerusalem Post*. November 2, 2010, 2.

Hoffman, Gil. "Ben-Simon to be Punished for Budget Vote." *Jerusalem Post*. January 2, 2011. www.jpost.com/diplomacy-and-politics/ben-simon-to-be-punished-for-budget-vote

Hoffman, Gil. "Ben-Simon Barred from Leaving Labor Party." *Jerusalem Post*. January 11, 2011. www.jpost.com/diplomacy-and-politics/ben-simon-barred-from-leaving-labor-party

Hoffman, Gil, and Claire Sheera Frenkel. "PM Vows Consequences against Rebels: MKs Vote Down Bar-On, Boim Bids; Approve Olmert." *Jerusalem Post*. November 8, 2005, 1.

Holden, Alice M. "The Imperative Mandate in the Spanish Cortes of the Middle Ages." *American Political Science Review* 24, no. 4 (1930): 886–912.

Honig, Sarah. "Was it Kalanterism?" *Jerusalem Post*. May 19, 1982, 1.

Honig, Sarah. "Five Liberal Defectors Ready to Talk Coalition with Labor." *Jerusalem Post*. March 29, 1990, 1.

Honig, Sarah. "Tsomet Showdown Expected on Sunday." *Jerusalem Post*. January 27, 1994, 14.

Honig, Sarah. "Shas' Azran Says He Won't Rejoin Coalition." *Jerusalem Post*. May 20, 1994.

Honig, Sarah. "Labor May Woo Shas with Religious Legislation." *Jerusalem Post*. June 20, 1994, 3.

Honig, Sarah. "Tzur Quits Third Way." *Jerusalem Post*. June 20, 1994, 2.

Honig, Sarah. "MK Salmovitz Wants Out of 'Marriage from Hell' with Yi'ud." *Jerusalem Post*. December 19, 1994, 2.

Honig, Sarah. "Yi'ud Party, Knesset Faction Disintegrating." *Jerusalem Post*. February 21, 1995, 1.

Honig, Sarah. "Segev Ousted and Yi'ud Chief." *Jerusalem Post*. May 18, 1995, 2.

Honig, Sarah, and Liat Collins. "Levy Prepares for 'New Way.'" *Jerusalem Post*. June 7, 1995, 2.

Honig, Sarah. "Salmovitz Accuses Segev of Fraud, Forgery." *Jerusalem Post*. June 21, 1995, 2.

Honig, Sarah, and Liat Collins. "Kahalani, Zissman, Seffi Call on Government to Resign." *Jerusalem Post*. June 12, 1995, 1.

Honig, Sarah. "Zissman, Kahalani Will Leave Labor for Third Way." *Jerusalem Post*. September 22, 1995, 5.

Honig, Sarah. "Third Way Rejects Oslo 2." *Jerusalem Post*. September 29, 1995, 2.

Honig, Sarah. "Yi'ud Shrinks to Last MK." *Jerusalem Post*. October 26, 1995, 12.

Honig, Sarah. "Labor Fails to Dissuade Third Way from Running." *Jerusalem Post.* November 9, 1995, 2.

Honig, Sarah. "Magen to Announce He Is Joining Levy Today." *Jerusalem Post.* December 11, 1995, 12.

Honig, Sarah. "Likud No Longer My Home." *Jerusalem Post.* December 12, 1995, 12, 1.

Honig, Sarah. "Third Way Officially Declares Itself a Party." *Jerusalem Post.* February 14, 1996, 2.

Honig, Sarah. "Netanyahu Sweeps Likud Party Vote." *Jerusalem Post.* June 6, 1996, 1.

Honig, Sarah. "Magen Resigns as Deputy Finance Minister." *Jerusalem Post.* May 21, 1997, 1.

Honig, Sarah. "Magen to Quit Government." *Jerusalem Post.* May 22, 1997, 1.

Honig, Sarah. "Rubicon Crossed." *Jerusalem Post.* June 19, 1997, 3.

Honig, Sarah. "Milo: We'll Split the Party." *Jerusalem Post.* November 18, 1997, 1.

Honig, Sarah. "Livnat Quells Anti-Netanyahu Mutiny by Staying On." *Jerusalem Post.* November 26, 1997, 1.

Honig, Sarah, and Dan Izenberg. "Tsomet Dissidents Charge Financial Irregularities in Party." *Jerusalem Post.* January 25, 1995, 12.

Honig, Sarah, and Michal Yudelman. "Despite Peretz-Deri Blowup, Shas Leans to Likud—Without Shamir." *Jerusalem Post.* March 19, 1990, 1.

Hopkin, Jonathan. "The Problem with Party Finance: Theoretical Perspectives on the Funding of Party Politics." *Party Politics* 10, no. 6 (2004): 627–651.

"How They Voted." *Jerusalem Post.* October 27, 2004, 1.

Hulst, Marc van der. *The Parliamentary Mandate: A Global Comparative Study.* Geneva: Inter-Parliamentary Union, 2000.

"I.L.P. Leader Wants Party to Join Labour Group." *Jerusalem Post.* December 26, 1967, 3.

"ILP Votes against Tie-Up with Labour; Only 8 in Favour." *Jerusalem Post.* May 24, 1968, 8.

Issac, Sueanne. "Summary and Analysis of Floor-Crossing Legislation." *Research Unit of the Parliament of South Africa.* July 24, 2008.

Izenberg, Dan. "A Doctor Turned Farmer-Politician." *Jerusalem Post.* June 9, 1992, 2.

Izenberg, Dan. "*Jerusalem Post.* January 13, 1993, 2.

Izenberg, Dan. "Knesset Debates PLO Contacts Bill." *Jerusalem Post.* January 19, 1993, 1.

Izenberg, Dan. "Knesset Repeals Ban on Meetings with Terror Groups." *Jerusalem Post.* January 20, 1993, 1.

Izenberg, Dan. "Labor Hawks Put Coalition on Notice." *Jerusalem Post.* January 22, 1993, 9.

Izenberg, Dan. "Human Rights Bill Compromise Collapses." *Jerusalem Post.* February 16, 1993, 4.

Izenberg, Dan. "Coalition Leaders Reach Compromise on Human Rights Bill." *Jerusalem Post.* January 26, 1993, 12.

Izenberg, Dan. "Basic Law Presented Despite Opposition." *Jerusalem Post*. March 24, 1993, 4.

Izenberg, Dan. "Tsomet MK Asks High Court to Block Treaty." *Jerusalem Post*. September 10, 1993, 3.

Izenberg, Dan. "Coalition Would Welcome Tsomet Breakaways." *Jerusalem Post*. February 3, 1994, 2.

Izenberg, Dan. "New 'Centrist' Labor Group Launched." *Jerusalem Post*. May 25, 1994, 1.

Izenberg, Dan. "Yi'ud Seen Split Over Joining Coalition." *Jerusalem Post*. June 22, 1994, 1.

Izenberg, Dan. "Yi'ud's Salmovitz May Refuse to Follow Faction Into Coalition Talks." *Jerusalem Post*. July 6, 1994, 12.

Izenberg, Dan. "Rafael Eitan's 'Wild Animals.'" *Jerusalem Post*. July 13, 1994, 12.

Izenberg, Dan. "Salmovitz Creates Interesting Anomaly." *Jerusalem Post*. July 13, 1994, 12.

Izenberg, Dan. "Azran Will Surrender Post, to Escape Shas." *Jerusalem Post*. November 8, 1994, 12.

Izenberg, Dan. "Shas Continues Battle to Remove Azran from Knesset." *Jerusalem Post*. November 9, 1994, 12.

Izenberg, Dan. "Law Would Remove Azran from Post." *Jerusalem Post*. November 16, 1994, 4.

Izenberg, Dan. "Yi'ud Cleared to Join Government." *Jerusalem Post*. December 20, 1994, 12.

Janda, Kenneth. "Laws against Party Switching, Defecting, or Floor-Crossing in National Parliaments." Paper delivered at the 2009 World Congress of the International Political Science Association in Santiago, Chile.

Janda, Kenneth. "Adopting Party Law," in *Political Parties and Democracy in Theoretical and Practical Perspectives*. Washington, DC: National Democratic Institute for International Affairs, 2005.

Karni, Yuval. "The Trick." *Yediot Ahronot*. January 18, 2011, 11. [in Hebrew]

Karni, Yuval. "Barak's Shortcut." *Yediot Ahronot*. May 9, 2011, 11. [in Hebrew]

Karni, Yuval. "Independence with Salmon." *Yediot Ahronot*. May 13, 2011, 6. [in Hebrew]

Karvonen, Lauri. "Legislation on Political Parties: A Global Comparison." *Party Politics* 13, no. 4 (2007): 437–455.

Katz, Richard S., and Peter Mair. "Changing Models of Party Organization and Party Democracy: The Emergence of the Cartel Party." *Party Politics* 1, no. 1 (1995): 5–28.

Katz, Yariv, and Yuval Karni. "Examination in the Pensioners' Party: Rafi Eitan is Olmert's Puppet." *Yediot Ahronot*. November 17, 2006, 6. [in Hebrew]

Kedzia, Zdzislaw, and Agata. Hauser, *The Impact of Political Party Control Over the Exercise of the Parliamentary Mandate*. Geneva: Inter-Parliamentary Union, 2012.

Keesing's Contemporary Archives. London: Keesing's Ltd., volume 31. 1985.

Keinon, Herb. "Two Shas Men May Abstain in Vote Tomorrow." *Jerusalem Post.* July 12, 1992, 1.

Keinon, Herb. "Shas Council to Meet Before Knesset Vote." *Jerusalem Post.* July 13, 1992, 1.

Keinon, Herb. "Force 17 Tests Netanyahu." *Jerusalem Post.* February 21, 1997, 7.

Keinon, Herb, and Gil Hoffman. "Sharon Appoints Substitute Ministers." *Jerusalem Post.* July 5, 2004, 3.

Keinon, Herb, and Gil Hoffman. "Netanyahu Quits Over PM's 'Blind' Insistence on Pullout." *Jerusalem Post.* August 8, 2005, 1.

Keinon, Herb, and Gil Hoffman. "Peres Quits Knesset by Fax after 47 Years: Enables Him to Return as Kadima MK." *Jerusalem Post.* January 16, 2006, 3.

Kenig, Ofer. "The Primary System in Israel: A Balance Sheet." https://en.idi.org.il/articles/6883

Klein, Elad. "The Personal Vote and Legislative Party Switching." *Party Politics* 24, no. 5 (2018): 501–510.

Klein, Elad. "Explaining Legislative Party Switching in Advanced and New Democracies." *Party Politics* 27, no. 2 (2021): 329–340.

"Knesset Passes Governance Laws, Electoral Threshold Raised." *Knesset News.* March 11, 2014. https://m.knesset.gov.il/en/news/pressreleases/pages/pr11193_pg.aspx

"Knesset Plenum Approves Bill Enabling Four MKs to Break Away From Their Faction, Even If They Do Not Constitute One Third of It." *Knesset News.* July 7, 2021. https://m.knesset.gov.il/EN/News/PressReleases/Pages/press070721b.aspx

Kohn, Moshe. "Dayan to Sit as Independent MK." *Jerusalem Post.* July 13, 1977, 2.

Kopecky, Petr. "Political Parties and the State in Post-Communist Europe." *Journal of Communist Studies and Transition Politics* 22, no. 3 (2006): 251–273.

Kopecky, Petr, and Peter Mair. "Political Parties and Government," in Salih, Mohamed A., ed. *Political Parties in Africa.* London: Pluto, 2003, 275–292.

Koren, Dani. *A Time in Grey.* Tel Aviv: Zemorah, 1994. [In Hebrew]

Laakso, Marku, and Rein Taagepeara, " 'Effective' Number of Parties: A Measure with Application West Europe." *Comparative Political* Studies 12, no. 1 (1979): 3–27.

Laver, Michael, and John Underhill. "The Bargaining Advantages of Combining with Others." *British Journal of Political Science* 12, no. 1 (1982): 27–42.

Laver, Michael, and Junko Kato. "Dynamic Approaches to Government Formation and the Generic Instability of Decisive Structures in Japan." *Electoral Studies* 20, no. 4 (2001): 509–527.

Laver, Michael, and Kenneth Benoit. "The Evolution of Party Systems Between Elections." *American Journal of Political Science* 47, no. 2 (2003): 215–233.

Lazaroff, Tovah. "NRP Split Over Leaving Government." *Jerusalem Post*. June 7, 2004, 1.

Lazaroff, Tovah. "PM Loses Majority as Eitam, Levy Quit." *Jerusalem Post*. June 9, 2004, 1.

Lazaroff, Tovah. "Eitam, Levy Weight Leaving NRP." *Jerusalem Post*. January 21, 2005, 4.

Lento, Tal, and Reuven Y. Hazan. "The Vote of No-Confidence: Towards a Framework for Analysis." *West European Politics* 45, no. 3 (2022): 502–527.

Lewin, Leif. *Ideology and Strategy: A Century of Swedih Politics*. Cambridge: Cambridge University Press, 1988.

"Lok Sabha Passes Anti-Defection Bill." *Time of India. Delhi Edition*. December 13, 2003, 13.

Lynn, Uriel. "In Defense of Electoral Reform." *Jerusalem Post*. December 12, 2000, 8.

Mainwarring, Scott, and Timothy R. Scully. *Building Democratic Institutions: Party Systems in Latin America*. Stanford, CA: Stanford University Press, 1995.

"Maki Central Committee Demands to Cancel Preminger's Mandate in the Constituent Assembly." *Kol Haam*. February 14, 1949, 2. [in Hebrew]

Malhotra, G. C. *Anti-Defection Law in India and the Commonwealth*. New Delhi: Metropolitan Book Co., 2005.

Martin, Shane. "Why Electoral Seats Don't Always Matter: The Impact of Mega-Seats on Legislative Behaviour in Ireland." *Party Politics* 20, no. 3 (2014): 467–479.

McKee, Seth C., and Antoine Yoshinaka. "Late to the Parade: Party Switchers in Contemporary US Southern Legislatures." *Party Politics* 21, no. 6 (2013): 957–969.

McLaughlin, Eric. "Electoral Regimes and Party-Switching: Floor-Crossing in South Africa's Local Legislatures." *Party Politics* 18, no. 4 (2011): 563–579.

McLaughlin, Eric. "Did Floor-Crossing Alienate South African Voters? Evidence from Municipal Legislatures." *Politikon: South African Journal of Political Studies* 41, no. 2 (2014): 289–310.

Mershon, Carol, and Olga Shvetsova. *Party System Change in Legislatures Worldwide*. Cambridge: Cambridge University Press, 2015.

Mershon, Carol. "Legislative Party Switching and Executive Coalitions." *Japanese Journal of Political Science* 9, no. 3 (2008): 391–414.

Mershon, Carol, and Olga Shvetsova, "Timing Matters: Incentives for Party Switching and Stages of Parliamentary Cycles," in W. Heller and C. Mershon, eds., *Political Parties and Legislative Party Switching*. New York: Palgrave.

Miskin, Sarah. "Politicians Overboard: Jumping the Party Ship." Research Paper No. 4. Department of the Parliamentary Library, Australia, 2003.

Mitta, Manoj. "Disqualifying Expelled MPs, Speaker to Decide." *The Times of India. Delhi Edition*. July 24, 2008, 11.

Mualem, Mazal. "Knesset Passes Land Reform and 'Mofaz Law." *Haaretz*. August 3, 2009. www.haaretz.com/1.5085713

Muller, Wolfgang. "The Relevance of the State for Party System Change." *Journal of Theoretical Politics* 5, no. 4 (1993): 419–454.

Muller, Wolfgang, and Ulrich Sieberer. "Party Law," in R. S. Katz and W. J. Crotty, eds. *Handbook of Party Politics*. London: Sage, 2006, 435–445.

Navot, Suzie. *The Constitution of Israel: A Contextual Analysis*. Oxford & Portland, OR: Hart Publishing, 2014.

"New Jerusalem Coalition Minus Orthodox Parties." *Jerusalem Post*. August 27, 1956, 1.

Nielsen, Marie Kaldahl, Ann Mogeltolt Andersen, and Helena Helboe Pedersen. "Balancing Costs of Legislative Party Switching in the Danish Parliament, 1953-2015." *Parliamentary Affairs* 72, no. 1: (2019): 42–58.

Nikolenyi, Csaba. "The Adoption of Anti-Defection Laws in Parliamentary Democracies." *Election Law Journal* 15, no. 1 (2016): 96–108.

Nikolenyi, Csaba. "Keeping Parties Together? The Evolution of Israel's Anti-Defection Law." *Polish Political Science Yearbook Special Issue on Israel Studies* 47, no. 2 (2018): 188–201.

Nikolenyi, Csaba. "Party Switching in Israel: Understanding the Split of the Labor Party in 2011." *Contemporary Review of the Middle East* 6, nos. 3–4 (2019): 408–422.

Nikolenyi, Csaba. "Changing Patterns of Party Unity in the Knesset: The Consequences of the Israeli Anti-Defection Law." *Party Politics* 25, no. 5 (2019): 712–723.

Nikolenyi, Csaba. "The End of *Kalanterism?* Defections and Government Instability in the Knesset." *Israel Studies* 25, no. 2 (2020): 95–114.

Nikolenyi, Csaba. "Government Termination and Anti-Defection Laws in Parliamentary Democracies." *West European Politics* 45, no. 6 (2022): 638–662.

Nikolenyi, Csaba, and Shaul Shenhav. "The Constitutionalisation of Party Unity: The Origins of Anti-Defection Laws in India and Israel." *Journal of Legislative Studies* 21, no. 4 (2015).

"Nissim Considers Law against Kalanterism." *Jerusalem Post*. May 23, 1982, 2.

O'Brien, Diana Z., and Yael Shomer, "A Cross-National Analysis of Party Switching." *Legislative Studies Quarterly* 38, no. 1 (2013): 111–141.

Odenheimer, Alisa. "MK Segev Asks Court to Cancel Rabinovitch Posting." *Jerusalem Post*. January 12, 1992, 3.

Owens, John. "Explaining Party Cohesion and Discipline in Democratic Legislatures: Purposiveness and Contexts." *Journal of Legislative Studies* 9, no. 4 (2003): 12–40.

Özbudun, Ergun. *Party Cohesion in Western Democracies: A Causal Analysis*. London: Sage, 1970.

"The Paritzky Affair." *Jerusalem Post*. July 11, 2004, 13.

Pasquino, Pasquale. "One and Three: Separation of Powers and the Independence of the Judiciary in the Italian Constitution," in J. Ferejohn, J. N. Rakove, and J. Riley, eds., *Constitutional Culture and Democratic Rule.* Cambridge: Cambridge University Press, 2001, 205–222.

Paz, Shely. "Labor MKs Pressure Barak to Rule Out Serving Alongside Lieberman." *Jerusalem Post.* February 6, 2009, 4.

Petreanu, Dan. "Likud in Uproar Over Unity Deal." *Jerusalem Post.* December 21, 1988, 1.

Radoszkowicz, Abigail. "Rabbis: NRP Can Stay in Gov't." *Jerusalem Post.* October 28, 2004, 3.

Rahat, Gideon. "Determinants of Party Cohesion: Evidence from the Israeli Parliament." *Parliamentary Affairs* 60, no. 2 (2007): 279–296.

Rahat, Gideon. *The Politics of Regime Structure Reform in Democracies: Israel in Comparative and Theoretical Perspective.* Albany, NY: SUNY Press, 2008.

Rahat, Gideon, and Ofer Kenig, *From Party Politics to Personalized Politics? Party Change and Political Personalization in Democracies.* Oxford: Oxford University Press, 2018.

Reilly, Benjamin. "Political Engineering and Party Politics in Papua New Guinea." *Party Politics* 8, no. 6 (2002): 701–718.

Resolutions by ANC, 52nd National Conference, Polokwane, December 20, 2007. www.sahistory.org.za/archive/resolutions-anc-20-december-2007-52nd-national-conference-polokwane

"Rivlin to Give Gantz Mandate to Form Government on Monday." *Times of Israel.* March 15, 2020. www.timesofisrael.com/liveblog_entry/rivlin-to-give-gantz-mandate-to-form-government-on-monday

Rubabshi-Shitrit, Ayelet, and Sharon Hasson. "The Effect of the Constructive Vote of No-Confidence on Government Termination and Government Durability." *West European Politics* 45, no. 3 (2022): 576–590.

Rubeinstein, Amnon, and Barak Medina. *The Constitutional Law of the State of Israel.* Jerusalem: Shoken Books, 2005. [In Hebrew]

Rudoren, Jodi. "Israeli Defense Minister Says He is Leaving Politics." *New York Times.* November 26, 2012. www.nytimes.com/2012/11/27/world/middleeast/ehud-barak-israeli-defense-minister-to-quit-politics.html

Saltan, Jeremy. "Kadima MK Breakdown: Who Supports Livni vs Mofaz?" www.jewish press.com/indepth/analysis/kadimamkbreakdownwhosupportslvsmofaz/2012/01/29

Sartori, Giovanni. *Comparative Constitutional Engineering: An Inquiry into Structures, Incentives and Outcomes.* New York: New York University Press, 1997.

Scarrow, Susan E. "Explaining Political Finance Reforms: Competition and Context." *Party Politics* 10, no. 6 (2004): 653–675.

Scheiner, Ethan. "Pipelines of Pork: Japanese Politics and a Model of Local Opposition Party Failure." *Comparative Political Studies* 38, no. 7 (2005): 799–823.

Smiles, Joseph. "Floor Crossing in South Africa: A Controversial Democratic Process." *Insight on Africa* 3, no. 2 (2011): 162–163.

Somfalvi, Attila. "Netanyahu Dissolves Plesner Committee." *Y-Net News*. July 2, 2012. www.ynetnews.com/articles/0,7340,L-4250215,00.html

Somfalvi, Attila. "Kadima Faction Votes to Quit Coalition." *Y-Net News*. July 17, 2012. www.ynetnews.com/articles/0,7340,L-4256736,00.html

Somfalvi, Attila. "PM Offers Portfolios to Kadima MKs." *Y-Net News*. July 23, 2012. www.ynetnews.com/articles/0,7340,L-4259030,00.html

"Split in the Tzomet Faction." *Yediot Ahronot*. February 3, 1994, 1.

Stoil, Rebecca Anna. "Ben-Eliezer Calls for Candidates Outside Labor to Contend for the Party Leadership." *Jerusalem Post*. November 4, 2010, 10.

Subramanian, R. *Developing and Testing a Theory of Legislative Party Fragmentation*. Unpublished PhD dissertation, University of Wisconsin-Madison, 2008.

Tepperman, Jonathan. "Levy-Netanyahu: The Latest Round." *Jerusalem Post*. June 30, 1997, 3.

Torgovnik, Efraim. "The Centre Party." *Israel Affairs* 7, nos. 2–3 (2000): 135–152.

Tsebelis, George. *Nested Games: Rational Choice in Comparative Politics*. Berkeley: University of California Press, 1990.

Tuchfeld, Mati. "This Could be The End of a Beautiful Friendship." *Israel Hayom*. October 5, 2012. www.israelhayom.com/2012/10/05/this-could-be-the-end-of-a-beautiful-friendship

Tuchfeld, Mati. "Netanyahu's Advantage." *Israel Hayom*. December 21, 2012. www.israelhayom.com/2012/12/21/netanyahuas-advantage

Tuchfeld, Mati. "Livni-Poraz Deal to be Urgently Investigated." *Israel Hayom*. December 21, 2012, 9. www.israelhayom.co.il/article/61519 [In Hebrew]

Uri, Dan. "What Makes Rafi Run." *Jerusalem Post*. March 2, 2006, 14.

Venice Commission. *Report on the Imperative Mandate and Similar Practices*. Strasbourg: Council of Europe, 2009,

Volpi, Elisa. "Ideology and Party Switching: A Comparison of 12 West European Countries." *Parliamentary Affairs* 72, no. 1 (2019): 1–20.

Vowles, Jack. "The Politics of Electoral Reform in New Zealand." *International Political Science Review* 16, no. 1 (1995): 95–115.

Vowles, Jack. "Systemic Failure, Coordination, and Contingencies: Understanding Electoral System Change in New Zealand," in A. Blais, ed. *To Keep or Change First Past the Post: The Politics of Electoral Reform*. Oxford: Oxford University Press, 2008, 163–183.

Wallfish, Asher. "Knesset Marranos' Danger of Anti-Floor-Crossing Law." *Jerusalem Post*. November 21, 1968, 8.

Wallfish, Asher. "Proposal Would Stop MKs from Bolting Their Factions." *Jerusalem Post*. September 7, 1982, 2.

Wallfish, Asher. "Shamir Asks Party to Back Moda'i Deal." *Jerusalem Post*. April 20, 1990, 1.

Wallfish, Asher. "Bill Targets Perfidious, Corrupt MKs." *Jerusalem Post*. June 22, 1990, 9.

Weiss, Shevach. "Explanation to a Bill Proposal," Eleventh Knesset, 03/0882/A/024. https://main.knesset.gov.il/Activity/Legislation/Laws/Pages/LawBill.aspx?t=law suggestionssearch&lawitemid=151847

Wootliff, Raoul. "With 'Paritetic' Proposal, Rivlin Looks to the Past for Power-Sharing Model." *Times of Israel*. September 26, 2019. www.timesofisrael.com/with-paritetic-proposal-rivlin-looks-to-the-past-for-power-sharing-model

Yadav, Vineeta. "Legislative Institutions and Corruption in Developing Country Democracies." *Comparative Political Studies* 45, no. 8 (2012): 1027–1058.

Yoshinaka, Antoine. "House Party Switchers and Committee Assignments: Who Gets 'What, When, How?'" *Legislative Studies Quarterly* 30, no. 3 (2005): 391–406.

Yoshinaka, Antoine. *Crossing the Aisle: Party Switching by U.S. Legislators in the Postwar Era* Cambridge: Cambridge University Press, 2016.

Yudelman, Michal. "Peretz Stands Firm—Shas Rift Deepens." *Jerusalem Post*. March 21, 1990, 1.

Yudelman, Michal. "Tsomet Splits, 3 MKs Form New Party." *Jerusalem Post*. February 3, 1994, 1.

Yudelman, Michal. "Labor, Yi'ud to Form Joint Histadrut List." *Jerusalem Post*. April 5, 1994, 12.

Yudelman, Michal, and Dan Izenberg. "Yi'ud, Labor Initial Coalition Agreement: Shas Expected to Follow After Tisha Be'av." *Jerusalem Post*. July 13, 1994, 1.

Yudelman, Michal. "Meretz Split over Whether to Veto Labor Agreement with Shas." *Jerusalem Post*. July 24, 1994.

Yudelman, Michal. "Yi'ud Still Part of Coalition Despite Court Ruling." *Jerusalem Post*. July 26, 1994, 1–2.

Yudelman, Michal. "Levy: Fix Primary System of I'll Quit Likud." *Jerusalem Post*. May 30, 1995, 1.

Yudelman, Michal. "Countdown to Likud's Self-Destruction Begins." *Jerusalem Post*. June 2, 1995, 8.

Yudelman, Michal. "Goldfarb: Nonentity Who Saved the Government." *Jerusalem Post*. July 27, 1995, 1, 2.

Yudelman, Michal. "Goldfarb Leaves Margins to Rescue Government." *Jerusalem Post*. October 6, 1995, 15.

Yudelman, Michal. "David Levy to Announce New Party in December." *Jerusalem Post*. August 13, 1995, 1.

Yudelman, Michal. "David Levy Launches his Gesher Party." *Jerusalem Post*. February 21, 1996.

Government Sources

ISRAEL

Central Election Commission. *Elections to the Fifteenth Knesset.* www.gov.il/apps/ elections/Elections-knesset-15/heb/index.html

Coalition Agreement Between Kadima and Gil to Establish the Thirty-First Government of the State of Israel. http://main.knesset.gov.il/mk/government/documents/ Coal2006gil.pdf [In Hebrew]

Coalition Agreement Between Likud and Yisrael Beitenu. http://main.knesset.gov. il/mk/government/documents/coal2009YisraelBeitenu.pdf [In Hebrew]

Coalition Agreement Between Likud and Labor to Establish the Thirty-Second Government of the State of Israel. https://main.knesset.gov.il/mk/government/documents/ coal2009Avoda.pdf [In Hebrew]

Coalition Agreement Between Likud and Kadima to Establish a National Unity Government. https://main.knesset.gov.il/mk/government/documents/coalition2012.pdf [In Hebrew]

Coalition Agreement to Establish an Emergency National Unity Government. https:// main.knesset.gov.il/mk/government/Documents/CA35-Likud-BW-200420.pdf [In Hebrew]

Constitution, Law and Justice Committee Protocols. No. 464. Thirteenth Knesset. February 21, 1996. https://fs.knesset.gov.il/13/Committees/13_ptv_476322.PDF 2022 [In Hebrew].

Knesset. Amendment No. 12 to the Basic Law: The Knesset. February 22, 1991. https://fs.knesset.gov.il/12/law/12_lsr_210826.PDF [In Hebrew]

Knesset. Amendment No. 31 to the Law on the Election of the Knesset and the Prime Minister. February 29, 1996. https://fs.knesset.gov.il/13/law/13_lsr_211239. PDF 2022 [In Hebrew]

Knesset. Amendment No. 62 to the Knesset Election Law. March 19, 2014. https:// fs.knesset.gov.il/19/law/19_lsr_301595.pdf [In Hebrew]

Knesset. Amendment No. 41 to the Party Funding Law. May 7, 2020. https:// fs.knesset.gov.il/23/law/23_lsr_570150.pdf

Knesset. Amendment No. 51 to the Basic Law: The Knesset. July 7, 2021. https://fs.knesset.gov.il/24/law/24_lsr_603565.pdf

Knesset. Proposed Amendments Nos. 18 and 19 to the Party Funding Law. May 1, 1996. http://fs.knesset.gov.il//13/law/13_ls1_292588.PDF [In Hebrew]

Knesset. *National Legislation Collection*. https://main.knesset.gov.il/Activity/Legislation/Laws/Pages/LawBill.aspx?t=lawsuggestionssearch&lawitemid=435177 [In Hebrew]

Knesset Arrangements Committee Protocols, Twenty-Third Knesset, March 29, 2020. https://main.knesset.gov.il/Activity/committees/Pages/AllCommitteesAgenda.aspx?Tab=3&ItemID=2086941

Knesset Committee Protocols. First Knesset. November 22, 1949. https://fs.knesset.gov.il/1/Committees/1_ptv_399113.PDF [In Hebrew]

Knesset Committee Protocols. No. 120, Sixth Knesset, June 11, 1968. https://fs.knesset.gov.il/6/Committees/6_ptv_425610.PDF [In Hebrew]

Knesset Committee Protocols. No. 130, Sixth Knesset, July 30, 1968. https://fs.knesset.gov.il/6/Committees/6_ptv_425630.PDF. [In Hebrew]

Knesset Committee Protocols. No. 2, Ninth Knesset. July 5, 1977. http://fs.knesset.gov.il//9/Committees/9_ptv_441705.PDF [In Hebrew]

Knesset Committee Protocols. No. 3, Ninth Knesset. July 12, 1977. http://fs.knesset.gov.il//9/Committees/9_ptv_441707.PDF [In Hebrew]

Knesset Committee Protocols. No. 100, Twelfth Knesset. February 26, 1990. https://main.knesset.gov.il/Activity/committees/Pages/AllCommitteeProtocols.aspx?ItemID=2051471 [In Hebrew]

Knesset Committee Protocols. No. 103, Twelfth Knesset. March 6, 1990. https://main.knesset.gov.il/Activity/committees/Pages/AllCommitteeProtocols.aspx?ItemID=2051471 [In Hebrew]

Knesset Committee Protocols. No. 104, Twelfth Knesset. March 14, 1990. https://main.knesset.gov.il/Activity/committees/Pages/AllCommitteeProtocols.aspx?ItemID=2051471 [In Hebrew]

Knesset Committee Protocols. No. 107, Twelfth Knesset. March 15, 1990. https://main.knesset.gov.il/Activity/committees/Pages/AllCommitteeProtocols.aspx?ItemID=2051471 [In Hebrew]

Knesset Committee Protocols. No 108, Twelfth Knesset. March 15, 1990. https://main.knesset.gov.il/Activity/committees/Pages/AllCommitteeProtocols.aspx?ItemID=2051471 [In Hebrew]

Knesset Committee Protocols. No. 105, Thirteenth Knesset. February 7, 1994. https://main.knesset.gov.il/Activity/committees/Pages/AllCommitteeProtocols.aspx?ItemID=2051471 [In Hebrew]

Knesset Committee Protocols. No. 373, Thirteenth Knesset. February 28, 1996. https://fs.knesset.gov.il/13/Committees/13_ptv_477527.PDF. [In Hebrew]

Knesset Committee Protocols. No. 377, Thirteenth Knesset. March 11, 1996. https://fs.knesset.gov.il/13/Committees/13_ptv_477584.PDF [In Hebrew]

Knesset Committee Protocols. No. 225, Fourteenth Knesset. February 23, 1999. https://fs.knesset.gov.il/14/Committees/14_ptv_486649.PDF [In Hebrew]

Knesset Committee Protocols. No.226, Fourteenth Knesset. February 23, 1999. https://fs.knesset.gov.il/14/Committees/14_ptv_486652.PDF [In Hebrew]

Knesset Committee Protocols. No. 230, Fourteenth Knesset. March 22, 1999. https://fs.knesset.gov.il/14/Committees/14_ptv_486664.PDF [In Hebrew]

Knesset Committee Protocols. No. 231, Fourteenth Knesset. March 25, 1999. https://fs.knesset.gov.il/14/Committees/14_ptv_486667.PDF [In Hebrew]

Knesset Committee Protocols. No. 232, Fourteenth Knesset. March 29, 1999. https://fs.knesset.gov.il/14/Committees/14_ptv_486670.PDF [In Hebrew]

Knesset Committee Protocols. No. 284, Sixteenth Knesset. February 1, 2006. https://main.knesset.gov.il/Activity/committees/Pages/AllCommitteeProtocols.aspx [In Hebrew]

Knesset Committee Protocols. No. 6306, Sixteenth Knesset, March 10, 2003. [In Hebrew]

Knesset Committee Protocols. No. 284, Sixteenth Knesset. May 18, 2005. https://main.knesset.gov.il/Activity/committees/Pages/AllCommitteesAgenda.aspx?Tab=3&ItemID=100211 [In Hebrew]

Knesset Committee Protocols. No. 233, Seventeenth Knesset. May 28, 2008. https://main.knesset.gov.il/Activity/committees/Pages/AllCommitteeProtocols.aspx [In Hebrew]

Knesset Committee Protocols. No. 144, Eighteenth Knesset. January 17, 2011. https://main.knesset.gov.il/Activity/committees/Pages/AllCommitteeProtocols.aspx?ItemID=2051471 [In Hebrew]

Knesset Committee Protocols. No. 301, Eighteenth Knesset. July 24, 2012. https://main.knesset.gov.il/Activity/committees/Pages/AllCommitteeProtocols.aspx [In Hebrew]

Knesset Committee Protocols. No. 412, Twentieth Knesset. December 30, 2018. https://main.knesset.gov.il/Activity/committees/Pages/AllCommitteeProtocols.aspx [In Hebrew]

Knesset Committee Protocols. No. 30, Twenty-Third Knesset. July 14, 2020. https://main.knesset.gov.il/Activity/committees/Pages/AllCommitteesAgenda.aspx?Tab=3&ItemID=2142496 [In Hebrew]

Knesset Committee Protocols. No. 102, Twenty-Third Knesset. December 28, 2020. https://main.knesset.gov.il/Activity/committees/Pages/AllCommitteesAgenda.aspx?Tab=3&ItemID=2151769 [In Hebrew]

Knesset Plenary Protocols. No. 250, First Knesset. April, 12, 1951. https://fs.knesset.gov.il/1/Plenum/1_ptm_250163.pdf [In Hebrew]

Knesset Plenary Protocols. June 20, 1977, 69. http://fs.knesset.gov.il//9/Plenum/9_ptm_254065.pdf [In Hebrew]

Knesset Plenary Protocols. No. 11, Ninth Knesset. July 12, 1977. https://fs.knesset.gov.il/9/Plenum/9_ptm_253917.pdf [In Hebrew]

Knesset Plenary Protocols. No. 113, Sixteenth Knesset. March 1, 2004. https://main.knesset.gov.il/Activity/plenum/Pages/Sessions.aspx [In Hebrew]

Knesset Plenary Protocols. No. 51, Seventeenth Knesset, October 30, 2006. http://main.knesset.gov.il/Activity/plenum/Pages/SessionItem.aspx?itemID=178107 [In Hebrew]

Knesset Plenary Protocols. No. 13, Eighteenth Knesset. March 31, 2008. http://main.knesset.gov.il/Activity/plenum/Pages/SessionItem.aspx?itemID=322083 [In Hebrew]

Knesset Plenary Protocols. No. 12, Twenty-First Knesset. May 29, 2020. https://
main.knesset.gov.il/Activity/plenum/Pages/SessionItem.aspx?itemID=2080595 [In
Hebrew]

Knesset Plenary Votes. January 19, 2011. www.knesset.gov.il/vote/heb/Vote_Res_
Map.asp?vote_id_t=15213 [In Hebrew]

Knesset Plenary Votes. December 1, 2004. https://main.knesset.gov.il/Activity/
plenum/Votes/Pages/vote.aspx?voteId=3430 [In Hebrew]

Knesset Plenary Votes, January 19, 2005.
www.knesset.gov.il/vote/heb/vote_gov100105.htm [in Hebrew]

INDIA

India. Parliament. *Lok Sabha Debates. Eighth Lok Sabha.* January 30, 1985.

India. Parliament. *Rajya Sabha Debates.* January 31, 1985.

NEW ZEALAND

Report on the Electoral (Integrity) Amendment Bill. New Zealand. House of Representatives Justice and Electoral Committee. www.parliament.nz/en/pb/bills-and-laws/
bills-proposed-laws/document/BILL_75706/electoral-integrity-amendment-bill

SOUTH AFRICA

South Africa. National Assembly. *Proceedings of the National Assembly.* February
25, 2003. www.pa.org.za/hansard/2003/february/25/proceedings-of-the-national-
assembly-tuesday-25-fe

South Africa. National Assembly. *Proceedings of the National Assembly.* Proceedings of the National Assembly, August 20, 2008.

"Address by Prime Minister Ariel Sharon at the Fourth Herzliya Conference."
December 18, 2003. http://mfa.gov.il/MFA/PressRoom/2003/Pages/Address%20by
%20PM%20Ariel%20Sharon%20at%20the%20Fourth%20Herzliya.aspx

Index

www.ingramcontent.com/pod-product-compliance
Lightning Source LLC
Chambersburg PA
CBHW020348270326
41926CB00007B/348